# HC WRESTLE A GRIZZLY BEAR!

### Demon doing it

With Gary Cooper leading the way, Larry "Demon" Edmon of Franklin college heads downfield Saturday after recovering a Georgetown fumble. Making a futile chase is Ed Moore (66) of Georgetown.

# CHAPTERS

| | |
|---|---|
| We may ask ourselves… | 3 |
| How to Wrestle a Grizzly Bear | 5 |
| How to Paint Your neighbor's car… | 14 |
| The Bike Race | 18 |
| Fire | 20 |
| Uncle Walter & 'Gary… | 23 |
| A New Start | 26 |
| The Unconscious | 39 |
| How to Really Wrestle a Bear | 44 |
| Franklin College of Indiana | 51 |
| "Make Me Play You!" | 58 |
| 1972-Franklin College | 64 |
| The Beginning-Janet's Starry Nights | 83 |
| The Telephone Call | 88 |
| 'How to Quit' and Get a Regular Job | 91 |
| The Conclusion… | 98 |
| Sometimes One Has to Wear Blinders | 105 |
| The Promoter | 111 |
| The Happening! | 124 |
| Let's Get Married with Flair! | 129 |
| The Winks from Jersey | 139 |
| Goal and Dream Planning | 150 |
| Maslow's Hierarchy of Needs | 160 |
| Vector Investment Corporation | 164 |
| Express Bond and Collection | 169 |
| My Arrest – Why? | 176 |
| Oil – Water & Racism | 189 |
| The American Movie Classics | 198 |
| Pete the Python | 205 |
| A&E Wild Justice | 211 |
| We Want you to be Snake? | 215 |
| The Day 'Our Time' Stood Still… | 216 |
| The Jumpers | 219 |
| The 'Middle '50s'… | 240 |
| The Heavenly Touch on me! | 245 |
| "Am I Superman's Cousin" | 249 |
| The Miracle of the Ones… | 255 |
| What about Us? | 269 |

# We may ask ourselves, why did I fail, or who can I blame? Others may say, "Go Figure"

**Was it too much confidence or too little effort?**

At times we may feel the pull of life's concerns and potential failures.

Some stop or quit and some never give up. Why? I have seen many people quit or just give up readily when they are facing 'BIG PROBLEMS'. The weights and balances of 'what to do now' and one's personal perspective really do matter. "If only I had not lost that____ and then I would have____." I have felt this way and would share it with a trusted friend or family member. Confession is clearly good for the heart.

My mind echoes, *"Excuses don't go on the scoreboard."*

'How do you win if you've never been?' In other words, let's consider our failures... Did we not learn something from our bad situations? Can't we use this new information in a new similar endeavor or skill? Can we afford to lose our attitude with a defeated state of negative thinking? Or in a bold mindset, can we remain positive in the midst of our storm? We all have or will have a storm. It's just part of life.

This story is one of not quitting, but hopefully kicking the dust off my shoes as life's circumstances evolve in ways that can truly challenge in some really tough situations. While yearning for the new day experience and asking God, "What's next?" I couldn't sit still. I kept busy. I was open to the next opportunity. Finally my mind gets involved; it's time to start critical thinking and dreaming! Possibly a great hope or a wonderful thought appears while always seeking and never stopping until GOD shows up! Now it's time! Submit to HIS glory on this earth and HIS eternity for me. Clearly, in time I experienced feelings/thoughts with a heartfelt direction for the best remedy. Overcoming? Formulate a plan; any plan with that special 'critical type thinking' that always seems to save the day for me. I can't waste it!

*Using faith, love and almost always, patience along life's way regardless of the obstacles, attempting to be 'dead to myself' while trusting and hoping for a specific direction, I developed a mindset for myself. It was one of expecting little and receiving much, in time. This is what I call planning for the worst (no one wants this, but sometimes you have to lose to win) and praying for the very best.*

**During this same period of time I longed to 'make a difference' with a sincere desire to help somebody change for the better. As I examine myself, it is clear that my down times served a purpose and God has used these times to grow and develop me into the man I am today.**

*I'm simply known as 'Coop'.*

**Enjoy my reflections and connections!**

# How to Wrestle a Grizzly Bear!

By Gary Cooper- Author

Edited by Susan J. Cooper, my trustful and loving Companion

It was 1954 my Dad had the radio on full Blast. Little Milan High School (school population 34) was in the Indiana State Basketball Championship Game. Dad was from little Edinburg High School (school population 25) 20 miles south of Indianapolis and simply couldn't believe Milan made it to the state championships against huge (3,500 students) 4 time state champion Muncie Central High School. Mom seemed upset/uncertain and somewhat amused at dad's reactions, all at once. After all she was a country girl from poverty stricken Eastern Kentucky and clearly did not know anything about the fanatical/competitive basketball fans from Indiana. Until now!

I was only 3 years old, it was the first time in my life I had any recall of paying any kind of attention to a radio program. At that time, hardly anyone had a television set, mass production of televisions and all concerned was just beginning. Regardless, even with this soon to be somewhat outdated radio. And the reason was very clear. My semi-calm dad was going absolutely nuts, crazy, sweating, and at times completely besides himself screaming all through the game. Especially when tiny Milan High won by two points with 14 seconds to go it was also the first time I had ever seen my father dance and Baptists with a Pennsylvania Dutch background just didn't dance…much. This may seem a little outrageous or boring to most but to me it made an incredible difference….sports means something!*? A Very exciting, mysterious and challenging something! I believe, at that moment I wanted to be or do something with my life that was exciting, mysterious and challenging like sports. At that point in my life I wasn't even talking yet at age 3. The doctor thought it could possibly be a result of birth shock. I was born breech birth with the umbilical cord wrapped around my neck several times. The doctor said it almost killed both of us, Mom and me. He told her, "I hope your child is worth what you had to go through." Maybe Mom felt sorry for me. Mom thought my two year older, very verbal and gifted with interpretative type skills (for me) sister, Susan, did way too much of my talking for me. As a result, Mom always made excuses for me. Mom was the champion of 'the underdog'. She was extremely unsettled at times, due to her neglected and impoverished childhood. This insecurity seemed to follow me in bits through most of my life. In comparison, Mom had reason to be somewhat insecure. She grew up in poverty stricken eastern Kentucky where her father was a coal miner (1930-1945) and unfortunately was gone most of the time. Her mother died traumatically, with ovarian cancer. Mom mournfully endured the drawn out extremely painful, hopeless bout with her mother's illness and subsequent death at the delicate age of 13. She also had to cook and clean for her four younger siblings. In addition, she even cooked for some of the coal miners Papa brought home after (2 week work stints). Life seems very disparaging, moments especially to a child when discouragement trump's hope. Mom often had facing the feelings of loneliness and fear while fighting depression throughout most her life, Due to the trauma and hopelessness of watching her mother slowly die.

This emotional pain mostly real and/or somewhat imagined, so it seemed; spilled over into each member of our family. She was clearly my champion. I was the 'underdog' and she was my lifelong personal enabler. In time I attempted to return the favor somewhat.

After years of research and DNA checks while finding new or lost relatives due to the search. I have come to surmise that my presumed Grandfather who whittled wood toys and figurines for each grandchild those few years near the end of his life when I and most of his grandchildren were only occasionally there was an absolute Hero! Henry Neal was pretty much unknown when it came to my personal DNA checks and other checking devices. It turned out he was not even my biological grandfather. Nevertheless he had a vision...

Elderberry Kidd was a preacher who had two wives and over 13 children out of wedlock. He was a carpenter and worked in eastern Kentucky and southwestern Ohio. He found himself serving time in prison. In Ohio, he was subsequently charged with bigamy 2 counts completed jail 'time served' and was soon to return to Crab Orchard. Mom was the perfect age for a lustful man like Elderberry and Grandpa Neal knew it! He got the entire family out before cousin Elderberry put his mark on several of his daughters; he was not to be trusted. He possessed unbelievable demonic manipulation skills misusing God on one side with his pastorship side and his personal lusts on the other. You might say he didn't let his 'right hand know what his left hand was doing'. I call this the Christian cop out when it comes to personal wants as compared to the true intent of this phrase pertaining to protective family/business dealings.

On the more positive side cousin James Denney was a veteran of the Revolutionary War and several Denney cousins fought in the Civil War. Often we find persons who occasionally have 'flipped coin side effect' personality traits which sometimes makes us wonder. Good vs. bad.

Henry Neal might have been the last of his line or somehow lost in the shuffle of any current DNA checks that haven't been posted due to lack of money or lack of computer access. As recently as I wrote this book and was privileged to meet for 'the very first time' Pam Sarles a second cousin who had been adopted and put through 15 foster care takers prior to the adoption. Pam told me of the extreme dire and pathetic circumstances that led to her and her brothers' adoptions. Once again Elderberry Kidd was right in the middle of it. In both cases unspeakable abuses occurred in the hills of Eastern Kentucky. I now know that my Grandfather Henry Neal was not only a man of insight but vision to move his children to Indiana not to just 'not be adopted' as the Kentucky Family Services suggested but to survive with better educational and employment opportunities, as acknowledged by all of Henry Neal's children and grandchildren thus far. So I applaud this man's historical actions for it has allowed me to excel and prosper accordingly. One of my personal frustrations with my DNA and family findings is that I didn't get the blessings of music and music skills like Pam Sarles, Charles Reagan-professional, Julie Neal, Walter Neal, Clyde Neal, Jimmy Buffett-professional and others in the extended family. I have to look elsewhere for my talent base. But none of this could have happened had not Henry Neal made a big move at the right time! Thanks Grandpa! *God knows this move wasn't easy..*

Mom and Dad married in the 'late 1940's' after just after returning from his former Army-Air Force pilots slot with her at age 17, 'way to young, with an eighth grade education'. It simply was 'that look' as he kindly peered in her direction. Dad met Mom in a car and this became our immediate family's acknowledgement the classic 'Love at first sight' very similar to the songs/movies coupled with emotional-relational thought patterns in the 1940's right up to current times as well. As a result, the emotionally geared 'ups and downs' of marriage for my young parents ruled. But clearly the greatest thing in her life was having two children 'she often stated her position as Mother, with great pride and pleasure'. She always tried her best to raise us healthy but lacked in various social/ relational graces that many people seemed to have, once again mostly due to her shocking depraved childhood. Jealousy and insecurity, whether imagined or real, seemed to have its' place in our home with hints of sexual misconduct. I often felt that Dad was the natural recipient of these jealous accusations from Mom's statements 'accusations and such, all about dad...True or not true'. Naturally as 'an apple from a tree' falling upon us 'my sister and me'. In our futures, this clearly affected both of our initial dating relationships even with marriage to some degree after a period of time. It's often said, "apples don't fall too far from the tree", what traits we inherit from our parents, guardians, day care workers and influential friends and relatives often times greatly affected our lives. Especially in the first 3 years of life where we develop 70% of our personality traits. Mom certainly had an effect on me...particularly from an emotional and social perspective. These effects appeared in my early pre- grade school and grade school and even high school somewhat.

I grew up near one living Grandmother on the Cooper side of the family. She resided up in Taylorsville and later moved to Edinburgh, Indiana after she got her retirement via Social Security which was a blessing considering all of the strife and pain during the Great Depression and World War 11 years. Grandma's real name was Elizabeth Hickey Cooper and all her friends called her Minnie. Of course I called her Grandma. She and my parents loved me but with Grandma it was somehow different. I think it was the large amounts of time and care she would share while babysitting my sister and myself. She would also read to me which I loved. I would sit on her lap while sitting in a recliner with a lamp stand beside us. This was a general occurrence because she only lived fifteen minutes away. She always seemed to have cookies for my sister and me. I loved her cookies. Grandma would also tell me stories about life on the farm, my Grandfather Cooper passed away many years prior to me or my sister's birth. Regardless they had 5 children and many grandchildren who were all girls except me and Don Bice of Chicago who unfortunately got killed in a car crash. But the one who Grandma talked about most was Irwin Cooper who was shot on her front porch when a friend/playmate grabbed the gun off of the mantle 'thinking it was a play gun' and shot Irwin directly in the stomach, he died after much suffering 3 months later. It was clear to me that Irwin was very special to Grandma. She spent hours with me telling how he led others in a way that was so special she thought Irwin would have been a great leader. As time went on I believe Grandma was telling me to do the same in her own way. I thank God for my Grandma and the time she spent with me. One evening when Grandma was reading, the time came to stop. Since I was sitting on her lap I reached up to turn out the light and the weight and balance in the chair shifted and we both fell upside-down and backwards. The light fixture fell and the light bulb exploded, Grandma screamed. Initially I thought 'I was in serious trouble'. But not with Grandma, after she composed herself she came over and hugged me and I knew we just loved each other no matter what ever happens. What a great Grandma!

Family relationships can become at times a testy formula for any marriage and it showed somewhat over time. Prior to working for The Oliver Tractor Company, Dad was a policeman. Even as a small child, I was always so proud to see him in that uniform and being a Columbus, Indiana policeman had its privileges; low pay 'the reason he wouldn't be a policeman long' but policemen's wives did receive passes to get into the movie theatre free! *The Crump Theatre* was the only theatre in town. Every now and then the large print lighted sign would get a burned out bulb with the sign spelling…RUMP or CRUM, I loved it! It even had a crying room upstairs. This was the post war solution for many stay- at-home moms with small children…many of the kids did just that 'cry'. I got to visit there quite often, like every other kid I hated it also. Mom really got involved in the movies; she named my sister, Susan after Susan Hayworth 'movie star' and when I came along 2 years later she named me Gary Cooper after 'Gary Cooper the movie star' with my middle name 'Wayne' after 'John Wayne the movie star'. Do you think that those movies had an impact on Mom?! Not to mention me, I consider movies to be at least one of my life's hobbies; I preferred movie & documentary learning without reading. My eyes were slightly pointing outward; this would greatly help me from an athletic perspective in the future.

What else would Mom do as a 19-21 year old female wife without an education or job and was in the beginnings of raising children do? Especially in a small 8,000-10,000 population in a 'two horse' town. The horses by the way were Cummins Engine Company and Arvin Industries, both would be greatly successful in time. From this point on my Mom called me 'Gary Cooper the Movie Star' and continued this sporadically for most of her entire life. She must have hoped and was certainly influenced by the movies that I might possibly develop some characteristics of these stars per their movies roles thus reminding her of the wonderful character and traits shown in those movies with Gary Cooper and John Wayne. Of course, I was shy and somewhat, embarrassed and all 'the above' made me very reluctant to be in any plays or shows because of my name. My personal perspective especially with my name made me feel that these actions would make me appear as a *'fake movie star wannabe'*.

I'll never forget the movie 'High Noon' starring Gary Cooper, which played in a special event period for my senior class year in high school. I had never even seen a Gary Cooper movie before this time. Most kids my age didn't really know much about Gary

Cooper, the movie star, at all as the credits ran they looked back at me and laughed. Later on as an adult, I would realize that Mom was setting me up to be the representative of the American Movie Classics via Gary Cooper the movie star. She spoke in a sense 'life in the tongue' which according to the word of God works. <u>In others words be very careful the way you talk to others or yourself</u>. No one could have helped me to imagine what was to come later on…just because of Mom's tongue! It sure wasn't my intent. I wondered, 'maybe somehow this was coupled with God's sense of humor…'

After flunking (failing first grade) all of my worst expectations came to pass and were unfortunately realized. My sister was smart and I appeared, not smart! This really frustrated me. Believe me there was no life in the tongue regarding the upside actions here except the opposite. I was bullied after school and called very bad names. The only kids who would play with me came from bad to worse circumstances. I was a kind of <u>Rudolph the Red Nosed Reindeer</u> type, before Santa appointed him to lead the sleigh. I got all F's, better known as one legged A's, on my first report card. I didn't even realize getting an <u>F</u> was a bad grade. I also thought this was in fact 'really dumb' later as I reflected to write this story. I showed all the local school kids my report card which I found shortly thereafter, *which was an extremely bad move*. I suddenly found that maybe I was just plain dumb. Afterwards, I took the report card home for my parents to sign off. The neighborhood kids helped me to believe that I was dumb with all sorts of hostile bullying as I walked the 4 block trek home each day. They were cussing at me, name calling, group sucker punches to the stomach, hitting me over the head with a coke bottle, etc. I found out what it was to be a perceived loser, 'one without merit and going down,' especially on the dangerous way home from school. Thank GOD that my 2 year older and bigger sister Susan often walked home with me. She provided safety and I considered her to be, 'my bodyguard.' What else could I do in Bedford and Lebanon, Indiana? I would learn how to ride a bike <u>and never ever show my report card to any kid again</u>! Even in High School or College! Hang up? No doubt! I had some rather strong negative reinforcement at a young age that made me hold my scholastic reports very tightly.

Bedford was a small town known mostly for digging limestone quarries. This was part of Dad's territory for my kindergarten-preschool year. Dad moved us to Lebanon in first grade and I met a kid named Artie. He was in my class and also performed poorly with his academics as well. We seemed to be on the same level, but I wasn't really sure. Artie would come to our apartment 2 story building after school and Mom would let us play around the complex. Artie had a much tougher life than me. He would steal apples and peaches from various porches. I initially thought he did that for fun until I noticed later how he ate almost every one he took. He was hungry. Afterwards, I would help him take some of the fruit because he needed it. Artie's circumstance was helping me create sensitivity towards the 'less fortunate' that would greatly impact my future life. Artie had a father, who was a lineman 'he serviced utility poles for the electric company'.

I remember the last time I went to Artie's house. It was pretty normal without his dad around except a little more dirt was left lying around Artie's house. There also seemed to be a lot of beer cans in the overflowing trash. When Artie's dad came home, he was very angry! We continued playing with some games after school. He quickly pulled out his lineman's belt and was going to whip both of us. I didn't have a clue as to 'why?' We were going to be whipped until his mother warned him not to touch me or he would be in jail again! His father paused as his mother hurriedly let me out. I couldn't imagine what happened to Artie? A brutal beating no doubt. As I ran home really scared… for the first time in my life I went home and told Mom. Bye Artie! Mom banned me from Artie's' house for obvious reasons. I still remember pleading and crying, "What about Artie?!" Could Artie's dad just whip him because he felt like it? This was my first real experience with abuse and I didn't like it at all. To this day, I have a short fuse concerning personal and societal abuse. He had no right to beat Artie! I stayed in touch with Artie at school but we never played together again. Somehow we knew our boundaries without a word between be us was spoken. He knew that I knew his bad situation, but I simply could not mentally or emotionally process his horrible life. I was just a kid or so I thought, so oppressed it. My thought process with the deep laden subconscious mind effect reminds me of Artie's life from time to time.

Boredom once again, was my biggest friend at this point except for the apartment boys and girls; I was now on 5 year old restriction due to my grades. Mom knew she was feeling a little guilty and unsettled because of her own horrific childhood in Kentucky. She would constantly tell me, "You are smart and will do better in school. " I really had my doubts but I really loved her faith'. Mom was like a type of friend/mother while Dad was very frustrated about me. My sister excelled and did very well in school. I think that Dad bought into the concept that I was <u>slow,</u> so I started to <u>act slowly</u> and I secretly knew the difference. I was named after an actor and I was now ready to use this slow thought mentality to make an impression, 'acting out' is an understatement! Please put on your mind's perspective and safety seat belt thought process.

# How to Paint your Neighbor's car and not get caught!

Today one hears about children who act out. I was the type of child who could somewhat skillfully stretch boundaries. I remember my Dad and his friends telling their war stories. What they did in the military, including stories of killings and tortures during WW2 made a huge and profound impression upon me. I wanted to kill every German/ Japanese soldier I could find; at least in my mind. Later on in junior and senior high school days, I semi-seriously dated two German girls who both 'descended from at least 3 generations back' girls in high school with the same first and last names! They were both very nice, sweet, and pretty and obviously didn't know much about my mentally confused historical mindset regarding WW2 background and I didn't want or know how to tell them. Mostly I probably had a latent subconscious response/programming on my part with zero reprogramming that I needed as they were both German and I was the mixed bag variety...Irish, English and yes German descent also. Even Hitler was partly Jewish.

They each dropped me as their respective boyfriend's, in their personally convenient time periods. Maybe I was acting as a type of 'confused double agent' with these darling girls mostly due to my inadequacies? My Mother's influence was abounding. The fear of rejection and jealousy 'showed itself' in me as a youth. Clearly I wasn't ready for any relationships, let alone serious ones. I could still imagine the possibilities of fulfilling type relationships regardless as my hormones were starting to rage? Pre teenaged and teenagers often find themselves greatly oppressed with intense feelings of all sorts and act out impulsively without any warnings at times.

Between my freshman and sophomore years in school, my girlfriend Debbie's grandmother died. I only had one really close grandparent, my beloved Grandma Cooper. I was somewhat curious, I hoped to be empathetic and planned on being somewhat understanding with Debbie's family as I went to the funeral. I had been to a lot of family and friends funerals up to this point. Much to my surprise I was told her last name was Grobengieser. I'm not sure I spelled her name right, but she clearly 'in my mind' was one of those Germans from Hitler's days. I was feeling uncertain and became somewhat upset as I switched my thought process. I then questioned myself, but what if she wasn't like Hitler and his following as she experienced the shame of that horrific era, without any expectation of what was to come, completely innocent!…Suddenly 'much to my shock and surprise', <u>I found myself at age 15, crying and sobbing, like a baby for somebody I didn't even know during her lifetime</u>! After a few moments of the normal funeral response's, usually somber, with glory filled statements and futuristic guarantees about that heavenly excursion from the preacher; Meanwhile I'm putting on this unplanned and unbalanced emotional show and I couldn't stop. I found myself giving a seemingly sincere response with deep sorrow- filled crying, and powerful moans. Eventually Debbie's brothers were nice enough to help me out of the building. They were very kind to me and I eventually composed myself. I asked them both," What happened in there?" They didn't respond except shrugged their shoulders. What could they say? *A truth I hope we all use in our lives is simply, 'You can't read your partner, mate or friends mind, this is a truth that may save a relationship in time.'* To this day I really wonder what I was crying about…was it Mom and Dad's confused relationship? Some awful thing I read about in school, The Holocaust? My beloved Grandma Cooper, the thought of her eventual demise? Maybe I truly felt sorry for my girlfriend Debbie for having a grandma with such a horrendous name? I simply don't know, but they didn't invite me to any more of their family funerals. <u>If they had wanted mourners I would have been one of the best in history. Maybe I was acting out a part, just like in the movies…of course unbeknownst to me! I would like to think that I got caught up in a type of hormonal transition from a 'boy to man' effect. Sounds good?</u>

Getting back to my childhood state of mind at age 6...Dad had an acquaintance in the apartment building who had a new pretty bright yellow sports car. He was very proud of his special automotive possession. Impulsively, one early afternoon, for whatever reason, I decided that I needed to paint the underside of his car's back bumper with German swastikas. In the garbage cans outside (a frequent stop for me) I found a slightly used bottle of Testers. This was a brand for painting plastic model cars, etc. with black paint. As I painted, I put every war symbol I could find on the lower right back fender area. When I was finished, I simply got distracted elsewhere and I forgot about it until he got home! Two apartments away I could hear him yelling at his wife for not watching over the vehicle while he was gone. Suddenly instead of getting accolades for my great WW2 artistry, 'Oh, no" I could be in big trouble'. When my father questioned me about it later, I simply told him I didn't know anything about it. Dad believed me, he didn't think I would do anything like that; he was convinced that his son was slow. When the neighbor in the apartment complex questioned Dad with me innocently standing beside him, Dad made a great example as to why I couldn't have done it, "Gary just doesn't spell or write that good, he doesn't do well in school either." Whew! This was possibly my first real test of stress with a touch of excitement. Being a traveling salesman also had its disadvantages; he didn't really follow what progress I was making at the time. This was the point even as a small child I silently planned when someday I would grow up, it seemed like forever, and get a job where I would be home during the weekdays and the weeknights. I had a lot of doubts as a small boy and in the near future I planned on turning my doubts into dreams. I somehow was going to be great! At least in my mind! The above events remind me of this phrase, "I would like to buy him at his worth and sell him for what he thinks he's worth." My value was low but I was dreaming way above my worth, somehow I still had hope...

Cousins are always somewhat satisfied, content, silly, funny, crazed and so forth. Each one knows they are related... somehow. Of course this group is 4 of my immediate cousins. My mom and dad Cooper 'deceased' in 1980's must have wondered at times. Don't all parents wonder at times....

Next picture is cousins: Gary Cooper on left is me with my Teddy Bear, upper right Aunt Donna Mouser, she is holding Owen Neal -deceased, straight below Owen is Diane Neal-deceased. Holding Diane is older brother Ernie Neal. Looking upward is Susan Cooper my sister and far right is Alvin Dewayne Neal - cousin. Date 1954.

Next picture are some of our grandchildren at Chick Filet in 2010 range: On left: Christopher Davidson kicking back with drink, beside Christopher is Emily Degoursey, across from Emily is her sister Lauren McClendon with a very spicy smile, across from Christopher is Robert Davidson the youngest but hanging in there.

# The Bike Race

Our family had now resided in Lebanon, Indiana about one year for 'as dad's job and transfer went, so did we'. I was now in first grade. That fall, the boys and girls in the apartment building were talking about having a bike race around the large shrub lined square block, typically I stood near the back of the small crowd of youngsters just imagining 'how I could ride!', if given the chance. Earlier that sunny Saturday morning, Dad was trying to teach my sister, Susan, how to ride her new 26 inch bike. She struggled a bit and finally gave up as she and dad went into the house. Now it was my turn! With nobody around 'within the hour' I learned very quickly by myself and was riding her bike all around while she was inside. About that time the boys and girls showed up for the big bike race, when I said," I wanted to race" they said, "You, shouldn't race you can't even sit in the seat!" Regardless, I insisted that I was ready to race! So the second race was on. I watched with intense awareness at age 5 1/2 as they flew around the block and a guy named Bill won. The first race was over; I was very impressed and was mentally prepared to win in the next race. Most everybody was (7-12 years of age). Obvious delusions of competitive grandeur were overcoming me, I was 'filled with confidence' in my mind. 'Talk about child like faith!' We all lined up and the race was on! Standing up and not able to sit in the seat, I was in the lead into the first turn around the rectangular block, pedaling hard and fast like a little wild man. The next turn had a huge oak tree 'beside the sidewalk-outside right edge' that I wasn't aware of. Unexpectedly, at full speed I went too far to the left and hit the tree head-on! As I faced apparent doom it was the first time in my life that my mind went into hyperspace... time wise I knew exactly what to do and even thought about all of it in approximately one second. Anticipating, I held on to the handlebars like glue with a dash of oil, my fingers were extremely tight on the handlebars seemingly at the speed of light as I hit the huge tree my body literally rotated vertically straight upside down while hanging on. I went upside down upon smashing into the tree. I instinctually somehow cushioned the blow by awkwardly, at impact, putting my feet, legs and back out while hitting the tree simultaneously positioned upside down, to hopefully cushion the blow, all within a half/split second. I was immediately stuck for one second approximately 10 feet off the ground as the force of gravity kicked in I slid downward quickly while upside down with my brain/body in a type of semi-shock and crashed at the bottom of the huge tree among the exposed roots and grass. Immediately the apartment kids went running to get dad. They found me unconscious/ semi-conscious under the tree and the bike was broken in half. Some of the kids were crying as they told Dad 'they thought I was dead'. As an investigator and former policeman, he rushed to the site and found me drowsy but alive! He kept looking at me, the bike and tree in absolute amazement... He couldn't believe I was alive either! I couldn't remember much except listening to my friends and sister's descriptions with her complaints about me wrecking her new bike. Dad tried to get the bike fixed by having it welded, but it looked really bad and had to be junked. I felt sorry. I did not mean to hurt her bike as I told her later. It took a long time for her to forgive me. The apartment kids reacted much differently and actually seemed to accept me somewhat... a little bit, maybe they thought I was tough? I think I had my first mini ego trip during those precious moments. The neighborhood kids sent me a message in a sense. <u>Gary paid the price, so he is worthy?</u> Maybe I simply earned their respect by my actions. I noticed several of the local kids hanging around the wreck site touching their bikes against the tree wondering what it takes to break a bicycle in half. None would even try to attempt such a feat... Sounds like the beginning of a gang and I certainly was looking for acceptance as a lot of people are seeking every single day. The two relational aspects that one needs are acceptance and purpose; with purpose seemingly primary as compared to acceptance which often is fickle with just about anybody, at times. I always seem to think of the song, Garden Party by Ricky Nelson, verses 'You can't please everyone but you've got to please yourself' often rings true. As a result individual confidence must be reserved for oneself in a special manner/ skill or occupation to attach. Being a good athlete, pilot, businessman, husband, father and counselor over the years, have worked for me at times. Most of us have certain gifts of 'defying the odds' or simply using 'my unconscious competence' would often times assist me as well in the future, or so it seemed.

# FIRE

Shortly after the big knockout/crash (tree and bike wreck), still in Lebanon, I was milling around the apartment complex (two story reddish brick building). As a young child, I found myself bored almost all the time (many years later I was found to be slightly ADHD). When checking my favorite haunt, the garbage cans and bushes, I always hoped to see a snake, anything exciting! I found a pack of matches. Mom always used matches to start the gas burners on top of the apartment stove and thought I knew what they did or could do. My slightly younger cousin Diane had died from playing with matches in bed so I stayed outside. I wasn't going to do anything except throw lit matches into the sewer on Main Street especially because I knew how to strike the match by observation watching Mom light the stove at home. This knowledge never occurred to my parents who did not have a clue as to my knowledge of the stricken match. Only one problem persisted as I struck the fifth match... the wind blew the lit match, set a small piece of newspaper on fire which blew up against the bushes 'in the dry fall air' which set the entire neighborhood shrub lined block perimeter on fire. No homes were in immediate danger due to a concrete sidewalk in between. So I quietly and sheepishly went upstairs to our second floor apartment, stood out on the balcony to watch the fire. I was shocked by the large plumes of smoke as the fire burned with a type cleansing of the bush areas, right down to the roots. I was possibly semi- involved in the first 6 year old controlled burn in Indiana, just like the Southerners do all the time. All of a sudden two huge fire trucks with sirens came screaming down right in front of our apartment! I felt a kind of 'heat on me' as I saw an older lady pointing up to me 'the boy in the Chesty potato chip shirt!' Oh, Oh, I was in trouble! I shrunk down and crawled into my bedroom. All of a sudden a seemingly very large fireman came knocking on our door. I stood listening and not in sight around the corner as Mom explained that "Gary must have found those matches outside". The fireman said some wonderful words, "No charges! We found the matches. Some smoker must have thrown them out of the car window and your boy picked them up". The next day Mom and Dad talked about how the newspaper article blamed the young adult or idiot who endangered the area due to negligence where a small boy 'like me' could easily pick them up. Whew! Another close one! I didn't tell them that I found the matches by the garbage cans. I didn't mean to do that, but I did it! I was somewhat confused about myself at this point. The question was...am I ...Evil!?

After all of my troubling actions, the apartment manager Mrs. Bertrand didn't seem to like me very much at all. I think she was terrified of all the 'possibilities of danger' regarding me. She would anxiously complain to Mom, "Gary is destructive and must be watched!" During that period of time, my mother started talking about the movie: 'The Bad Seed!' It was about a very evil, bad, girl who was so mean she got struck by lightning and died. Mom let me see that awful movie! Oh no, I thought the movie must be about me! I had to convince myself to 'cool it'. I didn't want lightning to strike me like that bad girl in the movie! School slowly wound down and I finally flunked the first grade my sister swears 'I flunked kindergarten'! You can't flunk kindergarten, no grades are assigned...just reports, really bad reports regarding my progress. I really flunked first grade and I never forgot it!

One last event had to occur before spring came. The fellow kids and I were playing tag and ran into the adjoining apartment building. As I was playing tag running and trying to get away from the taggers...I closed the door very quickly while trying to elude the tag as the next kid smashed his head through the large window in the wooden door. Thank God, no injuries. Dad had to fix it since the extremely upset Mrs. Bertrand was holding Dad accountable, the father of the wild child to fix the window. Of course as he fixed it I was there as Dad didn't seem to hold me responsible 'maybe he was just tired of everything that had happened' Dad put the glass in and just as he tested it before the final fastening of the putty...suddenly the window crashed to the floor again! Dad got another window and reinstalled it with an adult neighbor while I stayed at home. Maybe Dad was sensing I might be bad luck. I would have to agree but, he never asked or made the statement. Whew!

Regardless, the good news that spring was turning into summer and Dad got transferred back to Columbus, Indiana (goodbye Lebanon, Indiana), the place I was born, but more importantly a new start in school, without much of a record! This was the first time in my life that I actually formulated a plan. This time I wasn't going to flunk ever again. Never again!, I knew what would happen otherwise, it hurt way too much! In a greater sense, my competitive bar was raised. I had already turned my situation around somewhat and everything was looking up and I refused to look back! I could not give any better advice as so many people, even though I was only 6 years old and going on age 7 with a record of sorts. Even a child is known by his doings and this kid is gonna do much better.

# UNCLE WALTER & 'Gary-the Race Car Driver' with the 'Fascination of Wheels'

Uncle Walter was clearly one of the most talented men I have ever known. He was the only relative I knew that built his own motorcycle, his own airplane, his own 35 foot boat, his house and Lord knows what else. He was inventive and clearly reckless. He was a natural musician and would drive my Dad crazy because he would put his cigarette in his guitars fret bar. It would start out slow because of the long shaft of the cigarette but by the end of the jam session there would be a big burn spot on the wood near the frets. He would always buy expensive guitars and do the same thing every time. That was Uncle Walter.

Uncle Walter was Mom's brother and just like Clyde, Helen, Donna 'the other siblings' had their individual take and memories regarding their share of trauma from their early poverty stricken Eastern Kentucky childhoods. Mom was always cautious when we went out to Uncle Walter's house. One of his children died of burns from a match found on a drawer near the bed as Diane my little 5 year old cousin lit a match and was burned as her little nighty clothes caught on fire. Diane's brother, Owen also died later, at age 17 from various drug overdoses and results, brother Wayne wound up in prison for selling drugs and Cindy got run over by a riding lawnmower. Which permanently damaged her leg? Meanwhile Ernie, Wayne and Reba remained 'vertical' while Cindy adjusted the best she could. My cousins and I always had fun times. There was always room for a certain sadness as well.

Mom and Dad would take my sister and I to the Indiana State Fair almost every year. Dad would always have a booth at the fair displaying his tractor company's lines and benefits for perspective farm accounts and sales. We would ride the various 'kiddie rides' and have a great time, while Dad worked. I liked to ride bumper cars and stationary cars that went slowly in a circle. Our family went out to Uncle Walter and Aunt Eva's house for dinner shortly after one of the many Indiana State Fair events. I thought, 'I know how to ride and drive cars'. I tended to have 'little boy' fantasies quite a bit regarding race cars and such. During the visit, I found myself wandering out to Uncle Walter's track he built for himself, his friends and kids. They could all race and drive go-carts pretty well and timed each other quite often. He had an eighty horse power Adult Go-Cart that could really go fast. I asked Uncle Walter if I could ride. Uncle Walter's personality was one of risky possibilities. After questioning me a little bit. All of my cousin's exclaimed, 'Gary can ride', "He's our age!" We were all 13-14 years of age. I faithfully convinced Uncle Walter that I could drive his eighty horsepower Go-Kart because of my naive- imagined experiences through pure childlike self confidence and State Fair kiddy rides.

Uncle Walter took me out to the middle of the track. He built a quarter mile track right by a convenience store in a place called 'Jewel Village' as people would get snacks and watch the 'speed trials' with the spectators cars parked all along the west side of the track. It reminded me of a small carnival type event and my show was just about to start! He positioned me in the roomy go-cart and showed me the brake and throttle positions. He told me to take off slowly and get the 'jist of it'. Next he stepped back...

I don't really know what happened at that moment. I didn't take off slowly at all; I took off like a 'bat out of hell!' In my mind, instantly I intended to break the track record without any experience! Somehow that 'competitive spirit' arose up deep within my being. I went down the ½ mile stretch and into the first left turn very fast as I kept the throttle 'all the way down'! As I streaked down the back straight away I swung way too far out on the back side off of the track and drove at full speed between the parked cars! I could see people throwing their children into to their car trunks and on top of the cars and running out of the open undesignated auto lane like it was for their lives, because it was! Just as quickly I somehow got back on the track. I have no idea how I didn't wind up crushed under a car! As I got on the far side of the track Uncle Walter was running like a deer to catch me but I sped faster down the backside of the track, went through the turn and spun out on the main stretch while somewhat running over Uncle Walter as he flew over the top of the cart and grabbed the roll bar as I was slowing down after a complete stop. Uncle Walter was possibly famished, bewildered and exhausted and I was somewhere between terrified, elated and depressed. I couldn't believe what I had done without any comment. I immediately went back to Uncle Walter's house and restricted myself in a back bedroom the rest of the day. I wanted to stay out of lightning's way. 'The Bad Seed has struck again'. I would occasionally look back out at the track through the bedroom window hoping nobody was watching me. Earlier as I walked from the end of my race track excursion, Cousin Ernie shouted out, "Hey Dad, I think Gary broke the track record!" When Mom found out, I think we didn't show up for at least a week or two. Family was just about everything to Mom and Dad so it wouldn't be long. I didn't go anywhere near that track again.

Cousin Ernie and Uncle Walter were accomplished mechanics at Cummins Engine Company and Ernie raced stock cars at the 'Gator Nationals' in Orlando, Florida. Meanwhile Uncle Walter remained as the 'top experimental engine tester' at Cummins Engine Company. Walter was the expert's expert, a true natural with a taste for risk.

# A New Start

In my mind, all I could think of… the chance of a new start a new future! I was really pumped up, all by myself and I occasionally looked outside for lightning. I did not want to be the 'Bad Seed'! Without realizing it, I was obsessing about my upcoming scholastic future. School did come; I made decent grades this time. Always good enough but (very seldom outstanding) as I moved along from 1st-'my second time around', 2nd, 3rd A boy named Dillon pulled out my school chair and I hit my head without complaint. So, I waited patiently and returned the favor 'pulled his chair' as Dillon hit the floor he almost immediately cried like a stuck pig. Regardless of my pleas for 'an eye for an eye'/fairness/mercy I was sentenced accordingly. I got my first paddling by the principal with the loud speakers on and the whole school heard me screaming! I really wasn't sure what had happened except I got a sense that life wasn't and isn't necessarily fair for people in general..., from that point on History studies and books took on a greater meaning for me. In 4th and 5th grade 'some of my fellow 5th graders decided to make pipe bombs', they would cut off match heads and jam them into a tight pipe. I had a pretty good idea what would happen when I observed them blasting near our grade school. I made a terrific decision compared to my recent past as to not make any of those dangerous bombs. The next week one of the kids blew his hand almost off and another kid blew one the school windows completely out! After the FBI checked into the event we found schools are federally protected. That was the end of pipe bomb making for all of us. I was now into 6$^{th}$ grade with friends, good grades, making money passing newspapers, my own money!

Often times we would go over to our friend's house named Jim Potter. We would all be on attack mode in the winter packing and throwing snowballs at each other. We would also go to the back of Jim's house in the alley and throw the snowball bombs onto the cars passing by. We often found ourselves running to get away from some of the unhappy drivers who had just cleaned their cars. In the meantime, my other neighbor Randy and I became very used to getting up at 4:00am every morning passing papers for the

Indianapolis Star paper route for the next 2 years. In the spring of our 7th grade year our entire neighborhood gang would go to Jim's house and climb all over their huge oak tree. We would play tree tag and literally jump and grab from limb to limb. We were little pretend Tarzan 'King of the Jungle' types. It was a lot of fun. One particular weekend morning we were all once again playing tree tag and Jim made the statement, "*I'll probably fall and land right into the middle of my little sisters baby pool.*" Within 5 minutes from his infamous statement, Jim fell from 30-20 feet hitting limbs as he fell and landed right in the middle of his little sister's half filled pool. All the climbers found it to be absolutely hilarious and didn't realize how badly one could be hurt falling from a tree. After the laughing died down we helped Jim into his house. I was still somewhat humored until his mother looked at Jim's pale face and said, "What has happened?" I told her, "Jim had predicted his fall into the baby pool 5 minutes before while we all were in the trees. We weren't laughing at Jim but what he said happened exactly as he said and that was humorous. I'm sorry I laughed but I couldn't help it." She took him into the house and I left. The next day, Jim was in arm and leg casts positioned as he hung with metal supports in a hospital bed with an outside view from the picture window in the front of their house. That was my second incidence of encountering life or death in the tongue. At this point in time it appeared to be another 'death in the tongue' moment. I found myself somewhat watching my own tongue as I got older. I continued my early morning paper route.

I bought a brand new beautiful purple Schwinn bicycle- 26 inch with all of my earned money. I was proud of myself. My Dad threw a fit! He claimed I had a bike with a 'nigger purple color' I really liked the color without any association of race whatsoever. He made me take it back and get a green one. I almost had a fit but maybe he knew something? I played along. I parked my new 'green bike' in the racks at school for 6th grade basketball practice and shortly thereafter somebody stole my new bike! Dad somehow got an insurance policy property insurance contract to buy me a new bike and this time my newly replaced 'Schwinn 26 inch bike was purple!' Dad didn't say anything. I think we both figured out a little more regarding racism colors and why we didn't need it. All through my bike experience! Clearly our paper routes gave us disposable incomes at our youthful ages resulting in opportunities.

- I was very careful with my new Mossberg rifle 22 caliber and target practiced in the nearby woods with my best friend, Randy Nentrup who also passed papers and bought his rifle also. While finally getting to play my first time with organized 6$^{th}$ grade basketball! I had become accepted and socially centered in a relational way with my school mates and finally felt a part. Basketball was a big deal; in grade school you tend to visualize what you might be in higher grades. My friends and I thought we were State Champions when we won the city 6$^{th}$ grade championship. I started at the center position and remember making several game points, the Coach named Mr. Adams took us all out for milkshakes and hamburgers as a reward! Once again positive competitive reinforcement prevailed. I was given an inch and was ready for a mile. In the same period of time while in 6th grade I told my father boldly, "I'm going to earn a college athletic scholarship and own an airplane!" He laughed (I was a 5'6" chubby kid) and said, "Gary, you will have to be very good at sports and have to make a lot of money for a airplane" I was truly and inwardly shocked by Dad's statement. As a result, I never told anybody my goals after that but I never forgot that moment and really wowed my father later on. I hardly looked back again (for this wonderful positive reason) as I had become an outstanding athlete until I played my last play in college football. In my early days with Dad, competition-winning had great results and I was in....I was totally convinced of achieving my goals regardless. Whatever and whoever might get in my way! Including all the kind and cute girls of my youthful future life. Whether it was Debbie, Carol, Lisa, Suzy, the other Debbie, Marianne, Jenny, Karen etc. I felt as though I was not going to let anybody stop me, including myself.

Accordingly, I was known as the guy who really got up and did well in my conference/ high school track events (I ran the 440 yard dash and was on the record setting mile relay team that held our record for over 40 years). I really liked football also. We had very good football teams in high school and I had over 15 scholarship opportunities at various Midwest colleges including the Coast Guard Academy. I had become someone to be reckoned with, an athletic overcomer -a commodity of sorts or a person who did better than most people in his or her particular endeavor/ sporting and athletic events was my jingle. As a 6th grader we would anxiously watch the many players that participated in high school athletics before us. My friends and I would watch and verbally dream 'what we might be' as we got our chances to play in our small town which had recently built an 8,000 person gym! The basketball players seemed to have an almost God like-hero stature as they all got big time scholarships all over the country. This made a huge impression to me! I once again was reinforced accordingly. <u>I was also very fortunate to be considered a 'gifted athlete'</u>. Clearly, It's very important to emphasize qualities that makes one do well and <u>everybody has something they do well</u>. All one has to do is find it- the vision the desire and the-have-to or gumption to finish it, no matter what happens. If you can't find it or find yourself giving up find a substitute career while always believing and searching

'I have found that your first thoughts prior to waking up may give you insight'...please, get up and write them down; this is your subconscious revealing what you might become. Finally stating after a healthy 8 hour minimum sleep period. So you might say," <u>Eureka, I've found it!</u>"

I've had few problems with attempting to always seek: not only to look but plan on finding it. Find it! Be ready! Make the adjustment necessary, sometimes while just getting by until 'the day comes'. That's it, providing that one has planned accordingly with education, attitude and social abilities various and given times. The Boy Scout's motto says, "Be prepared." Keep your eyes open! Upon finding our destiny we often say, '<u>Eureka, I've found it! - 'I did it!</u>' We all find ourselves as salesman and promoters at times, at least in the interview process.

<u>On a humorous note in my eighth grade year of school short mini skirts were hitting the scene in middle schools and high schools everywhere.</u> Administrations at various schools were changing rules right and left. Indecision ruled. One sign read 'no mini skirts' while another touted 'pant suits only' or 'no suggestive outfits allowed'. A lot of girls got sent home during the various interpretations of the female dress code. Parents also got involved and were frustrated

accordingly. This continued all the way through high school as well. Between my seventh grade and eighth grade years girls started taking on a greater sense of importance to me. The short skirts made a huge difference due to more accessibility to all kinds of legs. My eyes often saw more than I 'at this time in my life' could handle. Up and down stairways in the school and walking into classes late. These female viewpoints caused my heart rate to pulse rapidly, at times. It seemed to me that the whole room was enveloped in temptation, at least in my 'guilty mind'. I was having the struggle between looking and not looking which led to most young men's confusion and delight at the same time. I often found myself looking 'down at the ground'. I wasn't really sure what I might see next. I have found myself doing this at times as a way of coping.

During these 'crazy times' is when my science teacher asked me to give a presentation to the class. I worked on the presentation very hard and was prepared except for one thing I hadn't expected at all. When I got up in front of the class I saw what appeared to me was 25 girls all showing their panties at once, on purpose! I got so excited that I knocked off an entire row of glass test tubes that were elevated on the science demonstration desk as they were breaking all over the floor. Of course, I jumped down to rescue what I could and I never did have the chance to give that science report. I think the teacher knew exactly what had just happened because she told all the girls to wait after the class dismissed. I watched from a distance peering down the hall as they departed the class. Many were just giggling as they confidently and powerfully walked in their various directions. They all knew exactly how they messed me up. For I had just been had by a bunch of abundantly sorted female underwear exposures! I recalled what my Mom told my sister," You girls just don't realize how you look to boys and men when wearing such revealing skirts". You can say that again as I realized that I was a small part of the women's liberation reaction movement in southern Indiana. Seemingly our Indiana Governor had just banned the song, 'Louie, Louie' it was hardly selling, until after the Governor's ban, the song went to 1,000,000 dollars + in sales. In a great sense 'no' often meant 'yes' boundaries were being stretched.

Opportunities often at first glance, aren't recognized; in fact we often don't believe. Many years later my son-in-law Zac showed the

<u>real</u> 'Rudy' around the space command, this guy had an unrelenting faith and belief system at 5'6" and a 'huge heart'. This giant of a little man, the movie 'Rudy' via Norte Dame who was a speaker at the Air Force missile base 'Rudy is a motivational speaker for the Air Force and other organizations' better known as Malthus Aerospace Command where Captain Zac and my daughter Captain Amy were respectively 'educators and evaluators' for missileers 'those who man our countries nuclear missile arsenals- sites' in Great Falls Montana and surrounding areas. Zac was appointed to show Rudy around the base. He couldn't get over how much the real Rudy of the movie 'Rudy' acted and talked so much like me. We both came from Indiana and played football 2 years apart. I did very well in small college football and often displayed more desire to play than ability to play; in a great sense/much like Rudy! I have a picture of the real Rudy tackling the quarterback from Georgia Tech sent to me by my son-in-law Captain Zac and signed by the real Rudy! "Rudy simply wrote his phrase as It sits on the inside wall in front of our school. I have found it important to outperform, in whatever you do, if possible, regardless in any situation that is worthy of one's interest. In-other-words giving my best effort must be the standard, for any situation or circumstance; whether at work, play or with friends. It always pays dividends with almost everyone involved. Sometimes it's best to just believe. Ruby believed and accomplished his dream. How about yours? Did it take time, yes. Did anyone else believe him, no. Did he continue anyway, yes. Did he play one play for Notre Dame, yes (and was carried off the field). Did he influence his siblings, yes. They all graduated and completed their dreams at various colleges. One person, Rudy changed his entire family's perspective of one another. Not to mention the movie goers. Rudy signed the picture my son-law gave to me of the game between Notre Dame and Georgia Tech where the Rudy miracle occurred he wrote, "Gary...Believe" With faith of a mustard seed the scriptures tell us, we can move our mountains.

"Nothing really can be completed without a goal, while dreaming with faith and the various actions offered to accomplish it" Gary Cooper. I stand by this statement!

<u>The power of a coach!</u> The Vietnam War was just starting up when I was in my first year of junior high school $7^{th}$ grade. By this time

my various coaches were almost super human like symbols of leadership and authority. I knew that I needed this kind of authority as no one else was giving much of anything except my Boy Scout leaders in the period prior to Jr. High School. Scouting taught me many things regarding camping, leadership, sacrifice as we accomplished many scout type walks up to 50 miles. During this time period I witnessed so many dismal events. I had friends and relatives get killed and injured in all manner and various ways. Every one of them seemed shocking, depressing and useless. One cousin got killed flying a powered model airplane with a wire string as it hit an electrical power pole in the large lawn at Grandma Cooper's house (Linden was literally fried alive as he held the line) Prior to this horrible accident, I begged my Dad to let me stay and fly Linden's plane (Linden had promised that he would let me fly the plane) but Dad emphatically said, "We have to get home!" I didn't want to leave. Dad saved my life! Goodbye Linden. This was my first realized close call. I also felt really sorry for Grandma Cooper who had lost her son Irwin(my Uncle), many years before when her seemingly most promising child was innocently shot with a real gun that was thought to be play gun, tragedy happened again with Linden and Grandma left that house shortly thereafter as I recall.. My 5 year old cousin Diane died while playing with matches and dove into bed with her plasticized dress stuck to her which embedded into her skin over 70% of her little body, I will never forget my young age at 6 years and my sister 8 years of age. Waiting at a White Castle Hamburger Restaurant across from the Indianapolis hospital, while Mom and Dad did their part and sit with her in the burn unit (no kids allowed) It took Diane several months after intense suffering and pain providing for a merciful death/ no more pain. I'll never forget Diane she and I played a lot before her gruesome accident. Her brother, Owen Neal was 2 years behind me in high school. In Owens's sophomore year I was very interested and proud that my cousin was a wrestler. I remember wishing him the best but he didn't seem much interested. Later, as a high school dropout at age 16, after getting hooked on drugs(Acid-LSD) cousin Owen put a pistol to his chest and pulled the trigger after spending months in mental hospitals with drug intervention. Fellow Boy Scout Ronnie Dunn got killed as a drunken driver ran over him while riding his bike on the highway coming to our scout meeting. That was the first time I had ever had a part in a funeral.

The scout troop all showed up in uniform representing our friend Ronnie. The week before he died, Jerry Diewert told me at $9^{th}$ grade football practice, 'He would probably get killed this weekend with his crazy driving cousin' and that is exactly what happened. I saw my neighbor and my sister's friend Lorrie die the $2^{nd}$ week she got her driver's license in a car wreck as her car flipped over as she received head injuries near a railroad track. When I was in high school several people I knew vaguely died but I too had another extremely close call my sophomore year when my good friends, the Paul brothers, Charlie and Bill asked me to go skiing with them out at Grandview Lake, normally I would happily fly out the door to go…this particular time I told them I was behind in my homework and I just couldn't go, otherwise I wouldn't have missed it. They had a sporty convertible Ford Mustang they were driving, on the way to the lake they swerved and flipped the car over a log ( I would have been in the back seat, exactly where the log stuck as the car flipped) they were not hurt and they afterwards said, "We are very glad you didn't go with us." Whew, I could have been on the above 'death list!' *Life can be dangerous to your health, be careful.* One's will must be used with great care while measuring risk whenever possible. I have also learned that 'Driving is the most dangerous thing most people do on a daily basis!'

The halls in my Jr. high school were always social and at times challenging. A new arrival from California made his entrance. He was one grade above me in school. He was 9th grade and I was in eighth grade. He told everyone, "I'm a black belt in karate". He for whatever reason did not like me. One day on the hall stairs he intentionally bumped me (in front of my girlfriend) and said, "I'm going to kick your butt!" We both agreed to meet on the football field after school and fight. He had the edge: higher class, karate expert, skilled in battle? I didn't know and was genuinely concerned this guy just might kick my butt. So we met. Kids were everywhere and I told him, "You started this, you have to throw the first punch."

The rest is history. I brutally beat this guy so badly he was hospitalized for several days. The school officials were clearly upset and I thought 'He started this and I finished it'. Not true, the police were called in and contacted me saying my hands were now considered '<u>extreme deadly weapons</u>' and I would be charged if I got in another fight. They explained to me, "We don't care who started the fight because you almost killed that kid!" I tried very hard not to get in anymore fights I once again was dangerous no one wanted to fight me anyway. I could have been a felon just because of my hands and maybe my feet. Once again I was still somewhat enabled this time by circumstances.

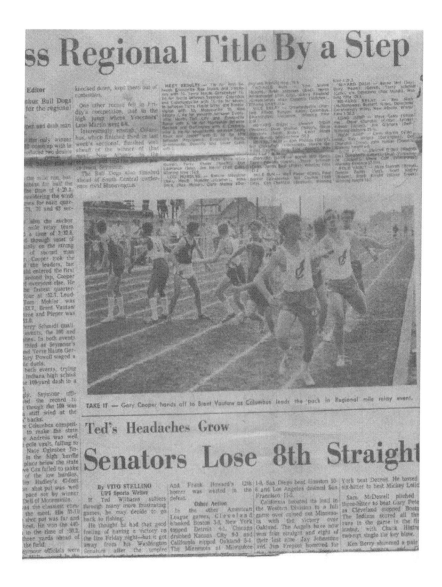

*Grade school, Jr .High School or High School friends gave me a picture and much to their surprise, I kept them. I didn't have any brothers and only one sister. I used to look at these pictures and imagine the possibilities. Football, Basketball, Track, gym, the school hallway of a really big school, the walks all around the school between classes, class rooms and breaks. I still remember each picture's (above) name and faces. There are still a lot of friends that aren't up there either. I suppose they didn't give me their school photo.*

<u>Sometimes Mothers have to leave.</u> During my sophomore year my mother and I simply were not getting along very well. I was trying to grow up 'with some slight rebelliousness' Mom had a person down the street name Mary. Mary was clearly an alcoholic. Mom had great compassion for drunks/alcoholics and I felt sorry for them as I wished I could help them at times, at this time in my life, I had a feelings of a certain type of hopelessness, possibly because of Mom...

Without any warning Mom and Mary impulsively decided to take a train trip. I was president of my sophomore class and serving on the student council, doing well athletically and I was licensed to drive a car. I thought I could somewhat take care of myself. So Mom and Mary decided their worthiness as parents was declining. My sister was gone and married and it was clear I would soon be out of the door...so to speak. I was not given any notice of this event except one day after football practice Mom met me at the back door and said, 'Gary, Mary and I are taking a train trip and nobody knows including your dad." I was somewhat shocked that Mom would take off with Mary. But I didn't let on 'I really did not know what to say' and drove Mom and Mary to the train station. I said a faint goodbye and she kissed me and told me 'She loved me'. She also asked me 'to not tell Dad until he returned from a business trip on Friday'. I said,"OK" and she gave me her car keys and left. Suddenly, I felt a sense of tremendous independence! I convinced myself to not feel sorry for myself. In a way I felt that Mom possibly needed a trip...

I proceeded to tell my fate to my friends. Accordingly I walked into a liquor store and with a 'face of a serious man' bought 3 big bottles of wine, liquor and beer. I had priory decided with my friends to have an impromptu- last minute party! With my friends putting out the word the party was on! Anybody and everybody was welcome and everyone seemingly had a good/great time. I took money for the alcohol and bought more as needed. No one could believe I had the confidence and looks to buy alcohol at age 16. The house was quickly filled with many fellow students from school. It lasted 2-3 hours and I had a work crew for cleanup. Party over. I never heard the first comment from any kids at school. I may have had one of the cleanest drinking parties in history no wrecks, no parents, no cops, and a beautiful clean sweep. My girlfriend Debbie didn't even know of the party. She really did care about my 'lack of a Mom'.

Debbie was considerably more shocked that Mom would take off. She was truly concerned and begged me to come eat at her house. The food was great as Mrs. Scheldt cooked 'short ribs' I felt as if I was in 'temporary heaven'. I mostly ate junk food in comparison. Although, I didn't like anyone feeling 'sorry for me'! When Dad got home he didn't react except to make sure there was food and money for me. I think he must have somehow expected this but didn't tell or forewarn me. School/sports and my busy school life went on. I just couldn't see Mom hanging around very long with

Mary due to her illness. Mom returned home the next month and she and Dad quickly made up. I could tell I was the only one out of the communication regarding this event while Mary went back to her family and died over the next several months. I couldn't help but sense her family's hopelessness also.

I'm not really sure I understood what really happened except that I had become somewhat lonely and simply glad to have her back. Mom's only comment to me was 'staying in the same room with a drunk was an experience she never wanted to happen again.' For once in my life I felt that maybe 'Mom learned a lesson'. Normalcy of life continued. The trust issue did present a bigger problem at times. But this was my mother! About this time in our lives the women's liberation movement was becoming known. A lot of traditions particularly in American families were now up for debate. I remember discussing 'my hair length' with my dad. I relented and cut my hair with an emotional protest. *After all Jesus had long hair! Why couldn't I?*

During this period of time I learned several things regarding my mortality. I surmised, life is short, make the best of it and 'Life isn't always fair'. To this very day I still believe this and hope to remind others accordingly. I find that almost every person has good intentions for their respective families especially their own children. I have learned the difference between being' infamous' especially with self centered individuals concerning evil thoughts regarding others mostly due to man-revenge/woman-sex/money-power, misguided belief patterns, etc.

Conversely as to one becoming famous (being known for some good idea that you have provided for others) are in many ways very similar except for the motivating goodness through God's love and/or having truly good intentions for others. I also believe that most people want to be known for something…the big question is what, who or how. My young life required me to either get <u>bitter</u> (due to semi intelligent excuses, etc.) or get <u>better</u> whether good or bad events occur regardless of outcome, because of a simple faith that God himself will lead me otherwise. We are all combinations of mind, spirit and body and hopefully each of us will keep each aspect balanced and healthy. My and your life will truly be in a sense famous because you will affect others individual/group in a good manner with a positive intent. My mother, father and many others are somewhat ' famous to me' because of their positive and kind responses regardless of circumstance or the many challenges of life.

# The Unconscious Competent

There comes a time in your life when you must make a life or death decision. Some of us do it often with high risk occupations/life styles like deep sea welders, high rise welders and steelworkers, close tolerance crop dusters/aircraft pilots, emergency room doctors and staff, military forward personnel, race car drivers, mountain climbers, etc. Due to enhanced wisdom with some close calls while in grade school and high school I felt relatively secure from any outside threats except for two fellow upper classmates who played high school football with me. Enter Larry and David; both were excellent upper class football players who were now playing football at relatively large colleges. Larry was a 3rd string tackle at Purdue University and David was a starting linebacker at Miami of Ohio. My senior year had gone very well athletically, except for my girlfriend breaking up with me. Although this time, I was temporarily and almost crushed emotionally much more than I expected for a longer while. As a result, it was time to do something!

*The faces of kindness, possibilities and great school life friends...memories never to be forgotten. They have become fading memories of fondness...*

I liked to go out cruising (riding around in the car) with one of my best friends who also played football. He was our football team's quarterback, we both had great football scholarship offers during these times weighing and deciding which College choice we should each make. Possible tough choices may seem easy but in reality were some of my toughest decisions to make <u>at this time in my life</u>.

As a hoot or nutty frustration release over our mutually crazed period during these times, we didn't really want anybody else to have a good time with their babes. Especially because we didn't have any 'babes', so to speak. We figured to hassle some kids who were 'parking in the corn rows' and laughingly in our opinion, lower the teenage pregnancy rates. By crashing the scene and disturbing the intense boy/girl parking processes. Since I knew almost all the back roads 'I drove a large tractor/mower in the summer for the county highway department' would play fiendish type jokes on the county parkers 'the boys and girls who parked hoping to not be disturbed while kissing, fondling, etc.' Without saying we were interested in the etc. My teammate Dave and a few friends on occasion would go out with us, we'd slowly pull into a narrow corn row and suddenly turn on the lights and yell. "What are you doing with my daughter?" or "It's candid camera!" Almost all of the time we would hysterically laugh while pulling the vehicle out backwards and take off while we saw skin and clothes flying all around the car from our car's high beam headlights, beaming on them while frantically attempting to put their clothes back on. As they didn't know 'who was out there and for what reason?' 'God forbid their parents were really there!'. Somehow our former high school football teammates, (David and Larry) heard about our humorous and ridiculous pranks and called us 'Dave and me' to go out with them. They were both on Christmas break as we were also. They wanted to show us what they did or would do? We thought to ourselves, we were the 'pro bushwhackers' and they would clearly learn from us. We met with the other David and Larry in town and off we went into the boondocks, the back roads of the county. Dave, my friend and I rode in the back of their car as we pulled up to a car 'running the engine for warmth' parked on the pavement in the middle of a very cold Indiana winter night, on a very, very lonely road. We thought and whispered quietly how bold they were pulling and creeping up to a car on a paved road with the headlights off. We had never done a paved road bushwhack, we couldn't believe their boldness. They pulled out a red hot cigarette lighter and lit a very large M-80 firecracker while throwing it on the roof of the car 'that was truly scary different' and much to our chagrin, we both whispered," That might damage the car!"The fire blasted across the car's roof with a thunderous boom as the M-80 mini bomb blew up and instantly the other Dave pulled out a pistol and yelled, "What are you doing with my wife!" and started shooting the gun as the car tore down the narrowly paved road. Immediately we were thrust into a true 'life or death' car chase....Dave and I looked at each other and whispered, "We need to get out of here, how?" Every time he shot the pistol. The car at speed would plunge into the ditch back and forth, left and right, with each shot: Every single time they heard and saw fire from the pistol! Dave and I in the back seat were completely shocked and surprised but nothing like the half dressed 'stuck in the mud' looking recipients in the completely destroyed car! The chase -shooting took place down the straight of this country road. They wound up crashing off the road into an open field 'just past the T in the road' with tremendous body damage as the rear door of the car was missing while apparently stalled and the engine and radiator was fuming up in the air with laps of smoke! We, 'the four of us' just slowly turned right at the turn, looking at our 'victims total disaster' while still on the pavement, sped up and kept on going. Dave and I really wanted out that car as soon as possible while we were insincerely congratulating the two main offenders David and Larry for bushwhacking far beyond anything we could have done. We stated," You both outperformed anything we could possibly have imagined". As they dropped us off at our car sitting nearby. We each had visions of front page news the next day regarding a 'Vicious and brutal terrorist-type attack on a Bartholomew county road'! The news never came and we were so very, very glad as we would have been charged as accessories to the crime! We didn't want to' forfeit our futures' over such a dangerous and high risk prank. As a result, we never in any way disturbed parker's again. We both pondered whoever those horribly abused 'obviously guilty of, only God knows ???' People might be waiting for us with payback in mind, most likely with a shotgun! Many years later my father died and Dave, my friend came to the funeral. I had never talked with Dave very much about this event, as it happened near the end of our very busy high school days. We both had completed our football and scholarships, while attending different colleges, fraternities, girls… afterwards our dreams/plans had somewhat been met, we were both married, had children and were for the most part 'living our dreams' as time had marched on. As the funeral parties 'families and friends' were getting out of our cars for the graveside rites. Dave walked up to me and said, "Coop, do you remember David and Larry?" I tried not to laugh but no one could have said anything any funnier than my buddy Dave at that moment in time 'while the crime in college was so recent, we still might have been implicated'! But now 30 years later. What a great relief from the pent up anxiety filled memories which I know were completely repressed. That memory still held almost current in both of our conscious/subconscious minds as we exchanged one of the most shockingly-traumatic insane experiences we had ever experienced. I think we both thought the law was going to catch up somewhere but it apparently didn't. Surely, it was a major crime to say the least. Thank God. Laughter is likened to good medicine and Dave with his presence, knowledge and keen remembrance didn't necessarily honor the moment but definitely honored me with his presence and of course my father's memory during this time of humble rejoicing with God's promise that Dad will not suffer any more. It rang especially true that life is full of uncertainty and yet let's not forget to put all of this in perspective. The funeral ended, all parties had to go. And my precious father is much better off, no more suffering from the pathetic effects *of* dementia; he was a believer as was my mother, 'who predeceased him'. They each left a heritage of love, mercy, care, concern and my sister and I am better off because of it. One other thought grabbed me. 'My sister and myself are the oldest now....we're next!' And thanks be to God the infamous 'Dave and Larry' wasn't at the funeral...

# How to Really Wrestle a Bear

At this point High School was basically over as Dave Andress, Terry Schmidt and I were the only athletes in our class of (1100 students) elevated and slated for obtaining 'Senior Blankets' for winning and earning points due to participating in multiple athletic endeavors such as football, track, basketball, etc. in addition all the other Seniors were presented with academic, drama, etc. and social awards were given also with diplomas. All of this while the typical High School graduation was taking place. It was now late summer/fall. The Bartholomew county fair had made its appearance once again. This was no ordinary fair. It had all kinds of rides, events, politicians, farm equipment displays, field displays, auto displays, musical tributes, car crash events and so on. My sister and brother-in-law were visiting from Atlanta where he had recently played basketball for Georgia Tech and was now in the Army. We all decided to go visit and revisit our old stomping grounds at our big hometown county fair. This fair reminded me of the state fair of Indiana, it seemed bigger every year at least during my High school days.

Enter...with shock... at the fair! <u>David and Larry,</u> 'these were the maniacs who fairly recently engineered the blow up the car, gun chase', I in my gut… shuddered when they saw and approached me, I thought to myself as they came closer "Oh No!" David said, "Coop you've got to see this!" I immediately remembered...One of the winning coaches in my life was my $9^{th}$ grade coach, Mr. Russell Owens 'this man was the winningest Jr. High coach in Southern Indiana where 10-0 seasons were expectations not just hope(s) with words, but action'. Coach Owens said," <u>Excuses don't go on the scoreboard</u>". We all really bought into his concepts '<u>somebody might beat us but nobody's going to out condition us</u>'. In one ninth grade football game we weren't executing properly and he made us review and run plays at halftime. Regardless, we beat that team and were turned about from our bad play.

This was certainly one time in my almost adult life, that I really used an excuse 'Flat out lie or do anything' to throw Dave and Larry off. As I nervously with energy stated, "My sister and brother-in-law are with me." I thought this would somewhat misguide or throw them off. They said, "That's Ok, bring them along too". Susan my sister said, "I don't mind going" she didn't mind because she didn't know anything about 'the criminal mischief almost near death shooting- bushwhack event' I hadn't told anyone at this point and off we did go. I just knew somehow, in my gut, things weren't somehow going to go well. We all walked the back way through the fairground towards the apparent end lot of the fair; we all finally stumbled upon their find. I couldn't believe my eyes! Here was a huge brown/ black bear on the stage extending its big body and paws while sitting on a stool relaxed and stretching out slightly above the very large observant crowd as it sat there drinking one Pepsi after another. Within the same glance I saw a very large farm boy with overalls walk out of the arena side ramp looking disheveled, beaten up and worn out. He clearly was one of this bears victims. I immediately turned to my sister and laughingly said, "What kind of idiot would wrestle that bear". As I continued to really 'lock on' while I was truly fascinated with what I saw on the stage 'temporarily forgetting about the fiendish David and Larry' all eyes were forward to the stage events, David and Larry said, "Coop come up here so you can see this a little better!" Without thought or hesitation I impulsively moved visually-mentally locked on the bear. Almost immediately I jumped up on the smallish side elevated platform I suddenly felt myself starting to wonder... why we were the only ones up here?... A few seconds later my wonders would be horribly confounded. It was dusk and getting darker as the stagehands <u>spotlight suddenly beamed</u> on us as the ringmaster boldly stated, <u>"These three college football players are going to wrestle Gentle Ben!"</u> while he was touting the crowd to buy tickets as they were about to enter the large tented arena. I thought to myself I can't believe this. 'They got me again!' referring to the '<u>almost criminal auto event</u>' with two of the craziest/maniacs I have ever known. There is a saying, 'first mistakes their fault, second times my fault' I see this happen all the time especially in marriages where either party marries the same type person with similarly personality traits of the former spouse that he or she divorced in the first place with nothing really much changed, except the body.

I just fell into the same hole with a different venue that 'got me' just like the first time! Dave and Larry!!!! Initially I almost took off running to just escape but just then I boldly stated 'In the meanest, totally sincere and most disrespectful way I could, I am not going to fight that damn bear!" Immediately Larry said, "Coop, we need you! '*Now they were at my mercy!*' They have to have three people. Anyway you won't even have to wrestle the bear, I'm going to win the $1,000 dollars" David chimed in the same statement except 'he was going to win the money'. After all, I was now somewhat 'keeping my cool' while the spotlight was on us 'peer pressure' and I figured if they are so highly motivated I schemed,' I will be the last participant to wrestle Gentle Ben as they really needed me to fill the roster for the event.' Much more calmly with confidence I said, "Ok I'll wrestle the bear only if you two go first and tell me exactly what you are going to do before you wrestle." They agreed. I was now somewhat, getting a little bit excited about this event. Bear wrestling! I must be crazy! Entering with these unstable thoughts of desperation 'valley of death' or 'very anxious' 'or 'morbidly curious' this was the way I felt like prior to taking on this potentially hazardous unique event. As we entered the very large tent we were placed just outside the cage up on a platform overlooking the large audience. It reminded me of the set/cage in the movie 'Silence of the Lambs' and we were the lambs! I was particularly pleased to see that Gentle Ben had a muzzle placed around his mouth! Thank God! While the ringmaster was telling the crowd how one of these young men could win $1,000 dollars in addition to other various statements gave me the time to inquire as to, "How are you planning on wrestling this bear?" to Larry the first participant to enter. Larry said, "I'm going to bear hug the bear" 'I thought to myself. Larry's statement was a perfectly formed oxymoron, maybe the most ridiculous statement I had ever heard.' I told him 'he was crazy, that it won't work'! He said he knew it would work. I just shook my head and said "No way" 'The 270 pound ' Larry was escorted into the cage and put out his arms to bear hug the bear, The bear weighed 450+ pounds and the bear 'I think' kind of smiled and put Larry down like a sack of potatoes. 1, 2, and 3 you're out! Larry was gone! Immediately I turned to David, "Let me guess, you are going to bear hug the bear" David said, "No way Coop, I'm going to arm lock and throw the bear" I simply said, "I've got to see this" David was a very good linebacker who was obviously more creative than lineman Larry, but not creative enough. David entered the cage and for the first time 'Gentle Ben's eyes' looked a little bit concerned. David ran around in circles and grabbed Gentle Ben while locking his wrist and arm, big mistake! The bear stopped in arm lock position, simply stabilized himself and started twirling David in the air like a cowboy twirls his rope 'David was in the air, totally and completely helpless'. I couldn't believe the power of that bear he then crashed David down on the mat and pinned him…1, 2, 3 you're out! <u>I was next</u>! As they carried disheveled David out of the arena my mind suddenly went into hyper drive, similar to the time I had the bike and tree crash. It occurred to me one time as a small boy with my Dad, Uncle John Lynn and Cousin Leslie were on our way in the ballpark to see the Chicago Cub's baseball team play. In the stadiums walk up was a thick rounded rail about 4 feet off of the ground simply used to direct foot traffic. I somehow grabbed that rail and flipped about 4 feet away on the other side perfectly vertical on my feet. Dad and Uncle John were amazed and asked, "Gary could you do that again?" I simply said, "No, I don't think so" <u>Sometimes we all have signs of competence way beyond even our personal scopes of expertise</u>. It was now time to call on a competence way beyond the norm. <u>I needed to be a consciously competent (in this case) Bear Wrestler with a subconsciously competent response.</u> I concentrated, peered and completely scoured that bear visually just seconds prior to my Bear Wrestling Event (my mind was on hyper speed again) *until I noticed his little feet*. Yes that was it, Thank God, his feet! <u>Now I really wanted to sucker the bear into thinking I was another 'Larry the Dumb Bear Hugger'</u>. I now had a <u>quick plan that might work</u>. Later on in my life, quick thinking would be very helpful as well. Particularly if one decides to plan and utilize the 3 basics of a good life… None of this comes without solid well thought out planning with action. At the time I was not using anything near the 3 basics of life. Sometimes we just get undeserved merit…grace, especially if we choose a low risk lifestyle. Unfortunately, this night was not low risk! This was what I thought might come later.

Spirit – a healthy relationship with God
Mind – Keeping a mind healthy requires exercise plus 1 and 2 as well

Body – Eat a balanced diet with vigorous exercises 3-4 times per week

And GRACE…undeserved merit. As I entered the bear cage, I had a simple plan and the bear just calmly peered at me like I would be the easiest, simplest, possibly fun wrestling event of the day. I possibly appeared weak or maybe even small...compared to the other two just before me! The bear literally appeared to have given me 'his eyes of compassion' and maybe even <u>pity for me.</u> I think that was probably much the same way as in the Old Testament where 'Goliath looked and toyed with David'. Regardless the bear moved slowly forward and I moved slowly forward with my arms straight out 'just like Larry'. The bear's large chunky arms were out to meet me. <u>As we got just close enough to touch. I instantly dropped to my knees and pulled as hard as I possibly could on the back his feet, 'both at once'! Bam! Ker plop! The bear hit the floor mat with a tremendous thud, the crowd went wild!</u> I jumped very quickly on the bear (holding on just as a wrestler would) as he was desperately flailing his paws around in large circles trying to grab something/anything! <u>With huge amounts of adrenalin, the sheer fact that I had this bear down 'on his back' was shocking to me, It worked! I had done it again! Plus $1,000 bucks!</u>

I balanced the bears pointy rounded back. It wasn't flat like I expected at all? I looked up turning to the ringmaster and said, "Where's my money?" He said "You have to pin the bear on his shoulders" right! A 450 pound monstrous bear on his shoulders! I suppose we should have had a specific legal and binding contract with the ringmaster prior to this incredible event. After a few long minutes of holding the bear up on his pointy rounded backbone, with no reward forthcoming I let go and stood up, the bear rolled over, he stood up fast and started running after me! I suddenly realized that payback might have a price, that is the bear was clearly a competitive creature and might try to hurt me somehow, I wasn't sure. After circling the round ring for a few minutes 'which seemed like hours' I decided to let him 'get me 'I really didn't like that idea of him 'getting me" at all, but I was getting tired. I looked around and he was gaining on me! I'm sure the crowd was also wearing down and getting quiet or concerned or both, at this point. With a very determined look on his big hairy muzzled face! Not at all like the way he looked at me prior to the wrestling match, much more serious! The tables were turned, it seemed like he was laboring to get a shot at me. The unanswered question simply was; in what manner? Was he going to maul me? Crush me? Pull me apart? I didn't have a clue and the ringmaster wasn't giving me any advice while sprinting each circular pass! <u>There comes a time when one just has to 'Give Up'</u>. I had reached that not enviable point. Oh my God! Another no win situation except to survive. I decided to just lie down and let him have a real shot at getting me back. Total submission was not my style but absolutely necessary. As Gentle Ben jumped on me, I didn't move a muscle at this point I was shocked once again. He was very heavy but I had 2 and 3 football players on me in the past, I could take that. I lay very still as to not incite additional physical actions from Ben. <u>He obviously didn't kill me but he did seriously lick me</u>, while putting all of his weight on me while extending his extremely long tongue through his muzzle and licked me like a 'car going through a mechanical car wash' nothing was missed not my eyes, not my ears, not my nose, not my face…I was attacked by a giant hard/soft tongue as wet as a towel. Somehow it suddenly ended as the trainer got him off of me. I had lain so still it probably concerned him-the Ringmaster. I finally stood up while he soothed the bear and once again brought out the bear treats.

The Ringmaster finally said something, "I had to let him do this or he would have taken his frustration out on you, in some other manner, which you wouldn't have liked!" I got up and walked toward the exit. I personally couldn't imagine a better outcome for me considering that I had been duped into this fiasco by my so called scheming friends who I gladly and literally never saw again. Those two nuts didn't even come to congratulate me after this semi shallow victory. 'I suppose their Bear wrestling pride couldn't or wouldn't let them'. Upon reuniting with my sister and brother in law they couldn't believe what they just saw either. <u>Truly I was once again a type of conscious or unconscious competent. It was almost as easy as flipping over the iron bar at the Chicago Cubs stadium as a small boy</u>. Except the fans/witnesses weren't there, the bear and ringmaster weren't there, and certainly the hope of a reward wasn't there. Ironically the ringmaster said, "You really did a good job with Ben, would you like to have a rematch? "I said,

"No…" with a couple of curse words without further explanation as I quickly walked out of the arena. Life is good. But it did give me a special perspective for college football. <u>No one is as big as Gentle Ben!</u>

I really didn't tell anybody what I had done at the time. I knew they wouldn't believe me, but my sister and brother-in-law saw it! Life went on as expected for me. College football, a full ride (full scholarship) 1) No college loans or payments, very nice! 2) The hope of new friends and girlfriends! 3) An education that would be unlike any other in recent times, my immediate family had never gone to college, except for my Uncle, Kenny Cooper, who played basketball at Franklin College but didn't graduate for whatever reason. 4) I didn't have to make any military commitment for 4 years, I had the college deferment and my draft number was 270 'the military draft board only took the first 100'. I felt very thankful to have a quality opportunity at this point in time for my life. All I had to do was play football, run track and keep a 2.00 grade point. The scholarship even paid my fraternity dues and/or percentage of room and board if I got married during the four year term.

# (THE LITTLE POND) Franklin College of Indiana

FC was the place for me! The choice was made, I took the full ride plus! After planning and plotting my career, 3 years via athletic efforts with 15 scholarship offers from either ½ term or full scholarships plus extra benefits/offers. I was challenged like never before. Two weeks before standard enrollment and classes, was the gruesome fall football practice. I was involved in a very intense summer/fall college football experience. The first thing that I noticed was how very, very small the college campus really was. My large high school down the road about 20 miles was bigger than FC and the high school population was 2.75% bigger than Franklin College. What had I done? From 2500 students to 900 at FC! And to top that off the school was 80% males. The girls seemed to 'have it made' at this place; of course, personally I had more competition than imagined in this uncertain world of college life for me. What have I done, football is starting very soon and almost everybody I had talked with was a split receiver just like me! They only gave 8 football scholarships per year and it seemed like the quarterback had his many picks. I really wondered could I hack it. The grades, football, lack of girls and little bitty FC. Maybe I should transfer and attend Indiana University's losing program and 'walk on' with a seemingly perpetual losing program, am I really able to leave before even starting? I put blinders on myself, I paid the price. 'Hang in there' I told myself...I felt very uncertain..I had to be careful and cautious about trusting my emotions.

Maybe I was in the wrong place and/or maybe I should just join the Army and go to Vietnam.... Football was the only thing I was somewhat sure of and here it was. I couldn't believe it I was becoming increasingly unsure of myself when I noticed just about everyone on the football team was bigger than me or so it seemed. How could this be, FC was a little place but we had some real monsters on this FC team? When Coach Faught 'one of the most famous coaches in Indiana' recruited me, I really wondered at this point, "What did he see in me?" He talked to me as having a choice of being a <u>'Big Duck in a Little Pond as opposed to a Little Duck in a Big Pond'</u> *I could be cooked duck before this thing was over.* Since I was a child my 'old friend fear' gripped me like crazy, although I felt this way only between me, myself and I, I was self guarded. I wouldn't outwardly admit it or show it. Was my foolish pride well in place? This particular year 1970 the coaches seemed like they wanted much more out of this group than ever before. I later found the FC Coaches, 'Coach Faught and Coach Chiarotti' coached the Indiana high school all-stars the summer prior to now, they really seemed motivated...to do us in? Fall football conditioning is always known as football hell but they seemed to want to find Hell's depths... After very tough routines, thrusts of all types, 40 yard dashes, pushups, three man roll ups, carrying players on your back, I liked all the hitting drills and a menu of other difficult exercises with extra conditioning, at the end of practice they decided the entire team should go around the tree lined practice field on all fours. In other words on your arms and legs without standing up as we all started, offense first and then defense. It suddenly hit me by observing the bigger guys were really starting to have problems. I even remember certain 275 pound lineman crying like babies after the first 100 yards on all fours. At this point, I became glad I was only 185 pounds as our 'receivers' were far more adept than others on all fours. Although at the end of the 600 yard trek we were all exhausted. I was overwhelmed as this 'Football hell' had just begun. In my heart, I knew I could take it but would this be worth it? FC had some 270 pound lineman that could outrun the 160-210 pound halfbacks and they had a fullback named 'Boomer' who weighed 300 and would hit the line like a tank, at little FC? I had two of my fellow high school ball players who also played at FC. One of them also had the same scholarship that I had, Gonzy. Then came Craver who had a full ride at University of Louisville when all of sudden the scholarships got cut and here he was, Craver was so mad that I think it made him one of the best middle linebackers in FC history. He was my friend and stayed mad for at least the first 3 years. Later the next year came a guy named

Hunsucker arrived from Austin Peay University another all star had landed and John Jackson an absolute physical specimen who was the Indiana High School 'heavyweight' wrestling champ 'this guy helped me like you wouldn't believe when we played later on.' How did these people get to FC!

Once again, I found it to be amazing that Head Coach Faught and Defensive Coach Chiarotti were the State of Indiana all-star coaches the year before and the players that walked off of the various big Universities, 'Everybody, including football players often have a hard time adjusting to college life anywhere' They respected the FC Coaches and they wanted their respective chance to become big ducks at FC. In time all of this recruiting wonderment was starting to make sense. For me it took at least 1 football season to figure this entire craziest out. We were in the big leagues with a small team abounding with special abilities! Gonzy, my roommate and almost everybody was bigger, stronger and seemingly smarter than me 'first grade experience was still in check-low self grade esteem'. I learned this after joining the same fraternity, SAE!

Fraternity Life had some lasting Lifetime Qualities - 'The True Gentleman'

As pledges we had to memorize this and 'state the entire document' below while holding a burning match. "I could say it fast!" While these magnificent meanings did last and last...

*THE TRUE GENTLEMAN IS THE MAN WHOSE CONDUCT PROCEEDS FROM GOOD WILL AND AN ACUTE SENSE OF PROPRIETY, AND WHOSE SELF-CONTROL IS EQUAL TO ALL EMERGENCIES, WHO DOES NOT MAKE THE POOR MAN CONSCIOUS OF HIS POVERTY, THE OBSCURE MAN OF HIS OBSCURITY, OR ANY MAN OF HIS INFERIORITY OR DEFORMITY. WHO HIMSELF IS HUMBLED IF NECESSITY COMPELS HIM TO HUMBLE ANOTHER, WHO DOES NOT FLATTER WEALTH, CRINGE BEFORE POWER OR BOAST OF HIS OWN POSSESSIONS OR ACHIEVEMENTS, WHO SPEAKS WITH FRANKNESS AND ALWAYS WITH SINCERITY AND SYMPATHY, WHOSE DEED FOLLOWS HIS WORD. WHO THINKS OF THE RIGHTS AND FEELINGS OF OTHERS RATHER THAN HIS OWN, AND WHO APPEARS WELL IN ANY*

*COMPANY, A MAN WITH WHOSE HONOR IS SACRED AND VIRTUE SAFE.*

The 'above' was an outstanding ideal for me to use the rest of my life.

## College oarsmen challenge Sugar Creek

The victorious Sigma Alpha Epsilon crew "champs at the rope" prior to the start of Thursday's annual Franklin college raft race down Sugar Creek. Crew members Don May, Mike Heppner, Steve Gonzenbach, and Gary Cooper set a new record of one hour and eight minutes in the seven-mile race from the State Road 44 bridge to Horseshoe Camp, breaking by nearly two minutes the record the same team set in last year's race.

(Daily Journal photo)

I had always dreamed and anticipated the excitement of being in a college fraternity 'my sister used to date a guy she later married named Vic of the Indiana University SAE house, the pictures of the parties literally made me imagine', great times ...dates, fun, air conditioning, study halls, etc. After a hot, grimy, sweltering 3 times per day football practice still prior to academic classes there was no place I'd rather be, it was hot in the autumn 'Indian summer' and this SAE frat house had a great air conditioner except I was now a pledge; In other words a gopher/ slave for the older members to boss around and such. Fortunately for me, they gave football players certain benefits due to our high esteemed college activity. Maybe that was what the coach meant about 'big ducks in a little pond'. The only thing I felt confident about was the SAE house, everything else was hard, football and academics. During practice I was not a standout at all. Everybody caught the football and ran various routes as good if not better than me. I was one of 9 receivers it was almost hopeless in getting a starting spot for the entire season. "I expected to play first year at FC; after all I was on a great scholarship and heavily recruited!" During the first year I found myself talking most with the Defense Coach more and more. Coach Faught was coaching the offense and he hardly said one word to me all year, why did he even recruit me? All I can assume is that maybe "I was insurance when and if others possibly might leave or get hurt", I remained $2^{nd}$ string and a brown chip. Coach Faught had names of players with brown, yellow and blue on the wall in his office. The blue meant you put out (110%Effort) all the time. The other colors weren't even in the discussion at least for me; my personal wheels were starting to turn. Maybe I could make it at this little/big place. Academically, the defensive Coach John Chiarotti simply told me to major in economics because that was as close to a business degree as you could get at FC. Chiarotti was somewhat mysterious; he was from Detroit Michigan and had a sixth sense regarding football. He was one helluva player at FC in the recent past. He was also very intense, I liked intense; during a corporate finance class he threw a piece of chalk at someone who was sleeping in the class. From that point on I never closed my eyes. Wow, I hadn't seen any teacher, instructor or anybody do anything like that since I was in $9^{th}$ grade football with one of my famous mentor/coaches Russell Owens. Coach Russ coined the phrase <u>"Excuses don't go on the scoreboard!"</u> He swore that some other team might beat us but never out conditions us. He was the only coach ever that made us run wind-sprints at halftime during a game. OK, let's get back to FC. Later on I found from my frat buddies ...'economics' was the flunk out course at FC. What have I done! Am I doomed to defeat at FC! I found myself getting mad, more mad, madder, I was merely making a 2.0 GPA the absolute minimum for the first semester to keep the scholarship, we, the pledges 'first year boys' just had hell week 'going through a variety of tortures, including a 1 mile run' No matter what they did, I thought it was fun at the good ole SAE house and I wasn't even Playing football much at FC! So in mid season at FC, I switched positions from offense to defense in football, not for this year but next. I now had a workable plan The same Coach Chiarotti who had advised me 'he really took an interest in me', told all of us who played defense after the last game of the year, meaning those of us 'like me' who wasn't invited. The rest of the team went to the Mineral Water Bowl in Excelsior Springs Missouri and I wasn't even invited, God was I mad! *"You had better make me play you!" the coach stated regarding the upcoming next year football season's defense.* With a 2.20 GPA average for the entire year, now an active member of SAE, and a challenge to make the coach play me was all I needed...

*My controlled anger was now in check and I had a plan!* My parents had recently been transferred... Memphis Tenn. It was hot and humid, perfect for physical conditioning.... and all I needed was a chance, I was not going to miss this one! 'Make me play you'. Was etched in my mind, even in my inner being... Just wait. Size of school had absolutely no bearing or relevance at this point in time...can't wait!

# "MAKE ME PLAY YOU!"

Mom and dad had just moved to Memphis Tennessee from my hometown Columbus, Indiana but in my mind I had just moved to Memphis State University, a big school with a lot of academic, social and fraternal benefits. I felt as though I knew my way around- after all I was a college sophomore.

I immediately signed up for business courses my first week at MSU and made sure the course was transferrable to FC. The manual job market was great! I got two jobs and went to night school; I was going to bump up my grade average. I was focused on one thought, "I was going to make Coach Chiarotti play me and no flunking out for me!" I worked first at Tayloe Glass Company and put glass windows in Holiday Inn units and window and glass installations; before I left the glass company I met the King of Memphis...Elvis Presley! He had broken his glass table and I got to deliver and install it with one other Tayloe Glass employee, I found it to be amazing, here was a famous man (mostly in the 50's and early 60's). The place was absolutely beautiful the landscape was perfect but the amazing part was that he built his mansion in the middle of the poorest section in town. Elvis found a way to relate to his meager beginnings. It was literally night and day from one end of the block to the other. When I saw Elvis I couldn't help but think of my 2 cousins back in Indiana, one in prison for drug dealings and the other dead from a drug-use self-inflicted gunshot to the chest. It just wasn't the right time for me to be in awe, Elvis looked slightly dirty with long dirty hair and a lot of hanger on friends, that later seemed to influence his drug problems most by enabling I suppose. I think he had just come in from one of his motorcycle rides, everybody in Memphis always saw him and his motorcycle gang, with a group like that big group they were hard to miss and Elvis would be right in the middle. He was also hard to miss, very flashy. Bye Elvis. Ironically, 25 years later I would appear on the Today

Show in New York with the other Elvis who hailed from Texas recruited by the American Movie Classics with me and various other famous named folks. Simply Google: 'Gary Cooper of Thomasville AMC Grit to Grace' as he shares with Paul Newman and Warren Beatty also via AMC. I'll tell the rest of the story later in this book. This event would cause my life to change incredibly. But I didn't know it at the time.

Shortly thereafter I switched jobs and went full time at the Tayloe Trailer Company in the fabrication and semi-truck framing business. My job was at the Mississippi barges- docks hauling fabrication materials 'very long heavy steel rolled bars' that had to be on the welder's racks several times per day at certain times. *The men mostly black looked at me with that sense of certainty and confidence in their eyes.* 'They sort of reminded me of the way that bear looked at me.' I could hear them thinking, 'That white boy is a yuppie-type, white upper income, clean cut little or no manual work history, he won't work much..." Boy were they wrong, within 2 weeks I had the entire welding crew begging me not to move any more steel bars 'just like the bear was flat on his round back flailing his arms' I would, 'in a sense get this bear'- hot steel bars taken off a barge on the Mississippi river and transfer onto the island ramps in a full power flying for the takeoff run and at various times pull and tug all the way to the fabrication center approximately 75 yards away in record time. They 'the welding crews' didn't ask the big question, why are you working your butt off pushing those steel bars? Later I did tell them I could get a great workout pushing those bars. They shook their heads like I was crazy but I didn't care. None even comprehended a college career was in their plans, but they sure liked to run the dogs at the Greyhound racing and betting in West Memphis, Arkansas. <u>I was on a mission</u>. No telling how many won as opposed to lost, but I'm convinced that much in the way of the workers family monies were lost in Arkansas. Some thought of the dog track as their only way out. Some still do. Thinking forward I could hear my NML District Manager Joe Anderson saying, "It's not what one makes is the difference but what one saves" He gave truly sound economic advice with that statement. Too bad I couldn't tell them, this part of my future was not yet mine.

The company boss heard 'part of the grumbles' regarding what I was doing and came out from the front office to watch me. He observed then approached me stating,"Son, I've seen very few ever work like you work and if you ever need a job any time, you just come see me." I fessed up with him, I told him "I really do appreciate the offer but I'm working so hard because I am going to start on 'defense at my college' and nothing is going to stop me and I appreciate once again the opportunity to push this steel on a very hot day!" As he turned away he looked back and said, "No doubt you are going to kick ass somewhere, don't leave too soon we still need you" I shrugged 'OK' as I confidently walked back, out to the barges. The welders feared me, very few breaks for them, when the steel arrived they had to weld! They couldn't wait for me to leave for college! This bear was clearly flailing on his back...

Wait till I get to FC! My goal to play was intense, I wanted my fellow athletes and opponents to fear/respect me and I was on a mission. Clearly 'my goal was to start and play football!'

After the day's work on the docks and before the Memphis State night classes I would run in a large field near a Bank Tower with a huge UP (United Planters) lighted sign hovering over it. That was my ever present point of reference that told me my Kaye Street house address was near. Memphis is big! Every day I would run that field at the highest heat temperature of the day, after work. I would run sideways and backwards all over the field. I didn't mind who or what was watching and I don't think anyone ever did. Who wants to go out in a large field at 98 degrees and 98% humidity? Except me! When I would return home I would do unlimited pushups. I literally would do pushups for ½ hour without stopping. I later would convince dad to come out and sit on my shoulders with a 50 pound weight on his lap. I could do about 100 pushups like that. I could think of nothing else except 'MAKE ME PLAY YOU'. In my limited free time I joined a strength and training gym in Memphis. That's when one Memphis State football player stated, "Steroids really help most of us on the team, they build us up faster and stronger" My cousin's death and jail time effects on the entire family allowed me to simply state, "I'm not going to cheat myself out of being the best I can be without shortcuts on my team" I stated this with a sincere and confident boldness. "I'm simply not going to cut any corners". And I didn't. Later that summer my former high school girlfriend Debbie flew into Memphis and I was going to meet her and show her all around Memphis. She had contacted me prior to and stated she was going to a 'Pi Phi Sorority regional meeting' before our meeting and she had the weekend free. Great, I got off work the welders were delighted for me to pick her up at Memphis Regional Airport and drop her off at home with Mom and Dad ' she would stay in the spare room' I would then go back to work, later expecting a great time with her as we would travel my haunts in Memphis. Wrong! Sometimes the greatest plans turn to folly!

When her plane landed and she got off the plane she met me ½ way on the outside ramp approaching the airport facilities/hanger. She did not look happy, "You didn't tell me you were pinned to Janet! I was sitting in the jet by a Franklin College Pi Phi named Kathleen Hodgens, Janet's best friend'' as I recently had given Janet my fraternity pin which is a big deal but Debbie was my old friend also. I didn't have any expectations. In hindsight it appears Debbie was also excited to see me, by her reaction. Maybe F.C. looked better than the Indiana University social life? Her breeding really showed up, Sorority-loyalty at all costs with that old friend jealousy. That's a great trait except I was leaving the door open to our relationship ever so slightly. I was kind of hoping she would possibly make me change my mind to reignite our mutual love or friendship for each other. If nothing else eliminate the former relational battlefield so we could just talk. Or so I thought….regardless, Debbie wouldn't come off the tarmac and after a very limited unsatisfactory decision mostly by her; she got back on that plane, never to see her again as a single beautiful girl. The reason I was very disappointed was simply because Debbie and I had some unfinished business as former almost major big time lovers, we broke up with her dating another boy and an ensuing emotional and jealous tirade displayed by me right in front of the dean of boys office, boy was I mad. The dean saw me through his big office window as my display of anger would have caused a much different response otherwise but the 'Dean of boys' didn't even come out. We had a regional track meet coming and I was one of the main runners.. He didn't want to chastise me; I was a former class president and student council participant. Politics man Politics….Debbie and I pretty much ran the Young Republicans organization of Southern Indiana, great times good and bad. Maybe we could just be friends and maybe not, either way I simply wanted to close or open the door with a little more ease of pain, if nothing else. As I saw this, I wasn't engaged or anything at least not yet. After all my high school days were the most emotional heart wrenching and moving ordeals with specific young women that I had ever been through up to this time. <u>Sometimes we miss our greatest catch by inches(whether fishing or with lovers), I would never really know this girl, bye Debbie.</u>

In a sense I had now 'wrestled the bear of love?' Whether I won or not if there is such a thing, sometimes all one can say is, "I tried and I just might try again..."

I thought to myself, redirect Gary. Get back on track you sure can't leave your heart in suspension with former loves forever and I loved Janet as well, especially with our shared goals. Janet was my 'little sister' most fraternities and sororities have the little sister, big brother designation, at least in the early 70's' in my fraternity and National Charters, as her big brother I was supposed to lead her with my best interests aside. Due to our mutual natures and personal characteristics, she became my girlfriend as I was somewhat trying to protect her from someone with sorted intentions. We later were pinned, later engaged and we were married by my senior year in college. Very few people really get closures from their former girl friends or boyfriends. I just moved on. Some people call this type relationship 'soul ties' I was definitely loosening this knot.

Summer in Memphis was coming to an end and I was enroute to pick up Steve Gonzenbach 'Gonzy' his nickname' my former high school teammate and present college footballer at FC/SAE House roommate/fraternity brother who now lived in Conway Arkansas. Gonzy and I thought it to be amazing that our Dad's were both transferred within 200 miles of each other in totally different professions in the mid south. It was about time to head up to Indiana. We both met each other in our new habitats as Gonzy had great rivers and nature in Arkansas while I had the Memphis night-life scene. One can only see so many bars and nightclubs, I really enjoyed going down some rivers and waterfalls in a canoe near his new hometown, and his Conway area river was full of fish and water moccasins. I brought my pistol and shot snakes right and left, I don't remember catching hardly any fish? Summer was coming to an abrupt end.

The time was now. Go North! Football season, fall and Indian summer, my sophomore year. I was due! I picked up Gonzy in Conway for the Northern trip to Franklin College. It was amazing as we were traveling north the song came on the radio, "Indiana wants me…" This would be a year of destiny for Franklin College and NAIA college football and we were about to embark upon a season to remember! Gonzy was the player of the year our freshman year at F.C., he was an outstanding athlete. I had increased my weight from 185 to 205 'solid muscle' over my summer blitz in Memphis and Gonzy really seemed to take notice. He was a linebacker and he predicted I was going to be either a linebacker, defensive end or defensive back. Due to his freshman year he had some authority regarding some input over limited futuristic player positions as team captain, of course the coaches were final. I didn't care; in fact I didn't want any political help as long as I earned my right to play! I told Gonzy all about my exercise program. He was very impressed and felt certain a spot would be created for me. Boy was Gonzy and the rest of the team going to find out! This just might be my best 'Wrestling the Bear' event of my life!

# 1972-FRANKLIN COLLEGE & THE NAIA NATIONAL CHAMPIONSHIPS

*1st football event of national prominence in Franklin College history*

*Deemed the winningest team of all colleges in Indiana 1972*

*Deemed the smallest team (890) student population to play in NAIA National College Playoffs -Wall Street Journal 1972*

*Longest Punt in NAIA history 'Big Cat' Evan Williams 'World Long Drive Champ'*

*Home of Terry Hoeppner Coach of Indiana University and Miami of Ohio*

*Home of Coach 'Red Faught' Indiana and Kentucky Hall of Fame*

*Defensive Accomplishment from 1972 - Phenomenal Historical Results:*

1) Fewest yards gained rushing in a single game (17) Anderson College
2) Fewest points in a single season (10 games) 106 points
3) Fewest yards gained by rushing for season (10 games) 1093 yards
4) Fewest Touchdown Passes by opponent for a season (10 games) 6
5) Fewest Touchdowns by rushing for a season (10 games) 5

- <u>Indiana University would not and refused to play a preseason practice game with Franklin College for fear of losing. 1972</u>

After a 7 hour mid south to Midwest journey we arrived in Franklin Indiana. The anticipation for our team was evident. Our first event was going to the wedding of Francis Knue, a large tackle on the defense. Of course, Coach Chiarotti was there and was he glad to see both of us. He stated to me that you have the appearance of

## Franklin Sets Sights on Saturday's NAIA Playoffs

FRANKLIN, Ind. (UPI) — Franklin and Northwestern of Iowa collide here Saturday in an NAIA Division II football playoff, and if the two teams live up to their regular season performances, the game should develop into an offensive battle.

Tickets for Saturday's game are on sale at all First National Bank and Irwin Union Bank branches of Columbus. Cost of tickets is $5 and $4 for reserved seats and $1 for children up to 12 years of age. Standing room tickets will be sold for $2 each.

Both the host Grizzlies and the visiting Raiders were tied for fourth place in the final Division II ratings of the National Association of Intercollegiate Athletics. Franklin with an 8-1 season slate and Northwestern with a 9-0 record.

The winner advances to the divisional title game Dec. 2 against the winner of the Missouri Southern-Doane game.

Franklin fans have been calling their team "Big Red's Machine," combining coach Stewart "Red" Faught's name with the nickname associated with the baseball Cincinnati Reds. Both the Grizzlies and Northwestern have top flight quarterbacks to spark their offensive might.

Franklin's Phil Powell in four varsity campaigns threw 59 touchdown passes, despite missing three games this season with an ankle injury.

Northwestern's Curt Krull threw 20 scoring aerials this past season as the Raiders gained more than 1,400 yards in the air.

Franklin, whose only loss was to powerful Ashland in the season opener, averaged 407 total yards per game this season—214 through the air and 193 on the ground.

Fullback Ron Doyle spear heads the running attack. He picked up 1,001 yards for an average of 5.1 yards per carry, and averaged 111.2 yards a game.

Bob Zerr and Mike McClure also tote the ball well and double as pass receivers.

The Grizzlies also have Joe Bath as a backup quarterback. He filled in for Powell this season and threw for five touchdowns and scored two himself in guiding three Franklin wins.

Tom Martin rates as the top Franklin pass receiver, hauling in 58 aerials for a school season record.

Northwestern has relatively small but quick lines which have displayed consistency, but offense is the Raiders' forte.

someone who has come to play defense this year. I was shocked! I was still in my suit coat for the wedding. How could he tell? Even Jeff Craver the big middle linebacker said, "Man have you made a difference in your appearance!" I couldn't believe the response before I took the field! I was really pumped now! I was very willing that my appearance would be more than justified by my effort during our football preseason practices. Two days later we finally took the field. Sizing helmets, pads, bandages, rib pads, neck pads, etc., I never could find a helmet that fit me right. So I compromised with the slightly bigger one as opposed to smaller tighter one. I told the coaches and they said it didn't matter. Boy were they wrong, It didn't matter with my play but my teammates in the later years all stated that when I tackled someone my helmet would be pointed backwards. They didn't seem to remember the 17 quarterback sacks I got that year or the refusal of not letting any offensive halfbacks ever get around my end the entire year! <u>But Coach Chiarotti never forgot!</u>

When practice started in fall of 1972 I found myself excelling in all aspects. I could do the drills without a hitch and joyfully handle anything they gave me. Coach Chiarotti always liked what he called the 'bull in the ring' this was a drill where one or two come at you with pads and the bull is the football player in the middle repelling the attackers. This was one of the drills I had dreamed about playing and proving (make me play you) since the last year. When I got in the ring I knocked the first guy totally out of the circle or ring on his butt. I did the same thing to the next guy and finally they attacked me with two guys and I knocked them back. This became so embarrassing to some that Coach wouldn't let me be the 'Bull in the Ring' anymore. <u>Make Coach play me</u>……I continued to ponder and dream of my next fall football event.

The sled drill is a steel sled that has two dummy pads on it for protection. Coach Chiarotti and/or Coach Lawson (the offensive coach) would stand on the platform while various players would hit it. When it came my chance I hit the sled so hard it knocked the coach over towards me. Thereafter, whenever it was my turn again they got the 300 pound players to stand on the sled. After all when they were standing on the sled they were heavier than that bear who was 475 pounds. I could not knock them off but gave them the best hit I could deliver. I got so good at it that Coach Chiarotti asked me to hit the sled without anyone on it. I did and flipped it over 360 degrees back on its top side. <u>The next day they asked me to go in Coach Faughts office. He happily pointed out that due to my efforts I was now a BLUE CHIP player. The Blue chip designation was the highest position resulting in the concept that indicated you were in the best athletic condition at your position one could be for himself and the team. I was now Blue Chip!</u> When we went into our respective units they started me at linebacker, later defensive end and even some play at defensive back. I never sat the bench the rest of my career at FC and played almost every play including kick off's where I tackled several kickoff return specialists inside the twenty yard line. I made them play me! And they did!

Coach Chiarotti loved it and it excited me so much that I would come off the field after a big sack and jump right into his arms! I was like a big kid with a load of hits and defensive mayhem. Total exuberance! That's how I played and was on the most successful football team in FC history. Every now and then when the football team was playing offense I would glance at times into the stands as I rested. I would chuckle to myself or tell Gonzy and Craver to look at our crazy fraternity brothers. At times it looked like they had more fun than we were while playing football...Appearance can at times be deceiving.

My fraternity brothers would load and shoot cannon every time we scored a touchdown. KA-BOOM! That certainly will get your attention but something else also got my attention. There were several frat members that were getting even more rambunctious and/or acting absolutely wild and crazed. They had obviously been drinking way too much and were putting on a type of 'far end of the bleachers show'. By this time the entire crowd was watching, including my parents and they were not impressed especially when someone stated, "Those guys are SAE's!" My parents had come up from Memphis to see me play and they knew I really liked the SAE fraternity. I just told them some SAE's partied really hard. I also said that even I hadn't seen them acting like that before as we watched from the football field. We called that..'Rare form"

Accordingly the new Dean of Students apparently approached them during the game while they 'showed themselves-rare form' in the bleachers. They still obviously had some brainwave functions somewhat and gave the new female Dean their supposed names. One week later our Frat President, Bob Weiss was called into the new Dean's office. She said, "What is the deal with these three insanely drunk crazed members of your fraternity?! 'She was exacerbated-very excited and upset'. They were acting extremely wild and were clearly so very drunk as they sat in the empty far bleacher section! Their names are Gary Cooper, Steve Gonzenbach and Jeff Craver!" After a pause, waiting while the excited Dean collected her breath and composure, Bob said, "Dean, it can't be those men's names, they were all playing football on the team." Sometimes and possibly even Dean's need to know how to wrestle a bear. I don't remember any more such displays in the far bleachers. I think most of the misnamed rambunctious frat brothers went to law school and received professional designations. They certainly should have developed empathy for some of their clients.

As I played football, the unconscious competent part of my play was three fold. 1) When they lined me up at defensive end I would look down the line and if the guard's feet/toes were pointing away from me, not showing he was headed my way except ever so slightly, meaning that he was pushing off my way. I would quietly announce my observation to the tackle and attack the pulling guard at full speed crashing into him while slowing him down, shed off him off with a powerful hand shiver, using my hands and arms while jumping or grabbing the halfback or quarterback. No one got away from me, especially with Big John Jackson beside me with Craver and Gonzy directly behind.

2) Indianapolis University 'Indiana Central' was its prior name; we always had super competitive teams between Indiana Central, Butler and Franklin. We were all 25 miles from each other and we personally knew a lot of each team's football players because of Indiana high school rivalries. As usual we were going to play I.C. it was very special to beat those Greyhounds of I.C.! Our coaches drilled us and warned us regarding their offensive line, the twin quarterbacks and the super quick halfback named Montgomery. Several years through the 1970 -74 era was our and my particular football playing years for many of us at F.C. Indiana Central from 1970-1974 always had this short 210 pound halfback named Montgomery, that man-boy could sure take your legs out on a sweep. He was an expert. After several past altercations with Montgomery, I had to figure a way out of this stocky challenge. 'I figured and pondered greatly as to what would happen if he came my way. I fully planned on jumping on his back. This seemed ridiculous! But I might be able to stifle his approach to my knees somewhat, I was gonna give Montgomery something he had probably never had to deal with before. I told Big John Jackson my plan so he could cover my spot, especially if I failed with my back jump attempt. So here he came, really fast and very low at my end! Yes, this time would be different the next time he came my way on this sweep. He was in that hard to block low run position expecting

to take out my legs while leading the play around my end due to his particular ability just as he arrived I very quickly jumped on his back with my feet, he instantly and instinctively pulled his body and back straight up while I jumped as hard as I could while being propelled straight up, as if standing on his shoulders! Balanced like a rocket! In that same split second, I was seemingly like a cannonball propelled approximately 12 feet straight up in the air! The stadium announcer, Don Treibic' stated, *"Gary Cooper had just completed the 'highest high jump' in FC football history!* The quarterback as he had a glancing-stare as he tried to comprehend what he saw looked hard at me and was so shook up while I was hovering in the air that he threw the ball in the dirt. Montgomery never went low on me again! I freaked him out, sometimes one can have a type of 'unconscious competence'. He was then easily handled for the rest of that game. Montgomery came up to me after the game and asked me," What the hell did you do to me?" I told him, 'I had to figure a way to stop those low blocks.' He said, "You sure did" and left while we celebrated our victory!

3) John Jackson was a giant of a man, God and Coach only knows how he got to F.C. when Coach Chiarotti made him the tackle beside and in front of me, 'that was the greatest thing ever!' John and I would talk about a certain number of scenarios and rushing positions and how we would literally attack, based upon

our findings. Our simple but effective analogies proved themselves regardless who was put in front of us. Size, speed & quickness really helped with an edge.

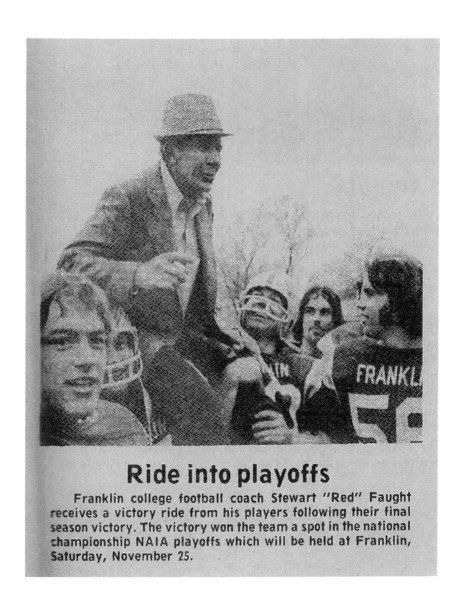

### Ride into playoffs

Franklin college football coach Stewart "Red" Faught receives a victory ride from his players following their final season victory. The victory won the team a spot in the national championship NAIA playoffs which will be held at Franklin, Saturday, November 25.

He would hold up two players while I rushed and often tackled or harassed the Quarterback. John regularly messed up many a running play. The competent aspect wasn't just the wonderful play but the fact that we once again recognized how we could help each other therefore it was always better working together than apart. We ruled the right side of the line in 1972. At times Jay Hunsucker-left defensive end and I would plan an attack on the quarterback such as 'you go high and I'll go low', the results were effective but not good for this one Quarterback, after 2-3 sacks between Jay and me. I actually felt myself almost feeling sorry for this one Quarterback, at least for the slightest moment. Our defense was really great! Jeff Craver always played incredibly consistent at middle linebacker. He gave everything he could give on every play. He was so skilled when he was hurt against Evansville University, I almost felt disjointed, it was first experience without Mr. Consistency? No one could come close to replacing Jeff. So what could I do? Their offensive line was doing a good job holding us out. So I faked the pass rush, ran backwards and got an interception by backing up as if I was an added defensive back and temporarily stopped the bleeding at least from my Coach's happy perspective, while giving the offense another chance. Steve Gonzenbach was the best of the outside linebackers and was hurt far more often than we could handle. But somehow 'we the defense' had to adjust. Just one time in our '4 college years together' all of these 'above mentioned teammates' were not playing defense due to 'injuries, exhaustion, cramps' I really noticed, felt lonely and readily petitioned our coaches for their reappearance. I fortunately never did get injured but I sure wasn't jealous of their individual injury plight, just needy due to their individual and our defensive group's dysfunction, while injured. One doesn't realize this need until, that particular group of defensive standard bearers are gone. Especially when it's the group that has calculated-planned, manipulated, pounded, tackled, jumped for joy, blocked, tripped, gouged and shedded more blocks, attacked, sneezing, coughing, spitting, wondering 'how we got here?', laughing, delivering 'high fives', gotten filthy, falling on our faces in anguish, intercepted a pass 'yelling Jo Jo', while completely exhausted and hoping the <u>offense can stay on the field a little longer</u> until it's time to do it all over again. And we never forget '*how truly great it all was*!

'WW 11'General Patton said, "Victory is fleeting" As a football player on a close knit football team 'on a dark night of reflection' feel 'thankful and filled with happy memories' Thank you Franklin College, Terry Hoeppner- my recruiter, Coach Faught's comments, awards and my beloved Coach Chiarotti who challenged me 'beyond my natural ability' I am truly a better man for this opportunity. I am always thankful, with great anticipation for a magnificent year. The athletic days are now over. I can truly relate to General Patton's comments but I have also used this inspiration, determination, team building and 'brotherly love' all enhanced and learned at Franklin College.

As a team we excelled and soared with a ranking of # 3 in the Nation! The announcers and boosters highlighted the huge stadium signs to read, 'Roar Grizzlies Score'. We scored! We presently hold several defensive records to this day! We had a stellar year with our lone defeat a 6 point loss to the NCAA Champion division with a final National ranking of #2 in our first game of the following year. In the last game of the year we lost by 6 points again in the National Championships of the NAIA. We were all very confident until a snowstorm of 3-5 inches fell. We simply weren't used to snow in November! Our cleats were possibly too short. Northwestern Iowa had size and stability which always beats quickness in the slippery snow. The Iowa team we faced was especially good as they had already played and won in 2 snow covered games that year. We lost, in spite of ourselves with just a couple of 'mistakes and miscues' but even with the shocking snow and slippery elements we almost beat them anyway. They were really the typical Midwestern 'big corn fed boys!' We had beaten these types all year long but they possessed a big offensive line push against a very quick and frustrated defensive slippery line of scrimmage, only if we could have gotten these boys on a dry field. The referee was my former 9th grade undefeated Coach. I had no idea that he was a big time NAIA referee! As fate would have it He was the former Coach who coined the phrase, "Excuses do not go on the scoreboard. You may get beaten but nobody will out condition us!" He worked our butts off and we won. Of course that was a building block for me in Junior High.

At Franklin College, nothing compares to that season and in comparison we continued to have winning seasons each year thereafter. Yet, not quite on the same level as 1972! But there's always hope and if you hear of the Franklin College Griz, that's the new shortened name. Score Griz Score!

Picture below: 'Oh those were the days!'

THOMPSON — RACINE — DOYLE — COOPER

Keith Thompson, another Woodburn, Indiana senior, returns as a starting tackle. At 6-3 and 220 lbs., his quickness makes him an excellent pass blocker. He will team with Racine on the right side to stabilize the offensive line.

Randy Racine, a 6-2, 210 pounder from South Bend will repeat as team co-captain from his offensive guard position. Randy, an All-NAIA player last year, ranks at the top among offensive linemen in Franklin's football history.

Ron Doyle, senior fullback from Indianapolis Ritter H. S., rushed for over 1000 yards last year and accounted for another 200 yards on 20 pass receptions. The 5-9 "statcat" is a real crowdpleaser with his many long punt and kick-off returns and his blinding moves out of the offensive backfield.

Gary Cooper, a senior from Columbus, Indiana, plays at defensive right end. A quick and very strong athlete, Gary is highly reguarded by coaches for his 'make something happen' ability and appears to be headed for a big senior year.

## GO BIG RED'S MACHINE

### THE MEN OF SIGMA ALPHA EPSILON

### 1973 Franklin College FOOTBALL SCHEDULE

| Date | Opponent | H/T |
|---|---|---|
| Sept. 8 | Ashland (7:30) | T |
| Sept. 15 | Rose-Hulman (2:00) | H |
| Sept. 22 | Evansville (7:30) | T |
| Sept. 29 | Indiana Central (2:00) (Homecoming) | H |
| Oct. 6 | OPEN | |
| Oct. 13 | Principia (2:00) | T |
| Oct. 20 | St. Joseph's (2:00) | H |
| Oct. 27 | Maryville (7:30) | T |
| Nov. 3 | Georgetown (2:00) | H |
| Nov. 10 | Earlham (2:00) | H |

Coaches:
Stewart "Red" Faught
Harold "Butch" Lawson
John Chiarotti

Left to right: Row 1–Bill Boltier, Keith Fiedler, Keith Thompson, Randy Racine, Steve Gonzenbach, Jeff Craver, Steve Welchans, Ron Doyle, Gary Cooper. Row 2–Coach Harold Lawson, Mike McClure, Terry Ruczkowski, Steve Harris, Dave Lyon, Gary Pate, Jay Hunsucker, Larry Edmond, Joe Beth, Tom Martin, Tim Mester. Row 3–Coach John Chiarotti, Mark Montgomery, Jeff Lombard, Keith Holland, Craig Messe, Steve DeVore, Jim Connell, Dick Martin, Greg Seanon, Brad Butler, Coach Phil Heller. Row 4–Jim Andrews, Carl Allen, Dennis Cooke, Greg Haworth, Brian Meeks, Joe Lire, Fred Weest, Kevin McBarnes, Bob Becht, Coach Rick Flacker. Row 5–Rick Martinez, Greg Phillips, Ken Andrews, Mike Wisley, Dave Bass, Jon Wagner, Bill Schwab, Mark Alexander, Mark Schuman, Coach Stewart "Red" Faught.

Once again, I couldn't have played with a finer group. We never gave up on any football games and always found room for improvement. Coach Chiarotti put this banner up in our locker room. In addition the large chalkboard also stated, <u>"Go wreck less, Stay loose , Enjoy Football"</u> No wonder we did so well. Perspective...helps. This concept was simple but gave us the concepts of 'flight, fast closing speed, the crash yet...it's all fun!

(above) The SAE house was a real blessing to me; Fellowship, academia, and fun.

74

While my senior year was winding down, Beanie and Barbie Broadhead 'Janet's parents' showed up to watch me play in one of my last football games. In addition while they were at FC Barbie was walking around the campus and by happenstance met the school nurse Mrs. Green. Mrs. Green had given me allergy shots for the past four years. She really liked me but, I didn't know how much. When Barbie was conversing with Mrs. Green she stated,"She adored Gary Cooper" and furthermore told Barbie that she would "offer her beautiful daughter to marry Gary Cooper in a minute." That was all it took, Mrs. Green's incredibly kind words offered the greatest approval that Barbie could ever muster concerning me. Meanwhile Beanie and Barbie reunited and attended the

football game and I played one of the worst game of my career, I wasn't doing anything right and even asked the Coach to take me out and he said, "Coop get your ass back in there!" I said, "Ok" It was very clear at this point that the coach regardless of circumstance trusted me. I was BLUE CHIP! Wow what a compliment to me! While Beanie stated to me after the game; "You didn't play a good game did you?" I somehow felt as if Beanie put a curse on me during that game or maybe I was trying so hard to impress that I did the opposite, I clearly did not have a 'lame duck attitude'. I did truly suck, to this day I still wonder about my effort during that game. Although in a way, I appreciated his knowledge and honesty, it kind of hurt but after all I knew he was right. But I also knew who the 'BLUE CHIP' player was, me...The motto for a Missourian is 'The Show me State'. I guess he showed me. Carry on Gary, as I remembered the meaning of the SAE Fraternity "True Gentleman' statements of great merit.

**Demon doing it**

With Gary Cooper leading the way, Larry "Demon" Edmon of Franklin college heads downfield Saturday after recovering a Georgetown fumble. Making a futile chase is Ed Moore (66) of Georgetown.

Beanie was a Big 8 Football Conference (Missouri, Kansas, Oklahoma, Nebraska, etc) fan. He also won the Missouri Amateur Golf Championships a few years before. I'm sure he thought as I originally thought also, that FC was small potatoes and 'in that sense' he was right. Coach Faught was right also, I had become a 'Big Duck in a Little Pond'. Take that Beanie! Perspective remains a lot of most everything. One person may think of a picture as a piece of junk, another may consider it a masterpiece. Attitude with just about anything or anyone makes a difference how's your attitude? By the way I didn't even know Mrs. Green's daughter. As Mrs. Green continued to give me allergy shots I said," If this doesn't with Janet I may need to meet your daughter."

When football for Gonzy, Craver, Hadley, Myself and many other seniors wound down, decisions had to be made. Academics had to be in order for graduation and career paths. For some it was grad school, for me it was, 'find a job'. I had an Uncle named Johnny Hickey who almost seemingly owned an entire county in Indiana back in the 1850's. He made millions in Insurance and Real Estate. I sought out to sell insurance and establish a new goal of eventually buying real estate as an investment. During my economics courses I had learned that '7 out 10 millionaires accomplished their goals in this manner. This appeared to be a good plan and was starting to set in me like concrete; it simply became more and more real to me over the next few years.

I was also completing the final review regarding my economics degree and preparing for Franklin College's Senior Comps with 4 economics/ business professors in attendance 'Franklin College was known for this challenge during the Sophomore and/or Senior year and made one summarize or review in detail his or her entire FC academic experience.' Clearly this was my 'Academic Bear Wrestling Event'. I was also planning on marriage my senior year. Janet had clearly become a great part of my life and we were married the winter of 1974. A Lot of my fraternity brothers trekked out to St Joseph, Missouri to witness and party over the cold winter parts of western Missouri. After marriage Janet and I would live in Franklin in order for me to complete my education. She was a sophomore and wanted to complete her education in Columbus, Indiana my hometown. But we were still in FC at this point and this was an exciting time for me.

Not coming from St. Joseph, Missouri had its downside at least for me. Janet's mother Barbie, her cousin Mary Brock and other various friends and relatives all pitched in to give Janet some terrific bridal showers, parties 'lots of silver pieces and trays, place settings, quality and sundry gift' and events. After all her father was 'H.H.' Broadhead President of the First Stockyards Bank of St Joseph, Missouri 'He had loans on many of the area's businesses and farms. Most of these individuals and wives were invited and did they give back, as the President's only daughter, Janet, was getting married and Beanie was their respective banker 'funding company for their business'. I hope you get the picture. First Stockyards Bank obviously near the Stockyards. It was also where Jesse James his gang got their start. Beanie's true love was golf. He was a huge member of the St Joseph's Country Club. They even had a tournament named after him 'The Broadhead Open'. Beanie was his nickname because he was lanky and skinny. What a golfer he was, the Missouri amateur golf champion. In addition he helped a young man named Tom Watson learned some of Beanie's shot patterns;

Tom's dad was also a Bank president in Kansas City, Missouri. Tom went to Stanford played great golf there and wound up being one of the greatest golfers ever. Tom knew Janet since she was a child and I thought to myself, he could have dated Janet, why not?

Janet's future daughter Kristi Cooper would stay in contact with Tom Watson and he greatly assisted her in raising money for charities in St Simons, Georgia.

What a golfer's heritage, Missouri amateur champ plus Masters Champion. I didn't fit into any of this. School was out during Christmas break and I worked to save money for our wedding. Janet called and said that I was going to be surprised when I saw her in February, just prior to the wedding. I was puzzled by what she said but not much as I secured a rental house near the campus. I thought new hairdo, fancy wedding dress, I'll just see when I get there. There was a bus load of folks 'SAE fraternity and Pi Phi Sorority accounted for at least 45 people' and other friends not to mention my immediate family (Mom and Dad, Susan and John and their children) that hailed from Columbus and Tom Broadhead, Janet's brother with his wife Anne Broadhead from the University of Tennessee where Tom was a paleontologist. In Franklin at FC, most people knew Janet and me so everybody pretty much felt a part. See you in Missouri several people quipped. I then thought I'm glad I'm not paying for this, let Beanie do it. Janet was his only daughter, one can just imagine. Without exaggeration I believe the Broadheads invested approximately $75,000 for this wedding and events. The biggest surprise was in waiting.

Seemingly everyone I knew had to come quite a distance to get to St Joseph, Missouri, on a late date in February, in the middle of winter 1974. The wedding date was Feb. 21st 1974. As people were arriving including myself we were all in a certain motel, I can't remember the name.. . Arriving one day before the wedding allowed me to have a bachelor's party 'I didn't want to get drunk, I partied and left it with most of my family and friends while I moseyed off to go to bed. This did not surprise my friends. They all knew I never got drunk or drank before a big game and this wedding was a big game type event! After the wedding, Janet and I were going to the Ozarks 'Tan-Tar- A Resorts'. They kept coming... greeting the

Franklin, Columbus friends and families. Everybody all seemed to have fun festive times for this great occasion. We had the wedding rehearsal dinner (close friends and family) the pastor had met with us prior to this event. In keeping with tradition I was not allowed to see Janet 'I did talk with her on the phone'. The craziest thing with the opposite sex occurred that night. As I was walking back to my room a very attractive slightly older lady literally grabbed me and begged me to come into her room. I immediately thought and stated, "Someone must have put you up to this". She then stated, "For what?" I told her," I'm getting married tomorrow and for whatever reason this would be really bad timing and why hasn't this happened before?" Thank God she let go of me. I slept fairly well except I was nervous because I knew Beanie was going to have a great event but I had forgotten about that Barbie influence!

*(picture above, Janet, Me and my frat brothers What a great and delightful group to come all this way)*

The wedding started it's procession.. The groom, the groomsmen and Janet's court were in place. Everybody was seated. The music started 'Here Comes the Bride'. As I looked I was completely shocked. It looked like Janet (though beautiful) had lost 40 pounds and appeared so skinny in this dress that I could hardly believe my eyes. In the first second as we held hands I stated, "What happened. You are so skinny!" She smiled and said, "I had to get into my mother's dress." I said "OK." We proceeded without incident. The reception was at the St Joseph Country Club. It was just for us! What a party, fraternal and sorority songs, statements of kind and funny quips. But I didn't expect the next item after things slowed down. Barbie with Beanie at her side gave me an envelope of stocks. I had forgotten that Barbie was the really rich one. She was a major stockholder and thereby owning Campbell Taggart stock, they were big players with Colonial Bakery as the holding company and had various issues for Janet and myself. We also had Bank Stocks from Beanie as well. These gifts were into the 10s of thousands from what I understood. I had never had stock until that moment. It suddenly occurred to me, as I would learn, there are only two ways to increase wealth 1) Save It (which I understood) 2) Inherit It (which 'they the Broadheads' understood) was I now a part of that team/program through Janet, maybe?

I later met with Beanie and Barbie and asked them, "What do you want us to do with this stock?" They said, "Just hold on to it" I put it in a lock box the next week in Franklin. Janet didn't seem to care either way. She was used to large funds by simply being a member of the family. I was not used to this, I didn't applaud this or deny it. I simply stored it and never ever pondered it, I knew that unearned inherited money would spend well but it could thwart the motivation to make my own money. I wanted to make my own money! Janet and I were married and now in the Ozarks. It was winter, cold and beautiful. The skiing was not very good, they had to make snow for the ramps and it was somewhat uncontrollable due to the ice. I planned on giving it my best shot.

This was the first time I had ever skied, so I had a very good time anyway. The room had a fire as Janet and I did the usual things that married people do. I was still amazed we were married. After the week in the Ozarks we returned to FC. I would finish my last semester and get licensed to sell Life Insurance with New York Life and shortly thereafter Northwestern Mutual Life. I only sold a few New York Life products. A former FC graduate Robert Dunlap, agent NML, in Columbus, Indiana my hometown recruited me. We had an office and everything one would need to sell life insurance. I sold life insurance to my friends, various business ventures and neighbors. I continued this while moving back to Columbus after graduation. I liked/loved people very much. Years later I took a color test-it measures emotional and genetic responses. I was found to be a lover of people. What I didn't like was bothering potential clients or pressuring anybody into buying life insurance. In most cases I didn't have to. Most just bought it, they were insured with a great company and I got a reasonable commission. It certainly helped with business and family financial needs. 30 years later I got one of the most backwards compliments from one of my fraternity brothers who bought an insured savings agreement which would have had dividends which are often more than the yearly premium. Apparently the NML insured savings plan after 30 years had been replaced by another fraternity brother who supposedly had a better plan buying term and investing the difference. Unfortunately and as usual this particular plan didn't work. I knew nothing about these events when attending the 30th graduation party held by the college. Except the replacement brother didn't seem to want to speak with me. The other frat brother simply said, he was the one who replaced it stating, "I lost big-time". I understood and didn't repeat anything until, this book. At least I didn't mention names. My older NML clients have huge savings within the insurance program which pays extra life insurance even if you are uninsurable. I've never had to say I'm sorry for selling NML!

It wouldn't be long before we sang the song 'Friends' for my last time in the SAE House with 60 brothers hand in hand as the Monthly SAE Chapter Meeting closed for the day. The memories last seemingly forever...

'FRIENDS' (I didn't look this up, it made an impression)

<u>Stated</u>: *The chairs are all empty the last guest has gone. The candles burn lower and lower yet sputter on and on. Yet after the last guest departed, in the smoke laden air remained a lingering presence, the ghost of good fellowship rare...*

<u>Song</u>: *Friends, Friends, and Friends you and I will be. Whether in fair or in dark stormy weather we'll stand or we'll fall together for SAE we will always be, our bond celebrating till death separating 'old pals' from me....*

The Senior Comprehensives were coming and shortly thereafter, Graduation. I was now married; football for me was over. My goal as a 12 year old boy had been accomplished, football and graduation-over! This senior year at least for me really seemed to really slow down, I only had to complete the minimal class hours 'I took the maximums my first year-21 hours as a freshman' and of course the senior comps. The day of the comps came, I reviewed almost everything I had memorized, applied and completed within reason regarding economics, my major. When I entered the Franklin College Administration building I ran into another econ major who said, "I'm glad I'll never have to do that again!" I now walked up the steps with great trepidation; I thought 'this might blow my career!' As I walked in I saw in one room every course professor I had in economics and related classes. I introduced myself to each one by name; thank God I remembered at least their names. Dr Launey, my main professor stated, "I'm glad you remembered our names and I can only hope you remember our curriculum of Economics and related fields." I said, "Well gentlemen let's get started." After 45 minutes of questions and answers with various graphs drawn on the board I 'couldn't remember some of them', it ended. They thanked me and I left. Whew. Comp grades were left on our last quarter report cards. All I remember is "I passed the comps 'C+' grade *Too bad they didn't throw FC football stats in the mix and reports regarding the tremendous amount of class time spent watching and discussing Watergate and Nixon.* Unbeknownst to me until graduation I was voted 'Senior Favorite' by the student Body. I was truly surprised and a little happier and very glad it was over, somewhat? Change is always disturbing. "What's Next?"

We moved to Columbus Indiana, rented in a new apartment complex and 1 building away was my former high school sweetheart, Debbie. She was newly married and we had one meal all of us together '2 hubby's and 2wives'. They say a 'baby changes everything' and I believe 'marriage does also'. Even after time, I still felt a little strange, although I was happy for her as well. The Bible says, 'Don't look back.'

# The Beginning-Janet's Starry Nights

Life goes on and opportunities took all of our friends elsewhere within a few months. I was now selling NML fulltime and Janet was working with Anderson's clothing next door, very convenient with one car and two jobs next door to each other. After selling insurance and Janet working everything seemed to be going fairly well until Mr. Anderson asked to talk with me. He said, "Gary I hate to tell you this but have you ever noticed Janet talking with herself? It concerns me greatly and also concerns some of my customers." I said, "I'm not sure you're talking about my Janet Cooper." He stated, "Yes." I responded, "I'll tell you this, I'll check into this because you are a man of great reputation and I respect your opinions. I promise I will give you a report." I then left and very cautiously questioned Janet who denied it to the last breath. She quit working there immediately. I continued on selling insurance. Since I had a good major medical insurance policy Janet and I agreed she could get her keloid scars taken off her knee, from a former tennis accident. They were unsightly scars just on her knee caps. The surgery took care of the scars but one of the knees needed padding surgery and she got that also. After a while, all seemed fine.

In the meantime, Janet went for a doctor's physical exam and came home crying. She told me, "The doctor said, 'I will never be able to have a child'!" I reassured her that if necessary, we could always adopt when the time came. I was disheartened but what could I do? I told her, "Quit taking birth control, at least we will save on that expense". Within one month Janet returned to the doctor and found out she was pregnant. At first I wanted to sue the doctor but then I realized this might be our only child. I became very happy and excited. Janet now had plenty of time to read since she wasn't working. Beanie and Barbie came and stayed with us during the last few weeks of her pregnancy. It became very obvious that in many ways Janet was still their little girl. I didn't know what to think except 'they must know what they are doing'. I found myself staying out of their way and did my work. One thing extremely important to Janet was her weight during pregnancy. She said, "All the books tell you to watch your weight for you and the baby". I said, "Just eat healthy."

Kristine Mary Cooper was born on July 21st 1975. Little Kristine was without any fat and seemed very healthy to me but my mother and sister stated, "She is the most muscular baby!" I said, "Maybe she took a little bit after me", as I really doubted their findings. This was my/our child and she was my "greatest responsibility!" That's exactly how I felt. At least at her birth. I found myself wanting to hold and watch over her from that point on. She was my baby!

Below: Kristi with Grandma Cooper, Flying into St Joseph, Missouri and Kristy's punchbowl shot.

Janet seemed to be having horrible times with nursing. She nervously smoked outside, which I demanded. I did not want Kristi's tender lungs damaged. I couldn't believe that Janet would start smoking because of her birth. I found it to be extremely disgusting. In college she smoked as my little sister with SAE. When we started dating she apparently stopped smoking to please me. I would rather have it been her idea. Everything with smoking was now reversed. Janet really seemed despondent and looking back this may be due to postpartum depression. When her parents left to go home things unraveled and it seemed like Janet couldn't handle any responsibilities. She sure couldn't work and I certainly had to continue. We survived for a while and started attending a Presbyterian church where we met some new friends. It was somewhat better for all of us. Kristi continued to be very much my baby. She could tell I was at ease with her and loved her, as opposed to Janet nervously doing otherwise.

After a brief period of time, Janet's next trip to the doctor stated that they found some problems with her hip and needed another operation. I said, "Make sure that doctor knows what he is doing!" She affirmed and after a second opinion and my warnings, had the operation. A much longer time period was needed for recuperation. A hip operation was quite rare for such a young person, Janet was confined to her bed for a week and Kristi and I assisted taking food, drink, etc as needed. As a result, Kristi and I grew much closer. What choice did she have? Her mother was needier than she was. Everybody always said, "That girl is your girl!" I happily agreed, but Janet's had a tough go of it. As time went on and Janet just partially recovered, I continued to sell life insurance. Janet stayed at home with Kristi. Janet was still having a tough time but slowly getting better, until the next doctor's news! This time the doctor said, "Janet needs shoulder surgery and a warm climate!" I said, "Doctors who are surgeons only make their money when they operate, and you are playing right into their surgical gloves! I'd rather take the warm climate as opposed to shoulder surgery." That was the sweetest and sour response I had ever heard. It was another cold, dark winter in Indiana and I was preparing to go to Career School with the NML. *She insisted on having her surgery done to her shoulder and a brief recovery time before my trip to Milwaukee, Wisconsin. The doctor's comments about the southeast appealed to me greatly.* <u>All my economic reports stated that the southeast had the greatest growth potential. I was certainly motivated with hope if nothing else.</u>

I believe in hindsight that I chose not to really look too hard at Janet's situation. She was my young wife, we had a child, and all I could do was just carry on. I had decided to plan for the worst and hope for the best. I made this bed and I would sleep in it. This would become a very hard road for our little family. Repression is not good, but nevertheless can be a temporary escape.

I believe this time of year had to be the worst time to have 'career school'! The temperature never got above 30 degrees below zero for the entire two week period in January 1977. The temperature was read at 60 degrees below zero near the end of the 2 week stay. I had to walk just 2 blocks from The Pfister Hotel to the huge NML Building. I almost froze to death each day due to the wind chill off Lake Michigan. I felt horrible with my insides/bad gut feelings and Janet's pain(s). Regardless of her condition, she was still my wife and I had a commitment that I did not take for granted in our marriage regarding 'sickness and health'. In addition to having Janet caring for our baby Kristine during this two week period, I was very concerned equally for Janet and Kristi's well being . I found myself having to be the 'adult in these matters'. Janet and Kristi were not normally together without me. Usually, it was Kristi and Daddy. Although I tried very hard to act like things were just fine, concerning these important family matters when asked, my heart had so much uncertainty regarding Janet during my absence. I was barely coping emotionally and was now even having a difficult time due to my great concern regarding 'both of their well being' while selling insurance right up to this great opportunity at NML Career school time. I was hoping to gain an extremely deep 'want to' selling attitude as opposed to being disjointed with the obvious cares of life while balancing my relationship with NML. Aside from life's cares for me The Northwestern Mutual Life had been a great professional training program. The school ended and I gladly returned to Indiana. Nothing shocked me more than what I saw on the Interstate Highway from Wisconsin to Southern Indiana in the winter of 1977!

I saw car after car stuck in the snow and pushed off in the ditches. There were reports on the radio of people being found dead in their cars due to exposure. Indiana was a mere 26 below zero as I carefully trekked home with loads of supplies in the event I got stuck in the snow. I was very happy that Janet and Kristy were in a warm house while I was on an uncertain road. No one could be seen wanting to come out in this frozen barren land. As I continued onward to Columbus just below Indianapolis I saw my first victim when I drove by on the side of the road as the emergency crews were removing her frozen body from her car. Most the people who got in trouble were found sliding off the road and dealing with gas line freeze or fuel running out. In addition, dangerous exhaust vapors were found entering the vehicle due to impacted snow in the muffler. Many were found with improper clothing and inadequate food and water. I made sure that I had plenty of fuel in the car with a can of gas line antifreeze, plenty to eat or snack on, lots of warm clothing and a commanding desire to get home.

Finally, I got home and was very glad to see everyone. Janet and Kristi were happy to see me as well. The next two nights everything seemed alright for the most part and then it happened. It was now January 1977 and the electric company's power went out in our immediate area of Indiana. It was overcast and still super cold. I'll never forget sleeping with all of us in one bed, while trying to stay warm in our all electric rental house, without electricity! Suddenly thoughts of a young family perishing from 'freezing to death' entered my mind and could possibly become a harsh reality. The next day the power was turned back on. I didn't forget that powerless feeling of freezing. Did I have the stuff to change things for my family? Looking back at what my Grandfather Neal had to do to change the Eastern Kentucky situation pulled on me as well to a certain degree.

# THE TELEPHONE CALL

Mom and Dad had just moved to Bainbridge, Georgia (30 miles north of Tallahassee, Florida). Dad called me and asked 'How did we do without power and 26 below zero?' I told Dad, "I didn't like it one bit and would do just about anything to not put my little family in that condition again."

Dad had just become the Sales Manager of a company called VADA Manufacturing of Bainbridge, Georgia. Dad was solicited by a big time headhunter job procurement person. He thought dad would be great prospect with his White tractor sales and management history. The Vada Corporation sold peanut wagons, various trailers for hauling, peanut ripper bedder ground preparation equipment, tobacco portable curing barns, etc. They had a full line and had recently gone from retail sales (individual farmer) to sales through a dealer organization that would buy at a discount and then sell retail. This was similar to the type of transitions Dad did with White Farm Corporation. Some of the farmers that had bought retail were not happy and Vada hired Dad to fix the problem. He was a dealer expert with White Farm Equipment for the past 25 years. His territory was almost the entire south. He needed help from some trustworthy men. Dad called me. He didn't waste words.

He asked "Son, how would you like to have the Florida and South Georgia territory for my company? You will get a company vehicle with benefits and a salary plus commissions." Perfect timing-I had just completed a Career School with NML in the bitter Wisconsin winter weather. After fearing for my life and my family's lives with the cold, and being told by a doctor that Janet needed a warmer climate, it just made sense. More importantly a job offer of great value from somebody I fully trust- MY DAD!

I, with my somewhat typical high speed thinking and the thought of an up and coming southern economy forecast along with the hope of a new President named Jimmy Carter from Georgia, a fairly local Chief Executive! Wow the possibilities, plus the fact that I will see the ocean for the first time! Overwhelmed with clearly a new beginning for me and my family I simply said, "Dad I will see you next week!"

I arrived making sure this was the right thing to do for all concerned. Expectations were everywhere. I was definitely new to this most unusual part of the USA-the deep South! Mom and Dad were located in Bainbridge, Georgia. My small family found a nice apartment directly down a busy street from the state capital of Florida, Tallahassee. Surprisingly, Tallahassee was very hilly. I knew that the Gulf of Mexico was less than 40 miles away. Where was the sand? My Yankee speech pattern and perspective were ridiculous and I would have to make and accept some changes. After time, I would realize the great benefits of being near the ocean as opposed to being close by the ocean, especially after you've experienced the effects of a hurricane! That will keep a lot of people 60 miles away from the ocean in many cases. Tallahassee was just 26 miles, as the crow flies. The fact that one has access to the beach as opposed to having beach property damage and numerous disastrous potential weather effects was important- decisions, decisions. I found that out after a normal tropical storm. Tallahassee, Florida is close enough to the Gulf of Mexico. On the positive side the area was teaming with wildlife and many streams, sinkholes, swamps and lakes.

After all the many questions and serious considerations, from family and friends, we nevertheless decided to leave Indiana. Janet followed my lead, in the hope and promise of a better future. Janet would not have that deep cold in her bones down there. I always wanted to be in the Deep South because that was one of my subtle business and dream type goals. I was pumped! Possibly a better way of saying it, "This is a major goal that I could only dream of, until now." FLORIDA! Truly, every Northerner's dream especially after enduring the long winter's super cold 'cabin fever' effect. All I had to do was adjust to South Georgia and I would be fine, or so I thought. As we were telling everyone and preparing to leave Indiana, I kept my promise with Mr. Anderson. I said, "Sir I told you I would report after Janet's actions and former employment with you because of your genuine concern, which I appreciate. Janet has had two more operations since our last conversation. She is more nervous than before and my only hope with this change is that it might turn her around. In all honesty, I don't know which way at present. Thanks for your interest and prayers." He wished me well as I left. The NML group hated to see me go, but understood my familial obstacle. The day we were loading and shortly would be leaving I was finishing my last bit of packing when my only sister, Susan, approached me and told me that she was divorcing her husband, John. The van was loaded and the keys were placed in the mailbox. There was simply no time to talk and I was completely befuddled and bewildered. I loved her kids, my 3 three nephews, and I considered John in a sense to be like my only brother, during their brief marriage. The timing of her statements hit me so hard that I hardly responded except to say. "I hope you thought this through Susan, I love you." Totally packed, I could only shrug my shoulders and hug my only sister's neck. <u>After 'the news' with the possibilities and problems, I couldn't help but wonder if this type of thing with my sister's circumstance might befall Janet and myself as well. Divorce was becoming almost normal in our society during these years. I had to chose to remain hopeful for our marriage.</u>

What an exciting feeling of new horizons where no one knows your name and the potential of a new life with no comments about my potential or lack thereof. Nobody knew me and I was delighted. I always felt due to my small community that I really couldn't reach my potential. Jesus even had that problem in his hometown, "He marveled at their unbelief" I was now feeling free and anonymous as we pulled into Tallahassee, Florida in January 1977. It was like a northern spring in the winter. WOW! I was impressed, the beautiful southern skies with puffy clouds! We settled into our apartment, once again, close to the Capitol building in Tallahassee. The next day we met some neighbors who asked if we would like to go to St. George Island with them for a day. We happily obliged with this offer and off we all went. I told them about my 'having not seen the ocean before'. They were very kind in taking the coast line route where I could and would get many looks along the way. I was filled with the excitement and wonder of a child. We brought picnic sandwiches and had a very good time, until we headed for home. My entire family of three looked like we were cousins to a boiled lobster. Sunburn Red! We quickly found that the Sun is really big and strong down here. Sunscreen rules.

# 'HOW TO QUIT' AND GET A 'REGULAR JOB'

Back in Indiana, during my NML life insurance career times a fellow agent named Bob Dunlap used to say, "At times, it would be nice to quit the insurance business and get a regular job." Over a period of time, 'that's exactly what I did!' The following week I started my new job as a sales representative for the Vada Peanut Wagon Corporation. I hadn't worked for anybody since college and selling insurance was out of the question at present. Thank goodness, new horizons, and Dad was my boss. That was just what I needed-stability through change, at least for awhile. Hopefully I could learn how to work 'the job' and adjust to the southern ways fairly soon. *'Hang onto your hat would be an understatement!'*

My first week at Vada Builders, Inc. was nothing like I had expected. When I got to the office I met the President named Bobby Jack and the rest of the office staff. Everyone was very nice and cordial. When I toured the plant that morning I walked in on the Morning Prayer meeting. I was surprised in a good way but it seemed so unusual. Furthermore, I was requested by the staff of Vada to see Mrs. Harrell and go to their home just a short distance from the factory. Mrs. Harrell was a very nice southern lady and asked me to herd in the peahens. I had never in my life herded anything called peahens. I figured they must be the funny chicken looking creatures running around in her yard. I went after them but I wasn't as fast as they were. I easily figured out that a Peacock must be around somewhere. Then she came back out and said, "Just run them into the pen." I did a very poor job of that, they were now running down the backside of the property and I thought to myself, 'is this really what I'm supposed to be doing?' I went to the house and told her that they were out of control and she just laughed and said," They'll be back when they are hungry I just hope the dogs don't 'git-em'." As I walked away I sure hoped the dogs wouldn't get them. I was led to the field office in order to get my truck. The new vehicle was white with the company logo on the side. After a few sessions with a map and learning about the local-immediate areas and concepts of selling to a dealer organization the day was done. As I arrived back to Tallahassee, Janet and Kristi seemed fine. I chanced the thought 'maybe this is the right move. 'A new start!'

The next day I couldn't believe what happened. As I traveled from Tallahassee to Vada I went around a curved road near the plant and hit a large vulture that broke and smashed the front grill on my company truck. I then had to use another truck until my truck got fixed. While waiting, I officially met the owner-top share holder of the company Levy Harrell. He was the one who hired dad, due to his expertise with dealers and such. He approached me and took my hand and rubbed his fingers over the inside of my hands. He said, "I can tell a lot about a man by shaking and rubbing my hands over the insides, particularly. You haven't worked much with your hands have you?" I responded, "Sir when I played football in college I worked on the Mississippi river and used my hands a whole lot. But, over the last year and half I was selling insurance, as you can certainly tell, I'm sure." He was the type of man that spoke his mind. He said, "That's probably true but most the folks we hire around here have those tough hands." That was the end of the conversation. I later asked Dad about it. He said, "Levy hired all the welders for the plant's jobs so he bases everything on that due to his past. After all, we (Vada) are nothing more than a large specialty welding shop." At this point I really needed some marching orders, in other words, do something. It didn't take long. Dad introduced me to Levy, Jr. 'the wayward son of the owner'. Dad said, "Levy is the field training representative and he will show you the ropes so to speak." I knew this program well. Coaches usually have their sons play quarterback, preachers usually pick their sons as the next preacher and owners naturally do the same thing. 'Often times it's not what one knows but who they know' Janet's Mom Barbie used to say this. It certainly rang true for me, my boss was DAD!

Levy and I headed out the first day in his truck. He told me about the company, where it's been and where it's going from his perspective. He continued to say, *"Ralph your dad' has been hired to save this company."* This was the first time I had heard anything about the company being near default from anyone including dad? Levy Jr. wouldn't and didn't elaborate regarding the 'state of Vada' as we rode on but his prior words regarding 'Vada potential problems' remained with me. Levy was giving me some kind of a confessional. I was the new unaware anonymous guy from Tallahassee in the truck. He proceeded to tell me the how's and why's he had been married to several women. He then stated that most were mistakes on my and their parts but we did get some good kids out of it. I agreed that some women and some men seem to make the same mistakes with the opposite sex regarding future relationships as well. "That's probably the reason for multiple divorces, don't you think?" Levy said, "That's what our marriage counselor said also." I kind of liked Levy Jr. He was showing me that people are the same wherever you go...Basically. Then he started on his life of being a 'dirt road spot' (sport) Levy implied that he was a wild man of sorts and we call it 'a dirt road spot'. I responded and said that I used to be a type of dirt road sport myself especially as a youngster. We met a few customers and possible future customers then returned home. I called Dad that night and asked about 'Dad being the last ditch savior for the Vada Corporation.' Dad said, "Gary, all I can tell you is keep your eyes open for other opportunities because one never knows in this type of situation here at Vada. I'm really disappointed with the big time headhunter- executive job procurement manager that placed me in this mess." Dad asked me to keep this information between ourselves. 'OK', was all I could say? I was so new in the deep south as I kept my eyes wide open as possible for any and all opportunities as they came along. I did not want to return north any time soon. I was determined not to fail regardless of the Vada Builders dilemma!

The next day Levy drove his truck and I drove mine, I followed Levy. Before leaving the plant site Levy Jr. said, "The dealer in Valdosta ain't very happy because he didn't like the dealer program especially the price increases." At this point all I wanted to do is get the flow of our company and 'move on' so to speak. We met the very large 'fat' dealer and his managers in a place called Shorty's Restaurant in Valdosta, Georgia. As we walked in I couldn't help but think of some 1960 era movie setting called 'Macon County Line' and such. Levy introduced me to the dealer and we all sat down to breakfast. The conversation was all about what the company 'Vada' was doing and the many 'why's' were put into doubt as he questioned and stated negative outcomes as a result.

Levy Jr. did most the talking. When the ordering of breakfast took place, all 4 men said, "I want eggs, bacon, grits, biscuits and coffee." When it came to me, I'll have the same also. They continued talking about Vada and the farm business in general.

As the order came all of the men did something I had never seen in my life, except for my Uncle Walter. Every person there took their knives and forks and mixed everything 'I mean everything' altogether in one disgusting ugly heap! Immediately my mind flashed back to my childhood when Mom or Dad mixed a couple of different foods on my plate and I threw up. I couldn't believe this was so, as I quickly grabbed the sugar and did the most disgusting thing a southerner will ever see, that I didn't not know anything about. I put the sugar on my grits. 'I used to do this with 'cream of wheat cereal'. Without any hesitation the dealer with a huge southern drawl slowly said, "Sooooooon(son) where you froooom(from)." Thinking fast I said, "Sir, I'm from southern 'I made sure I said something he could relate to was included-southern! I said, "Southern Indiana." He responded, "Down here in the south we consider grits to be ice cream and the only thing you put on ice cream is salt and pepper." I said, "I've only been down here a week and as they say, 'When in Rome do as the Romans do', so I apologize for my screw up." One thing for sure is that particular dealer never bought one dime's worth of trailers or peanut wagons or ripper bedders from my territory. He wasn't going to support this Yankee-Dad, _me_ or the company that just gave him a price increase! We left shortly. I got in my truck and Levy got in his. We headed west towards his place. He said he had to get something.

As we were heading west I found myself looking back and concerned because I had truly forgotten how my Uncle Walter used to mix everything on his plate. He was raised somewhat in Kentucky. Uncle Walt was the only one I knew who ate that way, until now. Anyway as we went towards the Bainbridge area I couldn't help but notice towns with names like, Quitman, Climax, Cairo, Boston, Thomasville, Repton, Whigham, Valdosta, Thomasville, etc. with lots of closed vacated gas stations and other empty buildings along the way. Looked like a tough place to make a living...

Finally we got to Levy, Jr's place in Decatur County. He jumped out of his truck and unlocked the gate and we pulled onto a sandy lane. Upon entering I couldn't help but notice how tall his chain link fencing around the property seemed to be. As we reached his nice looking clean trailer he had a hitching post with a horse attached which he unlatched and took around the back. He yelled to me, "Wait there, I'll be right back." As I leaned against the front bumper of the truck it seemed that his horse looked and acted very nervously as he trotted her back behind the trailer. I relaxed and looked all around from about the middle of the property and noticed the brown light sand where all the trees were perfectly spaced, they all had the same height and width from what I could tell. Then it happened!

Suddenly without warning, a large female lioness came bounding out from behind the trailer directly towards me! The lioness was running at full speed 'I couldn't do anything, she was so quick, I couldn't move or escape' right before one dies or has a traumatic event, the brain works very fast. My brain, once again moved at lightning speed and I decided to remain still leaning on the bumper to not incite this animal in any way. As the animal playfully pounced on me I could hear Levy Jr. laughing like crazy. The lion 'licked my face' and I quickly noticed that big cats like little cats have those rough tongues. At this point I had to think- <u>What is the deal about me getting licked by a bear and lion in one's lifetime?</u> It was over as quickly as it began. I pray that no one will personally introduce me to Shamu 'the killer whale!' Levy called 'Here Kitty' and the big lioness left me and went to him. He said, "That is one friendly cat don't you think?" The first thing I looked at was my pants to make sure I hadn't wet myself, thank God I didn't. I kept my cool just like the David and Larry event with the bear. With a deep breath returning, I then boldly stated, "Levy Jr., what the hell are you doing with a lion?" He proceeded, "I got this lion from the fair. The trainer gave me a price and I said, 'Sold America!' It was close to the end of day and I left and made it back home to Tallahassee. As I entered the front door Janet asked how my day was. I told her, "I don't know if I'm going to make it down here." I proceeded to tell her my day's story. She laughed a little bit and wondered also. A month later the Decatur Sheriff ordered Levy Jr. to get rid of the lion. The 'dirt road spot' (sport) did it again.

The next week I got my first peanut mill call. The owner wanted some more peanut wagons. The receptionist said,"Just head over to Doran." I didn't know how far away it was so I looked up 'Doran' on the map. It was in North Georgia far away... I went back into the office and asked, "Are you sure you want me to go to Doran?" She smiled and said, "Yes". I said, "OK"and then left the premises. After about 5 hours I arrived in Doran, Georgia. I looked 'I asked people in general if any mills were around?' I could not find any peanut mills so I called the office. I think her name was Sherry, "Hello Sherry, I'm in Doran and I can't find the mill?" She laughed and said, "Are you in Doran?" I said, "Yes, and I can't find the mill." I noticed she put me on speaker phone. The office staff could hear us talking. She said, "Gary let me make sure we have this straight. You are in Doran right?" "Absolutely" She then said, "Tell me about your surroundings." I said,"OK, it's a nice little town and there is a mountain in the northeast direction." At this point I could hear the entire secretarial pool howling in laughter. She said, "How far away are you from Vada?" I said, "About 270 miles I think." "Could I ask you a question?" "Yes." I said,"How do you spell Doran?" She said," D-O-E R-U-N". I said, "That's not Doran, that spells DOE RUN!" About this time everybody got it. From that point on they gave me written instructions regarding my calls, which I really liked. The next day I went to Doerun as it was written and made the call accordingly. I'll never forget meeting a stately attractive older woman on the Doerun road near the mill. I told her my purpose and she asked my name. I said, "Gary Cooper" I continued to tell her that I wasn't from here, she said, "I've noticed and want you to know I named my oldest son Gary after the movie star also. Do you know very much about the south? We call this place God's Country." Those words...'God's Country' would haunt me for the next several years. Years later one of my best friends who played lunchtime basketball at the YMCA with me was Gary Pitts originally from Doerun, Georgia. We both surmised that lady must have been his mother. Small world, nice lady.

I've heard it said that good and often bad events occur 3 times. I've had two crazy things already happen what else could occur? My next call was to take a trailer down to Creel Ford Tractor in Ft Myers, Florida. What a great call....Florida, my fantasy state! I was waiting near the front office while another one of Levy, Jrs.'s brother, Ronny, hooked up the trailer behind my truck. 'I planned on showing it all over the Florida/Georgia areas'. I jumped in the truck and asked Ronny the field manager, "Am I ready to go?" he looked at the trailer hitch and assortments all over and said,"OK, have a good trip!" I took off.

Finally, I was living my dream. Riding, 'flowing' down the roads of Florida! Wow! Everything was fresh and beautifully green. The southeast most of the time is a plush green, better known as 'ever green' particularly with the pine trees, not to mention the banana trees, ferns, palm trees, etc. I really enjoyed many trips down to tropical Florida. Although this day like so many others was different. As I was heading south close to the city of Tampa, it was mid morning and there were a lot of sewer works going on. It looked like the city workers were re-routing the pipes and in the very sandy white soil. It looked the way I thought all Florida would look like when I first showed up, in the north section'. I was in the middle lane due to sparse traffic that time of day, when suddenly I noticed the trailer I was pulling was at that moment...positioned right beside me going down the road! Somehow the trailer became totally unattached to the truck as I slowly but quickly got the truck away from the drifting trailer; in order to block it if it started pulling left towards the oncoming traffic. As it slowed down, the energy of the truck was lessening as I was now blocking. Fortunately for all concerned, the trailer drifted to the right edge of the pavement while clipping top after top off the sewer covers as it finally came to a rest and it stuck in a sand dune. Fifty yards ahead, one of the sewer workers had a forklift. He picked up the tongue of the trailer and put it back on my company truck as I attached the truck's back hitch safety chains, this time. 'I couldn't believe that Ronny didn't attach the safety chains'! I told the worker that I had trusted the field supervisor way too much. I told him that 'my trust for my safety' would be much more personal next time with a visual inspection from me with safety chains plus. I, with many more subtle type learning situations in the south would surely happen but if the 'bad times' were over and I was still alive, I was happy. The rest of the year would be normal and commonplace, thank goodness. Unfortunately, Janet's problems would reappear.

We hoped for a great future.

We had a lot of fun, particularly in college.

We had a beautiful baby, an absolute miracle!

 We moved south for health reasons, exciting. Bought a house!

We had some great plans. I continued to plan...

# The Conclusion...
# JANET'S STARRY STARRY NIGHTS

Time: during and after our college days

It's never expected when a very kind and loving young person seems to be recovering from an illness but simply doesn't. Janet didn't recover, in fact, she was now dealing with more pain and with deep bouts of depression. After a few months, it all started again. Pain, this time it was her back and due to her depression it was really starting to get ugly. I might find her hitting her head against the wall or simply acting out. I figured and tried to rationalize it might be the medications. The lock-ups are available for various emotional and mental problems. The facilities had names like Quinco, North side and Tallahassee Mental Health all of which I quickly became very aware of their various purposes, which for Janet and others mostly consisted of giving the recipients some medication and a safe environment for themselves and certainly for the rest of the family. Most were all clearly out of control for many reasons. Lockdown usually lasted for 2-3 days (the weekend). Due to my wife's bouts with unexpected outbursts, Kristi and I had many nights without Mom or wife. Needless to say the adjustment wasn't easy for either of us. Initially Kristi who was 2 1/2 or 3 years of age asked 'where's Mommy?' and I would say 'she is visiting some doctors but will be back'...As I thought to myself which depended on severity and slowing of Janet's emotional state or condition. Post lockdown reports from the staff social workers were usually sketchy at best as I inquired 'what happened?' Usually it would be the standard pat or bland response from the Social workers, "Some people get really stressed out with living in general and this is the result." <u>I never thought that our life together would be like this.</u> This was my life at present not knowing what tomorrow might bring and what if something happened when I was out of town on business? I remained committed with a great purpose and vigilance to the mutual statements made during our marriage ceremony 'in sickness or in health'. This was becoming very real, to say the least.

I was always fearful and 'really scared of flying' even though that was my goal way back at age 12. So during a return from business travels I decided to stop by the Quincy, Florida airport, just outside Tallahassee. As I pulled the car into the flight/road area a man came out from the hangar office. We met and I introduced myself to what I thought might be the flight instructor? His name was Lt Akins, the Quincy Airport Manager. I proceeded to tell him of my flight fears even though it was one of my personal goals. He had a relaxed manner and was very accommodating as he offered me a personal ground based presentation which greatly eased my flight fears. He proceeded to show me every one of the basic features of an aircraft parked at the edge of his field office. This information answered a lot of my questions. Although I found myself still anxious somewhat but I became very relieved as he actually flew me around the immediate area. His knowledge and professionalism while actually and personally flying ME around the 5 mile airport circumference was incredibly stimulating! I was suddenly hooked and realized the 'air possibilities' that I had only dreamed of until now. I started taking lessons every week for an hour or so each time as I was coming or going via my business travels. In approximately six months, I flew my first solo while he and his other student/pilots tore my shirt off and signed it. I didn't expect this at all. But easily chalked it up to...tradition! This reminded me of something my old fraternity brothers might do. Fun times. I really needed some good times to alleviate some of my family setbacks with Janet. Also since I planned on being a real pilot, in the future, I developed plans that would get me back a lot quicker 'based upon the weather' regarding my territory and my uncertain family situation. During this period of time I also contracted with a person to watch over Janet and Kristi as kind of a part time live in maid, only when I was out of town on business. She reported only to me. I kept Janet's condition very quiet socially, I was somewhat hopeful that somehow she would get better. Mental health problems are always weighty regardless who it is. She was so young just 23 years old. I also contacted a mental health counselor in addition to the doctors she wanted...orthopedic surgeons. Obviously you must have figured out I had a great health insurance company. The Aetna Insurance Group Health Policy. Due to my company's benefit package money was flying out of my policy as if it had winged flight privileges.

I decided that although Janet is having some really tough times I didn't need to feel sorry for myself and get depressed because my little girl Kristi is so very important! She was my light, a clear reason to continue on. Every morning Kristi and I would walk, talk and play around our block. I had bought a cute 3 bedroom cedar wood house that was brand new and the area had some great rolling hills and we had a steep driveway. Kristi would take her 3 wheeler and fly down the driveway 'with my supervision' and spin out at the bottom, man could that kid scoot. She kept walking up and then going down the elevated driveway like a little rocket and spin out. We had many Daddy and daughter fun times together. Kristi was also involved in jungle gyms, dance and gymnastics.

In our immediate neighborhood, just down the street, I actively recruited John Stocker as a fellow real estate investor. John was married and his daughter Jennifer would play with Kristi quite often. Due to my personal fear of buying that first house all on my own, I kept thinking, what if I couldn't make the payment or the house needed massive repairs. Most young folks have similar such thoughts. The owner of the house in question was the aunt of my sales manager for MFS. I met her in Hollandale, Mississippi while attending one the company's manufacturing site meetings. She was an elderly lady and complained to me about a house she bought in Tallahassee 30 years ago. She was concerned about the condition of the house and the renters were not paying her the monthly rent. Since I lived there, I told her I would check it out. I took the address and would call her as to what I found. Upon investigating the house, its condition and its renters, I responded and simply told her 'the house was brick, unkempt, and the renters were Hispanic and unapproachable'. I didn't emphasize the house seemed to be in a prime real estate location. I did tell her 'I wasn't sure if it was commercial or residential'. After a slight pause, I asked her if she would 'consider selling the house to me. I live there and could possibly take care of it better due to my location.' I advised, 'clearly the house needed some work, I would have to possibly kick out the squatters and try to find what the inside of the house looked like.' She directly responded, "I'm too old for this anymore. Would you give me $16,000 for the house and property?" We haggled from $13,000 my offer to an agreed on price of $14,500. OK, now I've got what I think is a good deal. I might need a partner to help me fix it up and spread the risk-payments." As fate would have it. I found that I just contracted for a house on one of the busiest corner 'Tennessee and Magnolia St.' in Tallahassee for $14,500'. I was so timid with this first rental house; I just had to have a partner due to my fears. The bank seemed happy to have two working men sign a mere $15,000 note. John, Becky, his wife, and I finally entered the now abandoned house. We spent two weekends cleaning, fixing, painting, etc. In just 1 year we had an offer for $80,000. We both profited quite nicely and I said to myself, 'I think I should do something like that again!' I suddenly remembered what I had learned in economics...7 out of 10 millionaires make it in real estate. I was in...! With this extra real estate money, immediately I started looking around for an airplane. I found one in an airplane shopper ad in my price range from an older gentleman named Hugh in Boston, Georgia. He traded his Piper aircraft for a recreation center (in Boston) that I had purchased immediately after my first rental house sale. I now had truly accomplished one of my childhood goals, an airplane! With the airplane in my possession, I hangered it in Thomasville, Georgia just 35 miles north of Tallahassee. This was a big deal to me!

I was now feeling somewhat empowered and made several points, sort of like a overview/matching game, viewing many business opportunities by simply observing just about any and every business and combining any other possibilities as I traveled my 5 assigned states. Many of my ideas were plotted on paper and filed in the spare bedroom where I also kept detailed medical files and records pertaining to Janet. The results were simple, Janet was now verbalizing and literally planning a 'back surgery' and Kristi was becoming observant while watching and noting when I had to work (leave town) therefore 'She had access to me' when at home , my car and hopefully more fun. My intentions were to entertain and lovingly engage my daughter as I felt very disjointed emotionally in my insides/gut with Janet's circumstance. I found myself dealing with this conflict especially when traveling was necessary. I was using combinations of day care facilities, friends and paid workers to watch Janet and mostly Kristi while I was away. Due to having the use of a telephone, an aircraft and certain day routes, I managed my life with business and family to the best of my ability, although it was always family maintenance driven.

A lot of my long distance dealers seemed to approve of me flying in to see them. I think it made them feel somewhat connected in a certain and special way. They liked picking me up at most of their small airports over my 5 state territory. I would always call ahead and owner, secretaries and/or foremen/mechanics would pick me up from the various airports. I particularly used the plane in Florida, Alabama and North Carolina. My company liked the access especially on big installations which required a great amount of detail, as I outlined my actions on my reimbursed company expense reports.

When Janet told me she definitely needed to have intensive back surgery I did not respond well. I questioned her motivation with the surgeons as well! Was her back really that messed up? What about all these other operations? I demanded we get an opinion from the best we could find in the south. We found one of the best back surgeons 35 miles north of Tallahassee in Georgia, a place called Thomasville. His name was Doctor Payne. Hopefully it wasn't a ticket name. It humorously reminded me the name 'Cooper' which meant 'barrel maker'! I sure hope his ticket name didn't mean 'pain' which means 'Payne' the Doctor. I had become extremely aware and very wary of what I perceived was scheming doctors and of course Janet; as he proceeded to give her a complete several day evaluation. I thought to myself, "Fine, let's see!"

His complete and intensive report was more shocking to me than I could have imagined! He stated, "Based upon my findings 'as he showed x-rays and such' Janet will have to be on her back for one year!" I said, "I am shocked and dismayed to hear this, I would have to quit my job and take care of two babies, one legitimate! Ok, let me think about this." Without the slightest hesitation, I called Beanie, Janet's father. "Beanie, this is Gary, You probably know about Janet, don't you?" He said, "Barbie had said something about Janet's back but we weren't quite sure what to do or think. It all sounds perplexing." I agreed and said, "This is no time for the little boys in other words DOCTORS!" I then very carefully described Dr. Payne's diagnoses especially a year on her back! We need to send Janet to the Mayo Clinic in Rochester, Minnesota, for a proper diagnosis regarding her orthopedic needs." He agreed and after a couple of days a twin engine aircraft showed up to take Janet to the Mayo Clinic. Kristi and I were as usual together again. The information we received from the Mayo was a 30 day complete physical assessment with results. She was off! I had absolutely no idea what was going to happen and I couldn't believe the results one month later. My head was shaking.

# SOMETIMES ONE HAS TO WEAR BLINDERS

Sometimes a person just has to 'put on blinders,' 'don't look it might mess you up' or get down on yourself and then hurt others unintentionally with statements of an emotional nature. I've had this happen in the past with 'Janet's illnesses' and 'put on blinders' I did not or will not knock anybody while they are down. I believe it's very wrong to knock someone when their down, 'whether fiction or fact'. I was now in the act of discerning what is fact and what is fiction. I was simply trying to be cool under my family's pressures.

After our goodbyes, Janet departed for the Mayo Clinic. Shortly thereafter I officially decided to leave The Vada Corporation. Dad had already left and the future looked questionable at best. I took a position in a similar 5 state territory with MFS (The Modern Farm Systems Corp.) out of Webster City, Iowa. They too had Aetna Health Insurance and I was once again very pleased. Janet's bills were adding up big time. Fortunately for me Janet's family had a trust for her college and medical bills in the past 'college days' which they used for the Mayo experience as well. I wasn't aware of this until I got the initial billing copies. Thank God I left Vada, they couldn't compare with MFS group-Aetna Health coverage. I may have mentioned being somewhat empowered in some former real estate deals, but no one could keep pace with the enormous expenses with Janet's medical condition and the Mayo Clinic. You'll see!

In the meantime Kristi and I traveled the entire five state territories together calling on dealers and/or grain bin installations and systems. We were quite a team, a very cute little girl and her big daddy who drove her just about everywhere and made a great big game out of it. We didn't really know about seat belts back then so she rode on my lap through the large territories of Georgia, Florida, North Carolina, South Carolina and Alabama. We called on existing and new dealer organizations and generally large grain installations. Almost every time a secretary would be at the front desk of the office. I always had coloring books and crayons for Kristi while I would talk with the superintendents, owners, managers, etc. I noticed that almost always the working girls-secretaries liked my little girl. Kristi didn't have an active mother but she sure enjoyed talking with the various secretaries. Every now and then one would ask, "Where's the mother?" I would say, "The Mayo Clinic in Rochester, Minnesota. They are trying to find out what the problem or problems are"; most of the time the ladies would wish us the very best. I was wearing my blinders very well.

As time moved along I would call Janet's ward/hospital number and she didn't know or wouldn't tell me what was going on. I thought this to be very weird. Why was she acting this way? In a couple of weeks I would find out 'the results!' Fortunately I was at home sitting down, relatively calm with expectations naturally low when I was informed. The telephone rang and I answered, "Mr. Cooper, this is Elaine. I am a social worker at the Mayo Clinic, how are you?" "I am fine, what's the word?" She said 'with a great humility, "Janet has been moved to the Psychiatric Ward". I emphatically responded, 'What are you talking about I thought I sent her up there for orthopedics!" "I know but did you know that Janet has *psychosis, psychosomatic tendencies, and schizophrenia?*" I was astounded and stated 'How could this be?' She informed me, "Over the past 30 days Janet Cooper has been moved from Orthopedic to the Psychiatric Ward due to the fact that she simply imagined the various orthopedic pain related problems. In addition she shows great schizophrenic tendencies so to speak in the way that she talks with many different accents and people...all in her mind." I said, 'after trying to calm down' "OK, how much time will it take to treat these problems?" She said, "One year at least, these are enormous problems." I couldn't stand anymore!'I thought my God the Orthopedic Doctor wanted her on her back for one year for absolutely no reason, according to the Mayo' . When I got alone by myself, I pondered these are all the terms I learned in basic psychology in college days. My question, this is REAL? Or Is this UNREAL? I had to find out! This was my wife?

I simply stated, while hanging up "I will see you in two days!" Fortunately Bob and Mary Cox were my very kind next door neighbors to whom I confessed the truth about 'Janet's situation.' I felt I had to tell somebody and they were most happy to care for Kristi (they had a young child, Robbie) while I drove up to the Mayo Clinic in Rochester, Minnesota from Tallahassee, Florida!

The entire route, 1,700 miles plus, my mind was going wild with the thought and horror of Schizophrenia, Psychosis and psychosomatic tendencies. I knew this part was real with the incredibly bad way and circumstance that Janet was confined to. My thoughts were questioning the diagnosis of Psychosis and Schizophrenia. Psychosomatic tendencies were the only symptom that I did agree with. Question- Is the Mayo Clinic Psych Dept crazy or is Janet Broadhead Cooper really this sick/crazy and why didn't I notice or pick up these traits from being around Janet? Once again, I could definitely confirm psychosomatic but the rest! I was almost crazed as she was as I drove an average of 90 miles per hour from Florida to Minnesota. I was stopped by State Patrolmen 2 times, ticketed, and I threw the tickets out of the window almost in front of them. Both of the patrolmen knew I was very disturbed enroute, I told them just like it was, talking with a bewildered heart. I really couldn't believe this is my wife, of course sick physically but now she's possibly completely crazed! I was so anxious that I couldn't sleep and drove all night, both nights, before I finally arrived at the Mayo Clinic. What a huge facility!

When I walked in, the Mayo Staff seemed happy to see me and wanted to give me a tour and show me around their terrific Mayo Clinic. They were so eager but I fervently declined any such assistance. I wanted to see my wife, now. They seemed very surprised with my attitude but I had to see my wife! It had been a 30 day stretch with one year in the balance of horrible news. They led me to an area and finally I arrived at the Psychiatric Ward of the Mayo Clinic. I must have looked a mess; I hadn't slept for 2 days and had driven 24 hours straight. Now I was waiting, seemingly for an hour or more. Finally Janet walks out in a patient's uniform. She seemed listless, not necessarily happy to see me. She had a social worker with her. I asked, "What's going on here?" She said, "We presently have 60 patients and are quite busy coordinating their medications and procedures." I stated, "I get it, Janet is very clearly heavily medicated" I said that right in front of her. The social worker said, "Yes, Janet has been prescribed various meds for her well being." Shaking my head I said, "Can I see the attending physician?" She responded and asked me to sit with Janet until he appeared twenty minutes later in the conference-waiting room. He was of an Indian or East Indian appearance and seemed to talk the talk regarding how mental health takes time especially with her combination of diagnosis. "That is 'the why' it will take at least one year, correct?" He responded, "Correct" and went back to the other area behind the wall. Conversation over! The social worker directed me to a local hotel and I left. Janet was there but <u>nobody was at home</u>. <u>I didn't know this Janet</u>. Who was I married to? I was ready to put 'my blinders' back on and leave as I made my way to the hotel. <u>I was having a very hard time accepting this unbelievable life circumstance.</u>

The next day Janet was only allowed to converse with me in the waiting room. I felt in a sense like I was back in college days sitting innocently in the freshman social areas at Elsy Hall, the girls' dorm at Franklin College where I first met Janet. I couldn't get over the fact that this person was my wife! It was uncanny and heartbreakingly sad as I cried like a baby after I left. I felt like a Martian. Our conversation was at best minimal and very unsatisfactory at least from my perspective. Janet and the social worker thought it would be good for me to play tennis with a fellow inmate. They both thought we resembled each other and the game might settle me down, '*I was still clearly upset*'. We met and went to the tennis facility. As we walked I asked 'why are you here?' he said, "I work at General Motors and recently had a nervous breakdown." I told him 'I was sorry and hope he recovers soon.' At that point I wondered why I wasn't more sympathetic for Janet and shouldn't I be more understanding. During the game, I'm not sure who won. I didn't care. He said something to me that I didn't expect, as we were leaving. "Gary I'm trying to overcome very strong homosexual tendencies." Suddenly I knew who I was and thought does he know who he is? Apparently not, I wished him well; my emphatically understanding or at least trying to understand was out of gas. I moved on back to Janet's ward. She was a little more aware during this next meeting 'they didn't medicate her because of me'. I tried very hard to be more understanding; I still had hope for her because Kristi and I truly needed her. She smiled and responded, "This has been a very difficult discovery for me as well. I'm just trying to get through this." I responded, "We will just have to get through this, I need to get back to Kristi. She is with Bob and Mary." She understood and I left. What a lonely life she must be having... I pondered all the way back to the south. Put on' my blinders', observed the speed limits, this time. Carry on, Kristi needs me! I focused rightly. It's been a long time coming I had to tell myself. Life isn't always fair. We just have to get through this.

After much checking in psychiatric journals, I found that schizophrenia occurred quite often in persons from 19 to 23 yrs. old. I found this illness to be the hardest to believe because she never exhibited this behavior in my presence. But at every clinic she was observed talking with other parties and/or groups of people without anyone in attendance. I must have been blinded to this but I once again really understood psychosomatic- I know that one! I had many general health orthopedic operations, procedures and such in my medical records as proof. To this day many years later, I still ask why? This thought process made me very leery of getting a hip operation years later. But after weeks of real pain, I got a new hip! And, "Yes, Doctor, I feel fine."

During our travels 'business and pleasure' Kristi and I were closer than peanut butter and jelly or bumble bees and honey or not quite but maybe 'even like a mother and her daughter'. Clearly I had to be the father and the mother, God helps me! I had one year with almost zero communication from Janet. 'She was not supposed to call in order to build her personal confidence. Of course I could somewhat understand the social worker's intent, with all the so called family guilt trips and such. I told her," I don't understand why, I didn't cause this!" Janet said, "The social worker is trying to find 'who did cause this' I know it's not you, they think it might be Tom, my brother." Being a rambunctious little boy and teenager he used to jump out behind doors and scare Janet. Every kid in America has done that! I ended the call and thought he is being set up for disaster. Her brother Tom is a PHD Paleontologist and has moved on. I didn't believe Tom did anything. The Mayo is simply looking for a <u>scapegoat</u> and the way, I saw it, just blame it on somebody? This was extremely dissatisfying to me, but standard procedure in Psychological clinics. Somebody has to take blame for this pain.

Kristi and I had 5 states to cover and we would look for motels/hotels with swimming pools and then a pizza place, if possible. We had our priorities. We also liked traveling Alabama because the song 'Sweet Home Alabama' was popular as we would sing it for many, many miles. We also had a small dog that would travel with us. Caesar was a miniature Chihuahua-poodle and was very spicy and fun. On a state highway I rolled down the window and fortunately had Caesar on a leash. After a mile or so I asked where Caesar is, he was found hanging on the outside of the car window. Literally bouncing off the car back and forth in the wind! I pulled him back in and we didn't let the car windows down after that event. Caesar was perfectly fine and seemed to want to do it again! We also liked to shop in the mall and grocery stores. At home we continued walking, talking and Kristi often played with other children and Caesar. I told all the neighborhood women that Janet was in the Mayo due to extreme back ailments, I knew if I told them the real reasons, it would not go well. I was in a kind of personality flameout engulfed with the process of absorbing 'our realities' as well. The neighborhood women seemed to see beyond my misleading talk. Psychiatric Analysis was often questioned and debated. I could explain Orthopedics and protect Janet's reputation possibly; providing that she would possibly someday return. For 1 year my blinders remained. I needed a healthy distraction. My mind was now geared on business opportunities. 'Sort of like my hobby' always asking myself, 'Is this profitable, workable and applicable within my context'. I was in the 'seek and you shall find mood'.

Enter: Kimball Harville of 'Concrete to Go of Statesboro Georgia. As Kristi and I passed by one day, I noticed a small concrete plant along the side of the road. I stopped and thought to myself,'Is this something a lot of people won't do for themselves? Such as mix their own concrete?' Kimball was clearly a welder, builder, adventurous type, and inventor all in one. "Sir, my name is Gary Cooper from Tallahassee and is this what I think it is?" He said, "This is a copy of 'U-carte of Kansas City, Missouri'. They pour small one yard amounts of concrete, put in on a movable cart and sell it. "I understood and said," Do you sell these systems?" He stated, "Yes, but I'm trying various chemicals for not drying the concrete out so fast." I said, 'Here's my card, figure a price and I'll get back with you." He responded 'OK". That was it!

# THE PROMOTER

When I returned to Tallahassee I had one main idea and business purpose. 'Find a group of people who have a vision, money and character'. I remembered my NML training. People who are 65 and older hold/own 70% of our nation's wealth. I was 24 years of age with $4,000 dollars in the bank, with just a car, my child, house, airplane and dog. I looked for the possibilities, at least two seniors (retired or near retirement). I washed my car at a very popular car wash, Ken Pogie, was the owner, He looked just about right! After many visits, I approached him with the Concrete to go idea. He seemed to like it and set a time for us to discuss it. We discussed and I went back to Statesboro with prepared questions and got more information from Kimball. This is what I found. The cost-entire unit, production requirements, chemistry- especially for slowing the maturation process with concrete, mixing procedures and various sales markets: Such as people with small yards where a concrete truck might crush the driveway especially with small application users. I told Ken we need another person to spread the financial risk. Here comes a friend, Harold Hill-retired of Ford Credit. He and Ken were very close friends and the next thing I remember, rather quickly Harold, Ken and I were signing notes at $800,000 initially and $1,100,000 later. These banknotes were required in order to start the newest Corporation in south Tallahassee, <u>Koncrete to Go, Inc of Florida</u>. Within 6 months we had a very nice concrete plant in south Tallahassee and I was president at age 24! Our markets were initially the individuals but then the State of Florida moved in. We got the contract for the entire state's manhole covers! Of which I had ironically knocked off manhole covers in Tampa with an unhooked and unmanned trailer in the Vada days. We were now signing $1,000,000+ notes and looking for a professional concrete man. Here came J. McDaniel's, concrete engineer 'age 56' from Kentucky, growing very fast at this point.

I was now president of a fast growing concrete company with a wife in a mental hospital, a representative of MFS and most importantly father of a darling little girl. She seemed to like some of the small preschools in Tallahassee that we previewed and only used for my business day requirements. The rest of the year went very fast. The Mayo Clinic called me and stated, "Janet is ready to come home." OK! I had a little bit of trepidation. What was this going to be like? Mayo sent the requirements ahead. 1) Janet must see a psychiatrist each week, mandatory. 2) All information must be kept confidential, 3) Janet will also be required to take various medications as directed by the local Psychiatrist. The bill breakdown also came. It was a mere $385,000 for one year at the Mayo! Thanks, Aetna Health Insurance. She would be arriving the following week. I wasn't sure what really to expect. Who would she be? Am I really in the picture? How about Kristi?..... I thought many such thoughts to myself and once again, to myself. I will not let Kristi get hurt by this, if possible. I decided not to tell Kristi that her mother was coming. I couldn't stand seeing her get a letdown, not to mention how Janet might feel as well. The week was nearing, Janet was coming....back.

## ADJUSTING, COPING, FITTING, ENFORCING, MEDICATING & COUNSELING

When Janet was released enroute to our Tallahassee home, she visited her parents first in Missouri. This was my first indicator? Husband and daughter #2, Are we as important? Is this behavior of seeing others a precedent? Upon her arrival she seemed to be like an old friend visiting. Janet had become in one year extremely small and skinny. She looked and appeared like she could have been my older daughter instead of my wife. I found this fact to be really weird. The word asexual 'one without sex' was introduced right away, by Janet. I think Janet told me this as to separate the thoughts of love on my part. With her emaciated look it was very hard to conjure up any love thoughts. Unless I viewed old pictures of WW2 starved Jewish concentration camp members. I told her, "I'm very concerned about how horribly skinny you are"... She assured me that was no problem but this is the effect of being in a hospital so long. She said, "I will get heavier." I had my doubts. She really looked sick.

Kristi wasn't rude but you could tell she saw Janet as a person, initially not after her return, her mother. Janet acted as if she's been here before, possibly Kristy subconsciously prepared herself with the thought 'don't get too close' clearly a defense mechanism. Almost instantly back in context was her next thought,'where's Dad,*my stable one?*' I decided to be very kind to Janet and try to understand, while hoping for the best. She toid me what a difference it made to read 'My Mother Myself' required reading by the Mayo clinic possible insights in the relationship between a mother and daughter. A lot has changed for all of us over the year while Janet was away. *I noticed that when Kristi played with her dolls, she was acting as though she was the doll in the middle and the father doll was next to her and the mother doll was near but not close.* Doll therapy was very effective with Kristi. As a small 3 & 1/2 year old this was the best she could do, at least in the beginning. I simply tried to play this new game-life adjustment with Janet and I really didn't like it very much. Janet was home, but not really back. This new person had most of her priorities, all about her care 'meds' and her doctor. Her medicines were high impact federally controlled substances. My commitment had to be paramount for the cause of getting her well 'in a sense' the chance of the close love we had in the past was simply not in the cards. With schizophrenia, a mental problem of not knowing with imagined, and multiples and real and unreal relationships, I began asking myself, 'who had I been dealing with? The former Janet doesn't seem to be home. I found myself wondering where has she gone?' I planned on asking the doctor these questions. In the meantime, food in the toilet started to back up. I knew it had to be Janet for sure, this time! I still couldn't figure it out and I started calling plumbers. I just needed their opinion. Janet had heard me calling the plumbers and complaining about the 'tiny bits of food in the toilet' and said nothing at all. I found these bits of food in the toilet very disturbing. How?

When Janet went to her new psychiatrist she seemed to like him. I talked with him on the phone to keep her stories straight, if necessary. The meds were always strong. I don't remember the names except Percocet with many other types of antidepressants. I felt these depressants did not seem to benefit anybody including Janet. Way too much 'out to lunch behavior' was now being exhibited almost all the time. When someone is truly mentally sick it is simply no fun at all. No more laughing or cutting up at such a young age, really sad.' They often can't help themselves and few patients come out of it....but, not very often', according to her

Doctor. I only had a slight shred of hope at this moment in time and then it happened.

Janet was now starting to try to kill herself again. She would beat her head on the walls in our house or talk about hanging herself. She asked and I refused to help her 'kill herself' and would 'rush her to outpatient lockdown' in the back of Tallahassee Memorial Hospital. This lockdown would only last 3-4 days and either start again shortly thereafter unless something major changed. Very little has changed since her return and this procedure was happening way too often- almost every weekend! This literally became routine. It was just a part of our lives. We had to accept it! Time goes on.

Janet's brother Tom and sister-in-law Anne came to visit us from Knoxville Tenn. Tom was a professor at University of Tennessee. The visit was fairly cordial as Kristi, Janet and I all seemingly had a good time. Kristi played with Anne and Janet, while Tom and I visited. None of us wanted to have Janet troubled. They were aware and had heard about some of her mental problems.

Thanksgiving went pretty well overall, thank goodness, and everyone eventually went to bed. About 2: 00 am Janet got up and tried to hit her head on the wall once again and I had to take her to lockdown. The next morning when Tom and Anne awoke they were surprised that Janet was in lockdown. At that moment Tom acknowledged his scare tactics as a small boy but found it hard to imagine that is what caused Janet to have these types of problems. I told Tom that he caused absolutely none of her problems. At this point clearly, "No one really knows, the Mayo was just shopping to blame and being her brother made you a suspect initially. It didn't last long and this abusing of herself has been going on since her return."

Tom and Anne felt they should leave and wished Kristi and me their very best with very heavy hearts. Tom was Janet's only sibling. All of this was very hard to make sense of. I didn't feel led to tell them that Janet not only wet the bed but soiled the mattress as well. Only aged seniors have this problem at times. The troubles just kept on coming and we all were desperately looking for answers.

Shortly after the holidays Janet returned to her doctor. Her doctor made a huge discovery. He explained, "Janet had a blister on her finger and she has anorexia nervosa." I said, "What' in the hell, is that?" He proceeded to tell me that Janet was sticking her finger down her throat and violently throwing up! He said, "Janet clearly needs some extreme mental health or death is imminent." Two things instantly came into my mind. 1) Janet was the one messing up my toilets and not telling me by throwing up and leaving bits of food!" 2) Janet is going to the best I can find and this is it! The doctor sternly stated this problem can be a death sentence. Impulsively, I once again called Beanie, her father. The twin engine plane reappeared and took Janet right to Menninger Foundation in Topeka, Kansas. I knew from past history with the Mayo experience that considering our traumatic life in Tallahassee, we would only go up to Kansas when everyone including me had a purpose/intent for her recovery. Somehow I was still slightly optimistic but very cautious as well. My heart was broken and I was numb. I couldn't quite feel emotions very well, I was expecting nothing. My wife was truly gone and Kristi's Mom was gone again which was the saddest part of all this, for me. Just before Janet departed she told Kristi 'her only daughter' "Goodbye! Kristi" This was the moment that I truly realized that you can 'goodbye' your child' unto unbelief. Upon Janet's departure, Kristi was also numb and went back to playing with her dolls. We both had different ideas about her dismissal but the emotions were same. All Kristi had again now was me. God help Kristi and God help me. I decided that negative thinking was of no benefit for Kristi and me! Let's do something that is fun!

One Sunday morning I listened to a preacher on television named Rayburn Blair at the Tallahassee Baptist Church, Tallahassee, Florida. His message to most probably wasn't over the top, but to me it was God! I watched the Reverend for the next several weeks and decided to ask him a very serious question. I went to his office and sought him out. He was dressed like a million dollars. I introduced myself and he did the same and we went to talking. Rayburn proceeded to tell me that he was in a foxhole in Korea and everyone was getting killed. There was no way out and he had a serious question and made a serious comment to God! Rayburn said, "God, if you will get me out of here. I will preach the gospel the rest of my life!" "And here I am!

I told The Reverend that I had given up on God in the 9th grade by not going forward to the church's altar and I haven't been touched by God since. My wife is in very, very serious condition at a hospital in Kansas. My child is at her daycare and she is my total responsibility. I am also a representative for MFS over 5 states. I work for the former Postmaster General under President Nixon. "My question is simple!" "Do you really believe that Jesus Christ is Lord?" He leaned back with his pure white hair with his beautiful black suit. He promised me "The same God who touched you is still on the throne and clearly wants you back. It's a totally free gift and all you have to do is receive it!" It was just this simple. He led me in a prayer of salvation and at this point in time. This moment in time! It was September, 1979! I'm on God's team! It doesn't mean everything is going to be alright but I'm still saved. This God is no Indian giver!

'Gary's on a mission!' Get ready I'm coming and God still sits on the throne! Kristi and I departed in my aircraft for St. Joseph, Missouri. Six hours later we were there. Upon landing at the airport Beanie and Barbie were both present. Kristi and I were happy to see them, and we were tired and hungry! We headed off to their very pretty country club condo on the golf course. After supper and a light conversation, we went to bed. The next morning we would travel by car to Topeka to see Janet. Prior to bed, they told me that we would be on TV at the clinic to observe our actions towards each other with 10 psychiatrists behind the glass structure. I asked how much? They said,"$10,000 per hour" I said," In the morning at breakfast I want to tell you all something." "OK"

The next morning all were refreshed and ready to travel from St Joe to Topeka, Kansas. Prior to our trip at breakfast I decided to tell Beanie and Barbie how God could possibly help Janet based on His will. I was greatly enthused with excitement in my heart, mind, and spirit. The table was dressed with beautiful silverware, real china plates and with a wonderfully green golf course right outside their dining room picture window. I said, "Beanie and Barbie, between our insurance company and ourselves we have spent very close to a million dollars regarding Janet's health. I almost feel like it's been a Humpty Dumpty experience and Janet is almost ready to fall from what the Doctors have told me. I believe it's time to ask God to somehow give her a miracle". 'I expected a negative heavy feedback from Beanie; he never went to church like Barbie did. Barbie strongly spoke up, "Gary, you really don't believe that Jesus was born from a virgin, do you? You don't really believe he was raised from the dead, do you?" I went from true/honest joyous/excitement to an obvious frown 'inside and out' with absolutely shock knowing that the church goer Barbie was talking just like the devil instead of the weekly churchgoer that made me think she was much more of a Christian than I! The Bible talks about 'Judge not lest ye be judged' I was more surprised & shocked regarding her response as opposed to the 'bear or lion' incident. I was shocked with a little emotional response of sorts. But with Barbie, there was no comeback. I held my peace 'I had nothing to say, there was no talking the entire way' from St Joseph Missouri through a 5 -6 hour ride to Topeka, Kansas. I gave Kristi a coloring book and she filled in the pictures while 'I was dazed' while looking at millions of tall Sunflower plants endlessly growing over the entire route to Menninger's Foundation. As we were nearing the facility it occurred to me that Janet 'my wife' really needed to know the Lord for truly no one else in her immediate family believed like me as compared to this demonic unbelief. I decided that I was the only one who could give her this good news at least for her salvation and possibly but not probable a type of spiritual healing! My spiritual battery was clearly on tilt!

As we pulled into the large Menninger Foundation parking area Beanie let everyone out. Beanie, Barbie and Kristy walked toward the center of the facility. I pulled the car around to park. I was still getting ready to 'lay it on the line' with Janet. My mind was whirling, thinking about how to tell her this news. In the meantime, much to my chagrin an attractive and problematic- type girl dove into the car through the side window and begged me to 'take her out of here'. Within seconds guards pulled the girl out and took her somewhere. I suppose this incident somewhat cleared my mind as I rejoined the family not telling of my recent crazy' experience. We were on 'appointment watch' to be joined with the 'Janet/ psychiatric TV intercession'. I asked to talk with Janet alone at first.

She looked horrible. I felt sorry but I still had to tell her, "Janet, did you know your mother does not believe in Jesus Christ?" She looked startled as she said, "What do you mean?" I told her the story in great summary.

I then told Janet, "I don't care how you feel about me but please allow God to help you. What choice do you have your electrolytes and synapses are completely shot according to your physician's reports!" She told me she would truly think about this and let me know. The social workers came and led us into the $10,000 dollar/hour room! Upon entering I looked through the opaque type glass and looked at many doctors and therapists with clip boards and writing pads. Inside the room they asked me to separate from Beanie, Barbie, Janet, and Kristi on the right side, while they asked me to sit on the left side. The moderator was off center from the middle of the room. Within 10 seconds, Kristi comes to me obviously feeling very disturbed. She begged me, "Daddy, get me out of here!" I turned to the moderator and he said, "Let them go they really aren't needed much for this interview." We were quickly whisked away and they put Kristi in a play area beside an office where I was led in to talk with one of the social workers.

She said," Mr. Cooper are you aware of the severity of Janet's circumstances?. As you may have read her electrolytes and synapse report didn't state clear results. Janet will be deceased within two years unless a miracle or change in her mind occurs. Even then she will not live very long due to such extreme self-neglect." I said, "I figured this much but am glad you have told me so we can plan accordingly." She quickly responded, "What do you mean we? Janet can't go back to Tallahassee and visit. Quite frankly our suggestion is divorce." I said, "That isn't your decision. We are still married and that is 'our decision' and 'our decision only'! I wasn't about let a social worker, doctor or anybody else make these types of decisions for me or her. I had never once thought like that because the entire time I honored our wedding vows 'whether in sickness or health' in a Biblical type way. I went on to tell the social worker about God intervening with Janet. At this point another counselor came in and took over. They seemed ready to put me into a type of therapy. She said, "I want to talk with you about religious beliefs and fallacies." I said, "Hold it right there, I've heard a lot of negative things about Jesus Christ in the past. I believe God could miraculously deliver Janet but it does take faith, that's something that psychologists often have problems with and I don't." She didn't waste her time and left. I got up walked over and played with Kristi until a few minutes later the group session opened and let out the rest of Janet's small family group. I asked everyone 'how was it?' Janet had no more time and was whisked away.

They rushed her out. They were obviously afraid that I would seriously harm her condition. They might have been right, I thought, as we left the large facility. How alone and empty I felt for Janet and myself. Was anything accomplished except an outsider's opinion of us which I rejected? I held little Kristi's arm and hugged her if not for her, then myself, and my emotional state. I was attempting to understand how differently I was viewing this entire situation. We eventually got back to St Joseph, stayed the night and left the next morning. The weather report wasn't very good; a lot of scattered thunderstorms were in the horizon. What a bumpy ride, thermals 'up and down pockets of air' were everywhere. The weather got so bad that we had to request the tower to bring us down in Memphis, Tennessee. We landed in a forty to sixty mph crosswind; I turned slightly right into it and landed instantly. We stayed in the hangar until the storms passed and made it back in much smoother air without incident. What a trip…

In a brief reflection of the entire trip I was shocked by Barbie, 'why in God's name did she even go to church'; Given very bad news re: Janet, given a forecast for our marriage that was unqualified at best and just glad to be back in Tallahassee with simple concerns which I could handle.

During the next few months there was little talk with Janet or her family. Then all of a sudden the Kansas City Memorial Hospital announced that they had Janet under their supervision and wanted to use electroshock therapy and shortly thereafter hypnosis. I had to sign off via my Health Insurance. Once again, I actually felt sorry for the Aetna Insurance Group. What a waste!

At this point in my life I thought and pondered that maybe putting her on a deserted island with palm trees and nuts might be good to bring her mind back to the true value of food, nourishment. I was floundering for ideas except for God himself to truly help her.

A week or so later Janet called and said, "The hypnosis really helped. I was raped in Estes Park Colorado by a young long haired biker who invited me to a party that didn't exist. He overpowered me, raped me and fled. I was so embarrassed that I didn't tell anyone and that is how all of this happened." I was very happy for her and she said she would call back. I almost told her it would be a great time to call her brother Tom so he could get off the 'he did it list' from the Mayo which tried to pin her illness on her brother. I was also glad I didn't tell the professionals anything regarding throwing Janet out on a deserted island. She didn't call me back. I waited a few more weeks and called the Kansas City hospital, 'I was told she had been checked out for several weeks!'

I thought where did she go? So I called Barbie who said, "I don't know where she is." I was getting angry and sternly asked "Look Barbie, I know Janet 'I really didn't know her', what a ridiculous statement. I haven't really known her for years, if she's not with you, where would she be? She is still my wife, I felt like saying child, and I deserve an answer." She said, "OK, here is her number." I immediately called her and was even angrier. Why didn't she want to be with her husband and daughter? Where were her motherly urges? "Why did you move to Missouri and not tell me? Do you realize that your little girl doesn't look for you anymore and only you can change that?" She didn't respond at all Sometimes psychiatric therapy teaches you to not to strike out emotionally, but remain silent. Once again, I felt completely and emotionally removed at this point as I stated, "If this is the way you want it maybe your caseworker was right." She responded affirmatively, not wanting to argue, stating,"That's right". I said, "After all this time and all this money, these poor results with our relationship seems pointless." She agreed, saying nothing. I said, "Have your attorney call mine", I gave her a number. She affirmed and hung up. The attorneys chatted. Our divorce was extremely simple. I demanded that I have the child. I hoped for at least a statement or attempt to demand her daughter's custody, for Kristine's record if nothing else. Only a very sick person would give up her child. Like this entire debacle, this divorce was absolutely abnormal and truly confirmed she must be very sick and crazy. Besides full custody of our child, I kept the house I paid for, any business's that I paid for, my car and the airplane that I paid for was mine without question. I committed to allow Janet to use my medical insurance accordingly and pick up any possessions within my household belongings to be taken. At this point in my life I really didn't care what they came and took. Divorce is very, very disappointing. I took this hard and vowed to not put my daughter and myself through this type situation again.

The divorce was granted and I had to appear in court with the honorable Hurley Rudd, an older Judge. It so happened that 'court day' was just before my 'basketball day' hardly anything stopped my B-ball day 'as my frustration over all of this was also very high, so I appeared with a friend in my basketball outfit. I had no regards for this divorce decree. I found the entire idea appalling. I told this to Judge Rudd. He asked me as he looked at the paperwork, "Son, do you have a job?" I said, "Yes sir, I am a representative traveling over 5 states for Blount Industries, Red Blount was the Postmaster General through President Nixon. Today I play and dress like this for basketball to reduce my anxiety regarding the pathetic situation where a mother can't even request her child, as she doesn't have the ability to do so."The Judge responded," Your case is granted and God bless you son." 'Thank you your honor" I left and played basketball. He should have kicked my butt out of his court and made me come back dressed more honorably, but he didn't. Judge Rudd knew something had to be very wrong for a man to have sole custody. I couldn't believe it either.

Shortly before the divorce was granted a neighbor across the street approached me 'about Janet' how much can you take? She was exclaiming, "Her ex- husband was an alcoholic." I think she conditioned me for 'going through with a divorce, thank God Janet left me...I suppose I could have handled it in my own way but I really do bend for the less fortunate. Regardless I was a free man! But I really didn't feel any different because for the last 5 years it certainly wasn't normal, to say the least. We haven't really been married for years. What an incredible learning experience, I took the long term pain for a long while. After all of this, if I ever remarried there are certain traits that must be met, spiritually and naturally. This futuristic female must without exception know God and show his love accordingly. I made that commitment to God because I was starting to feel sorry for Kristi. I noticed that she walked exactly the way I walked. I noticed that she spit exactly the way I spit. After this small fog of dismay disperses, I will possibly date for the both of us, but only with a special person.

I had been taking Kristi to church and I always sat on the front row and couldn't help but notice that everyone was nice but nobody spent any time asking because it didn't make sense for a man alone with a small girl. It was hard for me or them to hardly relate at all. I was now the third wheel. I had Kristi in dance class, tumbling class (she was a natural tumbler), and we walked and talked. We hadn't at this point joined a Sunday school class either adult or child. I was missing something and opening my eyes looking for it. A month had passed by and I got an invitation either in the mail or my newspaper slot it with a brochure from a church for a Christian singles-covered dish event. For some reason I wasn't quite sure what 'covered dish' even meant. So I just made note of the date and did my business as usual. Kristi was now in school and I had hired a lady to watch over her until I returned. The airplane sure helped, it was fast. I had various rice mills in south Florida move bulldozers off the track for me to land on little 8 foot wide roads with 4 foot ditches on each side. I became a skilled bush pilot before it was over. I also sold a huge 150' grain mill to Seminole Sugar as they flooded sugar cane to kill disease in the fields while planting rice...this is where I came into the picture. I spent several months flying in and flying out while crews erected the multiple tanks with in bin stirring devices. I also got to occasionally visit with my Aunt Helen Bice and her husband Graham. They were close by in Vero Beach, Florida.

The day of the single- covered dish arrived. I had just made it in from the airport, picked up Kristi, and scooted over to the St. Paul Methodist Church near a popular walking trail called ' Lake Ella' in Tallahassee. I timidly walked around the back rear of the church with Kristi and couldn't see in the windows because they were about 8 feet high. I picked up Kristi and said, "Honey look in there and see if they look normal to you." She said, "Daddy, they look very normal and there is an all night daycare right over there." I was shocked that my 5 year old Kristi knew exactly where she was. We left the church and went right over to the daycare and they knew Kristi by name! Kristi asked if she could play and I told her I'd be back shortly. Had the lady put her there often or at time for groceries? Either way I didn't like it, mostly because I wasn't made aware of this maneuver with my child. I returned to the church and walked right in. The time wasright, the meals were put away. They were forming into groups where I noticed this very attractive lady. So I went and sat at her table. It was really great to hear the message from the small group leader and I talked a little bit too much but they were all graceful. During the sessions there was a break as I remember. During the break the attractive lady named Susan and I conversed. She too was recently divorced had two children and was kind enough to give me her telephone number. She wanted to introduce me to another female close to my age that she thought we might like each other. I said, 'OK, thanks' and left. Kristi was having a good time at the night time day care and we left to go home. I thought it was interesting that Kristi was asking me all about the Christian Singles club meeting. I told her I really wasn't sure but I had met a real nice lady named Susan. I told her about you and she has two children. I asked her, "Would you like to have them visit?" She said, "Yes Daddy". It instantly occurred to me that I had never had any lady friends over with Kristi before. My reason was simple. I knew Kristi didn't have a mother and I didn't want to get anyone too close and then leave for whatever reason thus upsetting Kristi even more. In other words, I picked my female companions very wisely. The following week I called Susan and we had a very nice chat and I offered to have her and her children come over for some hot chocolate and snacks after dinner. I made my hot chocolate from scratch; I had to stir it for over an hour because Susan and her kids arrived really late. What a visit we had.

Since I hadn't exposed Kristi to anyone yet outside of family and child care persons Kristi was somewhat shy. When Susan, Melissa at 6, and Scott age 5 walked in, Kristi hid behind the couch. *We found that Scott and Kristi were just 20 days apart in age.* Kristi and I had not had any social life outside of a very close circle and my little girl didn't know what to do. It was humorous type of situation and Scott was a cute kid and had a funny laugh. He thought Kristi was hilarious hiding behind the couch. After a few minutes Kristi came out for casual introductions. Then shortly thereafter I noticed that Kristi, Melissa, and Scott were all playing in her room having a really good time. We both thought they all looked cute. Susan and I prepared the remaining snacks and we all finished the cocoa. Shortly thereafter everybody left and we wished them well. I continued to call Susan. She was really nice, in many ways. We had some really great conversations, our divorces, our kids, our relationship to God and families. I noticed she didn't say anything about the other lady close to my age. Could it be that she liked me or was I just imagining it. I personally thought Susan was very pretty and enticing. I liked talking with her also. So a few weeks later, I asked her out to lunch during business hours, at a place called Lucy Ho's Chinese restaurant. I believe that we thought that our lunch would be <u>just a lunch</u> (her job gave 1 hour for lunch) and that was it. Something had changed. Maybe there was a new kind of attitude. We both had basic assumptions regarding each other. We were both wrong!

# THE HAPPENING!

Sometimes things don't happen the way we expect them to occur. Susan was a few years older but I didn't have any problem with a slight age difference at all. I believe initially Susan was slightly concerned. Maybe we needed a sign.

It must have come through as we ate our lunch and I felt myself warmly gazing at Susan while easily studying the Chinese calendar placemat that we used in the Chinese Restaurant. It had relationship depictions based on birthdates and I noticed that with my birth date I was compared to a rabbit (very lucky and happy most of the time). I was very much like that! What was even more interesting Susan's date had a symbol which was called a 'boar' while finding factually that both dates said that Rabbit's and Boar's react really well together. We actually got a little insight/oomph from an old Chinese Proverb Calendar. *Could it be that God was working in mysterious ways or did I just react while consuming a sugar filled fortune cookie?* Regardless we left and I dropped Susan off at her work 'Special Ed Evaluator-Thomas County Schools'. I continued to call her. Once again I continued to call reasonably and consistently. Neither one of us complained when I needed someone to hear my story. 'Confession is good for the heart'. I believe we both really tried to hear each other.

Before we first met I remember hearing the old Frank Sinatra song 'Strangers in the Night' It reminded me of Susan and me. We had absolutely no friends in common, we didn't work anywhere near each other, I was a Sales Representative covering 5 States. She was a special education evaluator. Our children didn't go to the same schools. I was from Indiana and she was from New York, originally. I was a big FSU Florida State University football fan and she could care less. Our houses were over 10 miles away from each other. Her degree was in Education and mine in Economics. Except for this fateful singular Christian Singles meeting I would never have met Susan. The interesting part about the meeting was the brochures were not mailed or put in a newspaper. Somehow I got the news and Susan was on the Christian Singles board of directors and she didn't know how I was informed either. I had to believe that was either just an unbelievable chance or destiny was in play. Either way this adds to our relational-mystery at times. On the initial evening we met I didn't even notice that Susan had another man with her that night at St Paul's Methodist Church. They dated occasionally at best and according to Susan were slowly breaking apart. Nothing seemed to stop us. I wondered if God was acting on my prayer concerning a Christian wife possessing spiritual fruit with children playing happily. I didn't really know how to discern that something had happened. Our friendship had quickly moved from friendship into a serious loving relationship. We both seemed very happy and eager about it. A few months later I asked Susan to date only me in order to give us a chance. If possible to see how far our relationship would go. I would never imply marriage or any other ploy except dating as I quite frankly did not trust myself.

My first marriage was almost a total disaster except for Kristi which turned out to be a 'real miracle' considering her mother's health and eventual premature death. In the meantime I met some of Susan's family who also lived in Tallahassee. She had an Uncle Harold from St Petersburg, Florida, who was hospitable and accepting towards me which I greatly appreciated. She worked a part time job for Hal Herman 'her cousin' who had a sales order company in Tallahassee. Susan had a rigorous schedule when I first met her. She would drive from Tallahassee on a dangerous two lane road Hwy 319 which took many lives in auto crashes en route to Thomasville, GA about 35 miles north. Her full time job was clearly Thomas County School System. She would pick her children up from daycare and then work for Hal part time. I couldn't see how she had hardly any time for me or anybody else with a schedule like that. All of this was a definite issue in my prayer life. Was this relationship truly of any consideration? We also went to a few FSU football games and it was the only time I would drink except FSU allowed 'at the time' wineskin pouches into the football games. Probably to boost attendance, FSU football was really starting to 'take off' in the national sports scene, the booze freedom must have worked a little then. Can't do that now! Regardless, I would drink from the wineskin with my neighbors who had tickets beside us and get as close to feeling a 'little high' as possible. This did not impress

Susan at all and rightfully so 'Susan was thinking to herself about getting rid of me, especially after our initial football date. What if I was an alcoholic?' Or maybe just playful and this FSU thing was it? I found after her rightful communication I found through my historical soul searching that I envied persons that drank 'they seemed to have so much fun' when I played college football and couldn't drink. Could this be my personal fun time FSU football spectator fan rewind, only in my mind of course? Susan found out that alcohol had almost no effect on me except FSU games and a few weddings. I did drink responsibly most of the time. I clearly had the take it or leave it mentality. Thank God!

After this period of time with dating and shared life experiences I found myself infighting with a bit of confusion while telling myself, ' you're not good enough to further this or any relationship on your own'. This is what it boiled down to, "Who else can you ask except God?" I clearly asked God to show me if I'm wasting my time or in fact is Susan the person for me 'marriage'. I wouldn't and couldn't proceed without a direct 'OK' from the King of Kings. Nothing of course happened instantly, God just doesn't ever work that way for most. I think He wants us to forget and somewhat reduce our concerns and simply 'die to ourselves, while giving our problems/concerns to God' and then possibly work out my thoughts ending with His Will, possibly much later as I was hoping much sooner. After doing various fun and joint activities with the children, I did ask Susan something that excited and moved me greatly 'I tried not to let her know'. I subtly stated this in a gentle passing comment sort of like a nonchalant low key test as possible, "Susan, if you ever got married again would you consider having another child?" She said, "Yes, I would consider it." She had just given me an inch and I wanted the mile. I knew if we did get married that another child would tie everyone together and I really liked that idea. In the south they would say, "Everybody's kin, similar bloodlines...Meaning relational"

Our time had a certain bright and clear flow that particular upcoming Saturday after Thanksgiving. Susan and I decided to attend the large Market Day sales and crafts event held annually in Tallahassee. There we were, Susan, my girlfriend, and I holding hands 'I always loved to hold hands with this special girlfriend'.

The 3 children played as we were walking around the paved road/aisles looking around at various craft type objects. It came upon me gently even calmly to test 'the spirit of God!' In the natural I knew what I felt called to do would simply not work. I truly had a very small type of seed faith with this action. I sensed that God had inspired me to say 'two words'! At this point I figured maybe I had once again eaten something wrong. Then it occurred to me that maybe God is in this because this is completely absurd in the natural scope of most relationships. I had an unknown battle going on in my mind as we walked along holding hands. It was time to possibly 'test the spirit of God, maybe?'

I looked away from her beautiful eyes directly at the pillowy southern clouds. 'I was very sure she would respond, 'What did you say?' I proceeded and asked Susan 'W--- Y--?" Trust me they were ridiculous words, totally unromantic 'especially to ask a smart woman like Susan' She said, "Yes!" I reacted excitedly, was completely stunned and spiritually shocked while I almost physically picked her up with loving force and took her to a somewhat quiet metal building wall 'this time looking directly into the depths of her beautiful brown eyes' and very sincerely asked her," What did I say?" She quickly responded, "You asked me to marry you and I said, Yes" Only God could have given her this unbelievable 'non-romantic' spiritual discernment and I was absolutely thrilled because God answered my prayer. Therefore I knew! Susan was in fact my destiny! For the last 36+ years we return to The Market Day Event and I re-ask 'the question'. We have seen many vendors near this wall site in the past or present they either cry or laugh or both as I somewhat explain this annual mission a type of 'Mecca'. I'm truly glad many see it as romantic. I sure do. 'The happening' occurred when Susan discerned so wonderfully, as a result of prayer, the absurd question that only God could have given me. I can't begin to tell you what a difference this was for me, Susan and our children. A Christ centered marriage has a slightly better chance in our society and more significantly implies an eternal benefit as well for all concerned 'us and our children, etc'. A Christ centered marriage, if it truly is centered will never be in question when the world is telling you otherwise with the many temptations and all the challenging sinful pitfalls. Just like most preachers say, "What God has joined together let no man put asunder." When I advise young people I ask them this question very sincerely. Can you truly discern that you both are 'equally yoked in Jesus Christ' this question must be answered otherwise it's a crap shoot that you may fall into the divorce statistics and mayhem that have destroyed many families and greatly affected our country 'in a not so good way'. Sometimes one has to wait on God with much prayer. Susan and I also had a new joint basis for opportunities in Christ, business, family and helping others. The results are magnificent, two believing with power and faith. Now we are simply called to believe and act on the power of God. There simply was no great sense of guilt from our past lives, due to God's forgiveness while 'not looking back as opposed to going forward'. The future with our children has prayerfully been our greatest challenges and most rewarding as they 'their children and our grandchildren' continue to become our consistent #1 prayer.

We were now prepared to go 'full in'with our families and marriage; The hope of a fruitful combination of adults, children, all the many activities and challenges as well. Somehow all of this was going to hopefully be as good as possible for all concerned. Susan and I joined forces and together plotted our family direction as much as possible. We sent out invitations to close family and friends. We even challenged each other.

The book, 'Stepfamilies' was our chosen vessel for personal pre marriage requirements. We each read the book fervently 'eyes wide open' as possible.

1) Call each other's ex spouse and tell them that 'I will never say anything negative about you to your children for their individual self esteem and your honor as well.' We never did negatively comment regarding any ex spouse to our children. This really works and we live by this to this day.

2) Treat all children fairly without exception. Especially with money and economic opportunities, rooms, dinner rules, bathroom manners, etc. This worked beautifully also. Be fair. Talk out misunderstandings.

3) Adults honor each other by communicating at least 3 times a week for a meal, late night or early morning chat. Make this a

priority. Any preacher will tell you this is wise especially when counseling for marital problems. Communication is essential.

4) Forgive all. Or God won't forgive you. Once again essential for one's mental health. Please forgive me too! Thanks.

# Let's get married with a flair!

One of my near and closest friends in the southeast, my former FC college tutor Jack Sturdy, who always seemed a little different, was very kind. He was also an excellent tutor for English literature which I desperately needed help with in my freshman year of college. All through football-track, fraternity and balancing academics was a huge challenge for me my freshman year. Jack the senior with a 4.0 grade point average was very helpful and extremely important to me in keeping my grade point average, which was my scholarship requirement. I barely passed while Jack and I kept in touch as he was now a graduate heading to law school at Stetson University in Florida. Family and guests were now arriving for the wedding.

The first stop/shock for 'Jack n Al' was Susan's house in Tallahassee. Boy was Kitty, Susan's Mom, surprised when Jack told her he was my tutor for the football team. She didn't know what was going on? She did ask Susan 'Should I know something?', She responded in the negative(NO!). The classiest/craziest thing was when Susan and I pulled up in the La Quinta motel driveway/swimming pool area. We could see 'Jack n Al' playing and flitting around the pool. 'At this point we had talked with Kitty' and I personally was humored and they seemed like they were having a great time. Dad rushed from the other side of the chain fenced motel pool up to the car, he said, "Gary, do you know these guys?" I said, "Yes Dad, Jack was my tutor his senior year and vital for my freshman year in college for helping me with my grades and the football team." Dad said, "Did you know about the change in his life?" I said," I had no idea but he sure seems to be having fun." Dad walked away with shrugged shoulders. His generation simply couldn't relate. I had my doubts as well, I felt somewhat unsure, but Jack was still my friend and stayed in touch since our college days.

Unfortunately Jack died a few years later. Prior to his death he had summoned me to come to his place/hospital in South Florida and I didn't go. I was literally scared I might get aids possibly by association? No one in 1981 really knew how the disease was in fact transferred in those days; because little was really known at the time. Also Jack never told me he was dying. I might have gone otherwise. One year later Jack's mother wrote me a letter and stated that Jack considered you to be one of his best friends. Quite honestly prior to the 'public gay transformation' Jack and I were very good friends. Accepting Jack as he now was stretched me for sure but I have the gift to accept people the way they are. I treated Jack no differently 'my fraternity brothers felt as though Jack was gay-acting in college' He never made any gay or homosexual advances toward me whatsoever during our study times. Even though his life was very short he was famous with movie stars from all over the world. Jack Sturdy was my friend-he considered me to be his unofficial 'little brother' frat brother. Goodbye Jack. I think God wanted me to go south and lead Jack to the Lord, I'm sure HE used somebody else. I asked God to forgive me and promised regardless of circumstance, I will not prejudge again when somebody asks me, within reason of course. Jack was a well known

movie critic and a very good friend.

One more of my friends showed up and was not a problem at all. Suzanne Wild McGuire wore a bright red dress. I had previously dated Suzanne 'she was a travel agent' before I knew Susan. We were never serious but Suzanne must have meant something with the Red dress. I am just not sure. When I was first engaged to Susan her car battery was declining, as it sat in Tallahassee parking lot while we drove my car up north for the week. As we drove my car back from Indiana to Tallahassee we found her car battery dead. Suzanne gave us a jump from her car with the battery cable. Thanks Suzanne, 'That's what friends are for.' below...Mom & Dad Cooper, Kitty and Frank, Susan & Vic, Kristi, Melissa and Scott.

I was on cloud nine and Susan trusted the Lord Divine

Our kids seemed really happy and I was challenged at times

Our lives became a thrill with beautiful children and

A hope of a brand new baby sister, for Scott another girl! (3-1)

The family score. And we still had a lot of fun!

We were finally married and the following week moved the whole family to Thomasville, Georgia. The year was 1981. Susan and Gary Cooper; a new start with a new marriage and we shared and unified our family with love and fairness. Susan and I both reread the book 'Stepfamilies' and we got a lot of great points to inject into this marriage. There were several major items that we implemented immediately. Some of these requirements took guts:

Call each of our former spouses and tell them that 'we will never talk badly about you to the children' which would hurt their self esteem. That we welcome them into our new family and will do the very best we can do with Love, Fairness, Christianity and Unity.

We will do our very best to benefit their child's) lives with regular or semi-regular visitation as planned. 2) Each child is privileged to have their own rooms and responsibilities therewith.

Tim, Susan's ex husband was very easy for me to work with. We have had great relations over 35+ years. Janet my ex was very sick and she was so glad Susan was taking care of Kristi so well. It was really great to talk with ex spouses and assure them of their children's futures with us. It freed up all concerned.

Here we were in our new used house at 224 Glenwood Drive, Thomasville, Georgia. Each child had their own room; the house was huge and had a mother-in-law house. In the front was a large dining room with a formal room and library beside that. In the back of the house was a pool table and entertainment center with a half round couch and fireplace. Immediately the kids started searching for all the names under the stairwell written by mostly the Faulk children who were the former owners. They of course added their marks as well. We also bought season tickets for the next football season at Thomasville High right down the street. In addition we bought each child a new big wheel so they could race around the back red-colored concrete porch; although Susan almost immediately felt a little lonely after leaving Tallahassee. This is when I decided that traveling 5 states may not be good in the long term for the family, especially Susan. In our prayer time as Susan and I prayed each night fervently for our family's future and my job. How could I transition from southeastern travels to Thomasville? How much time did we have and how would I help provide for the family? These were unknown and unanswered prayers in the beginning. We immediately joined the local Methodist church. Everything was moving along fine until Susan's parents showed up for a visit. We all poured into church, Susan, me, Melissa, Scott, Kristi, Grandma and Grandpa Miller. We found out in very short order that seats were assigned and not 'first come first served'. We were literally booted out and turned towards the back of the church. OK, we understand each church has its set of rules and we will figure them out. Let's find the children's program and join a Sunday School class. Unfortunately the children didn't much like the present program and we didn't like some of the teaching in our married class as well. After a short while we decided to switch to

First Baptist Church of Thomasville, GA. I even played lunchtime basketball with the minister, Milton Gardner. We found our church home. Everybody liked it, the children's program was great and Susan and I were put in separate Sunday school men's or women's. We and our children flourished accordingly. They each grew

beautifully in time. The happiest nuclear family I could think of, ours!

Top picture: Susan's mother Kitty Miller, Susan and me with Kristi around my neck, Scott in middle and Melissa between Kitty and Susan- New in Thomasville Georgia 1981

Middle picture: Notice- 'Jamoca the German Shepherd' made them smile.

Lower picture: Kristine, Melissa and Scott all standing above their happy sister Amy 'who loved all of them' 1986. Other things such as business ventures changed quickly with our marriage and departure from Tallahassee. In 1981 there were no cell phones and Concrete to Go of Florida literally lost communication with their President (me). We had just attained the contract for all 'manhole covers' in the State of Florida. I had just jointly signed a $2.5 million dollar note for the upgrades and our south of Tallahassee business was really starting to boom. My life hardly at this point was concerned about the company to any great regard. We had a plant manager that reported weekly and I didn't think 35 miles would hurt me but before I knew it the other two owners age 65 had decided that I should sell my shares to Jim 'the plant manager'. Since I took myself out of the immediate equation and was therefore 'out of pocket' and since they felt that way about the co-inventor and initial provider of the company 'possible greed?' I gave them a dollar figure that was substantial and reasonable. Within the week they had a check for me and with the check; I bought or paid off some debts back in Georgia. There was something happening all the time as I bought a storage building in Boston Georgia. I decided to make most of my money in Georgia. Where I now live, <u>The principle in building companies is to know when one's usefulness runs out. Don't hang on when you are not appreciated...sell and move on. Don't look back.</u>

Unfortunately 1 year later, Concrete to Go of Florida Inc. was in a huge lawsuit when Jim 'the guy who bought my stock' loaded an open trailer with slag 'the bad part of concrete'. So Jim put the bulk slag, broken up irregular pieces on the guy's trailer. The trailer driver/or Jim the Plant manager didn't check the recipients load balance or the truck/trailer braking system. The driver took all he could so the slag was fully overloaded as he drove down the highway and being overloaded couldn't stop as he skidded running the stop light at the Capital Circle bypass/truck route and violently crashed killing a family of 4 as their family sedan was crushed under the heavy trailers load! After the lawsuits 'these were the days of unlimited lawsuits' Jim, Ken and Harold not only lost the company but all of their personal possessions 'house, car, other business, savings'. Boy am I glad I didn't feel sorry for myself, fight and lose everything. As it turned out I was the only one 'as they semi forced my sellout for their personal gains' really who gained financially? Sorry Jim, Ken and Harold. Remember a sellout is good if you are not needed and the sales price is right.

Our family's first summer together was ending and the children were excited about grade school. We had a cute dog that was fun loving. I decided to walk with the children and dog for the first day of school. Just as we were about to enter the school grounds our dog walked directly in front of a car and got run over right in front of our kids. The dog then started trying to run but couldn't as it twirled what we thought was a death spin as the local head football coaches wife quickly drove up and gently took and put the dog into her car while taking it to the veterinarian for me, especially since I was the only adult who was walking. So much for the first day of school, not to mention emotionally shocked kids.

One of the advantages of a family with kids 21 days apart; the result, Kristi and Scott were put in the same class. The teachers didn't know they were in the same family due to their different last names. This didn't last long. Their reports matched as they both emotionally told their teacher all about the family dog getting run over. Scary excitement for 2 first graders and 1 second grader the first day of school in a new town. They all came right home after school. The grade school was two blocks away. They all crowded around the family pet with a cast on his big front. This first year was relatively good as we watched local high school football. South Georgia high school football is fun to watch along with the cheerleaders and bands playing. Not to mention the large group of fans that way too often have a fanatical fan nearby where almost no one would rather not sit nearby especially as he yells on every play with extreme passion and noisy interpretations which often don't make sense. I would get excited occasionally with a somewhat emotional response. But, after all in most cases it's just a game.

Right! Unless it's FSU, then I needed a little bit of emotional outburst therapy also with their football games! Whether it's in person just 35 miles away, or on television; I became just like dad when I was a small child. My only boy Scott and I really enjoyed those moments. We loved to incessantly scream while the girls just mostly watched. The nicest thing regarding our Glenwood house was you could either watch football on the big couch in the back or you could read in the library or sit in the front formal room next to the kitchen. These were the days that I used to tell Susan, "I would rather not travel and just stay home with her and the children." Meaning that I was truly beginning to think about starting some type of business in South Georgia, the interest rates were very high and there were signs from other agricultural representatives that our jobs were in jeopardy. At this point I did want to change jobs but not necessarily quit until something better and local came into play.

By the end of the summer Susan found out she was pregnant. We were happy to find that this child would be a blood-kin- link to everybody in our new family. We were going to have a baby. The children were really excited when they heard. The news was now seemingly everywhere from friends to families. Truly this baby would be the 'link' from my child Kristi to Susan's children Scott and Melissa. We were all going to be blood linked. The great irony to this blood link process was further reached when Susan and I became members of '23 and me' which was a company that checked one's DNA. We were both shocked at the terrific response to the whole world through our individual DNA checks. I found that I had many relatives all over the world and some very close by as well. I found a cousin named Harold Reagan 'he was a trumpet player in Nashville, TN and Jimmy Buffett who had 6 out of 6 identical genomes with mine? But Susan had the real eye opener, she was found to have a cousin named Broadhead. Janet Broadhead was my first wife and this Broadhead lived in Kansas City just 50 miles south from St. Joseph, Missouri the city where Janet hailed from. There are just not that many Broadheads running around. In a way I suppose that all of us are brothers and sisters through our blood especially over long time periods.

Susan and I had planned our baby's birth at the right time. Summer vacation. Teachers always used summer vacations for similar events. Everybody was thrilled with our new baby girl named Amy Elizabeth Cooper. If baby Amy had been a boy I would have named him 'Link'. The fact is we were all quite happy the way it turned out. Never did our children say to each other,' you are not any of my original blood' because of Amy. To us of course Amy was the cutest of all babies...isn't that the way most of us think. Babies are beautiful and change everything. That is a fact. By the time Amy was born Melissa was age 8, Scott and Kristi was two weeks apart in age which was 6. We all knew we would have several in-house babysitters in time. Kristi was clearly most intensively interested in baby Amy. Often Amy would go missing but we knew who had her. Kristi would get her out of her crib and have her baby sister sleep with her. All in the family I suppose.

# The Winks from Jersey

When Susan and I were married with a total family reorganization which included our combined 3 children as we planned to move to South Georgia in the hopes of raising our children with a slightly slower pace than robust Tallahassee and with a very good school system choice in Thomasville/Thomas County Georgia. Though we each felt pretty good regarding each other it became very apparent...Susan and I didn't have many friends in Thomasville like we did in Tallahassee.

The difference was simple. In Tallahassee almost everyone was from someplace else. Very few of our friends and neighbors had been born in Tallahassee, which was becoming a major metro site as the Capital of Florida with a very strong population growth for business, the close proximity to the beach and the FSU football team growth and national stature. It was much easier to develop friendships because almost everyone was in the same boat, so to speak. In Thomasville the city council was very concerned and wanted a very slow and controlled growth. At least for a while time continued to march on and we finally began to ponder how best to 'get to know others'. That was our question.

I was somewhat concerned because even though Susan had worked for the Thomas County schools 2 years it didn't seem to have much effect when attracting friends. Work simply did. Like many small towns generally people might say hello and that's all. Trust or lack of trust question seemed to be ingrained in this small town. We were temporally lost in this little town of Thomasville, Georgia. So I bought football tickets and the tickets were placed directly in the middle of the stadiums black section. THE WHOLE FAMILY Even the black folks who were very nice did not invite or solicit any relationship whatsoever. Months had past and Susan and I was getting emotionally concerned with this area we called home, although not a problem for our children, she was questioning and wondering about our mutual abilities in acquiring friends. The children did have school friends at school. We had the problem. My old football coach would say, "Make em play you".

Enter Rusty's Convenience store right beside the YMCA across the street. I regularly played basketball every Monday, Wednesday and Friday at the YMCA. One of the day managers was Tony Wink. Tony was friendly and very nice as he had a very distinct New Jersey accent, he took change and assisted in the various duties of the store. One afternoon when nobody was in the store, I walked in and started a conversation with Tony. I had noticed his northeastern accent prior to this meeting. I asked Tony where he lived and also found that his wife, Barbara worked elsewhere at a food service-waitress job. After I qualified Tony regarding his background he said, "Were both from New Jersey, can't you tell?" I told him my wife was from New York and we might have a so called 'mother-in-law house' available to you both if you would like to get out of your trailer. Tony asked where we lived and when they saw the beautiful house with a separate 'mother in law house' they were thrilled with the opportunity to live in a nicer area while much closer to their workplaces as well. Game on! After the lease and monies were paid we *The Coopers* had renters next door connected by a long hallway with a locking door from their side.

Susan asked, "Why did you get these people to rent next door?" I simply responded at least you will hear some familiar northeastern sounds. After a short time period Susan found that Tony's wife Barbara was in the Mensa Society. 'The Mensa Society is the largest and oldest high IQ society in the world. It's a non-profit organization open to people who score 98 percent or higher on standardized, supervised IQ or other approved intelligence tests.' We also found that Barbara attended Indiana University and was Magna Cum Laude. We found it incredible that she worked as a waitress downtown? Why?

Later when Tony and Barbara were both off of work they came over and leveled our thought process. They told us they were both alcoholics and were very active in AA - Alcoholics Anonymous. At the time this didn't really mean that much to us. They had admittedly been sober for several years and had good intentions for their futures also. We agreed. They also had dedicated sponsors.

Both families would communicate and our children were fascinated as to 'how did they get here?' Regardless we all had several very good times and found out what alcoholics do. It seemed very routine, AA meetings weekly or biweekly, staying in close touch with an AA Sponsor. The Sponsor was clearly very important. Accountability was the motivating factor for both of the Winks. Our children were learning and naturally curious as well.

As Time passed we found that Alanon was a group for non-alcoholics like us to better understand the plight of an alcoholic. We also found that Barbara's son was my exact age and this became a problem when I had a Birthday because of her past and current pain regarding her deceased son. This almost restarted her drinking near the beginning of our mutual relationships. She had to spend extra time with her sponsor and their joint care for her not drinking accordingly. Our entire family quickly caught on, we as a family got so convicted that we let each child take taste of the various alcohol related drinks in our cupboard. We then allowed each child to open a bottle and flush its contents 'down the drain'! This made a profound impact on the children at this point. Our children would sometimes hear them fighting and verbally assaulting each other at times through our adjoining room walls. I was somewhat glad they heard the entire ruckus in order to let them plan out choices for their lives especially regarding their respective alcohol and drug choices which clearly affect futures. To fight or not to fight, that is the question. Our kids were getting convicted over the above matters.

One evening as the kids was now old enough to have friends over. Melissa had invited a friend over for the night. Unfortunately one of the friends brought/sneaked over a fifth of whiskey for her and our Melissa to drink. Melissa got wise and woke Susan and me up at 5:00am in the morning. Her friend was drinking by herself and she became drunk. Her friend's father had to come to our house to pick his daughter up. I was very surprised as he didn't seem upset. He told me he had to pick up his daughter in the past much in the same way as our situation due to her drinking problem at a very young age. The kids once again really took notes; Addiction? Many unanswered questions. How could this happen? How did she have access to alcohol?

A few years later Kristine and her friend Danica briskly entered the front door of our house shouting that Danica's boyfriend was badly injured in a car wreck; as they were engaged in the front of our house. At the same exact time Barbara our renter ran into our house while opening our back door shouting, 'Tony wants to shoot me!' I immediately called 911. When the mutual news hit everyone in the house quickly manned all doors, immediately locked with everyone away from the windows in the middle corridor of the house. Trauma!

A few minutes slowly passed while Tony in an absolute rage and complete state of drunkenness started shooting Barbara's car while I was once again dialing 911 this time with the gun shots blasting! Within seconds, 3 police cars pulled up. Policeman's revolvers were out! With their backs sliding along the concrete wall while one of the cops recognized Tony and talked him out of pursuing his dangerous shooting activity. They got his gun and whisked Tony out of the area, probably the state mental hospital lockup. This was not the Tony we all knew. Afterwards Barbara said, "We were up all night pointing pistols at each other!" I thought to myself, 'My God!' I couldn't imagine that. All night, what did he do?

Apparently, Tony had or almost had an affair with 'whoever' and proceeded to tell Barbara! This was a perfect formula for a disastrous circumstance with bad results with any normal family especially with this explosive powder keg potential combining two nervous feuding alcoholics who happened to be up all night holding guns and being married. Our family never forgot that particularly day, in addition two of Melissa's friends were brutally murdered at the beach while sunbathing and Dr Bill Hogan, a friend of mine apparently died in his sleep. Mysterious opinions still flare up at times through our community.

Eventually our kids got older and gone to various destinations and Susan and I made a decision to move to the farm. It was 60 acres and I had many septic tanks and separate properties in the immediate area as well. Tony and Barbara moved out of Thomasville and rented a mobile home lot on top of our farms higher ground plateau area on our property in Thomas County. After all this time, they had become like a part of the family, In spite of their history. And we simply accepted them as friends and tried very hard at times to get them involved in church without any luck. They never missed any payment of rent for the semi isolated lot. We really didn't see them much due to location.

In our final days with the Winks still in town two events occurred. The first was I convinced Barbara to take an RN nurses course at the local technical college. She academically tore the initial nurse's course up impressing everyone, maybe the Mensa affect had kicked in. I stayed somewhat in touch with nurses' supervisor and she couldn't find Barbara to take the very last step for the nurse's degree, the final exam. She was devastated due to her concern for Barbara as well, due to her tremendous intelligence. Barbara had simply left the area. When I finally caught up with her she simply said, "I have the brains but not the follow through." The Alcohol related effects had taken the toll over the many years of her admitted usage. Oh well, I tried. 'Horses and water' I suppose. None of this changed anything with our mutual dwellings; they were on the far upward part of the farm separated by a fence. Shortly after the nurse rejection by Barbara she told us," Tony has cancer". We prayed for Tony. Time marched on.

Months later I was walking around the fence line at the farm just checking around with a few valuable moments while trying to make a living. This so called free time was something I didn't have much of in recent times. But it was Sunday, our day of rest. I was surprised when Tony opened his mobile homes door and shouted, 'Hey Gary, can you come over'. I proceeded towards them as I carefully jumped over the barbed wire fence. The door was left open for me. "Hi" Tony and Barbara, 'what's up?' Tony never wasted words, "Gary I didn't become a Christian because I wasn't sure what God was going to do with my dogs. I've got cancer all over my body (as he lifted his shirt and cancer bumps were all over his chest and back) I've decided to give up on this dog thing, I don't care anymore. This is the day I've got to accept Christ." I thought to myself how many times over the years I had been witnessing Jesus to the Winks. The Bible says to be ready' 'in season and out of season' I was ready and truly excited for Tony. I proceeded to tell Tony when '2 or 3 are together God is with us'. There was Tony Barbara and me, no dogs. I told Tony how the man on the cross with Jesus had been promised heaven. I asked Tony if he wants the same for himself. He said, "Yes I do!" I was thrilled stating 'You are an answer to my prayers' I then proceeded to pray with Tony to 'receive the saving Grace of Jesus with the promise of salvation!' He accepted, I then told him to tell someone about Jesus, "For he who confesses me before man I will confess him to my father in heaven" Tony made the call on the telephone. I congratulated Tony and left. The next day Barbara called me that Tony had died 2 hours later. Stay vigilant my friends, God is at hand. I was very happy at Tony's funeral the next day or so. I told the preacher 'I knew about this one!' As I told him what happened. We both laughed with joy. Barbara sold and left the property and thereafter married a local farmer. Goodbye Winks.

As our family marched onward, we at times looked back, often with great pleasure. We were remembering how the children did in school. Melissa always achieved straight A's regardless of school situation or changes. Scott and Kristi often had B's and a few C's. When the children were in 3rd and 4th grades respectively they decided to do a short math quiz. Years earlier Melissa said, I'm 6 and 2 quarters. Scott said well, I'm 5 and ½. Kristi quickly responded I'm 5 and two dimes. Even though we tried to be fair, everyone had their own rooms, there is always competition, it's simply in us. We all laughed but not at Kristi except to say that girl sure had change on her mind'. She and Scott loved to go to the local mini mart convenience store and of course shop...candy bars.

I personally enjoyed watching Scott, Melissa and Kristi race their big wheels around the elevated concrete risers in the gated backyard. I would have each child peddle a pace lap and get their highest speed with my timer. Then I would stack the individual child in a stacking order to come as close as possible at the end of the race. The end of the races were incredibly close but usually Melissa the oldest would beat the other two by a nose. Great fun almost everyone eventually would grab a win, I made sure of that! Susan and I strived for fairness.

When Scott and the Morse boys got together they played a lot of Georgia and Florida State pretend football. We lived right in front of a spacious beautiful park and could easily observe most activities near our side between enormous pine trees. The three boys were woefully looking for a fourth player one Saturday. Kristi happened to come upon the boys and she was asked to play. Kristi said, 'OK' and game on. Scott and Kristi were initially tearing up the Morse boys. Scott threw the ball well and Kristi caught some great passes and seemed to be excelling in her galloping running style until Kristi got tackled (hit the ground and rolled) in the touch football game. She dusted herself off, got up and 'announced that was not fair' and marched off the playing field leaving, three boys. She never played football with them again. I think they mumbled 'poor sport' as they slowly walked off the park field, it just wouldn't work with most girls.

We would find various events or places in their early rearing; Wakulla Springs state park had some great swimming, eating and playing. So did Panama City Beach at various times. But the Marianna Caverns gave us a unique time as we were traveling for this one day event. Caves, caverns and such were discussed by all of the children. It seemed that each had their own description of what was in store. Of course I semi-jokingly said, "I'm just so glad that I am mostly bald so the bats won't attach on my head." When we all got to the parking lot while getting out of the van I had never seen Scott cram his head unto such a small rain flap in his jacket. You could only see his eyes as the flaps were pulled to the max. When we all finally walked into the various caverns and caves besides having fun he finally loosened his knot about the fourth cave.

During summer, spring, winter and fall vacations and/or holiday breaks the older children would at times depart and visit the other parent's which were generally coordinated/planned by the us, the parents. We called in the given times with the other parents so all the children would depart close to the same time and have pretty much the same return trip time as well. As I mentioned earlier the big three older kids would fly jets, with all the benefits of mini jet wing shoulder boards and the benefit of stewardess oversight. This was mentioned by Beanie, Janet's grandfather father, as he would particularly watch over Kristi as Janet was getting sicker in a very, very serious way. The Broadheads were planning, most likely Janet's last trip to Estes Park Colorado and of course wanted Kristi to come with them. I was very concerned and required/demanded that Janet would not be allowed to drive Kristi. That a mature adult would watch over Kristi constantly due to her dire state of illness. I had learned to be tough regardless of situations. My daughter was my complete responsibility for obvious reasons.

In this coordinated process I had the chance to call Janet and give it one more chance. I simply told Janet that her and my greatest achievement was in fact 'our daughter' Kristi. I went on to tell Janet that it might be worth her while eternally to listen to me. She agreed, "I said Janet, will you repeat after me" she said 'yes' Dear Lord we ask you to come into Janet's heart and spirit by faith and we ask you to take care of our forgiveness so we each will be touched by you. So right now I simply ask my former wife and sister in Jesus to come into Janet and give her life unto you Lord." Janet said, "Yes Lord and amen." Salvation in Jesus Christ is never by works. Only by 'faith' with the spoken simple words of her acceptance.

I felt much better/relieved and I knew whatever happened to Janet I would see her in heaven. Kristi, Janet, Beanie and Barbie all had a great time in Colorado and great memories resulted. Upon returning to St Joseph Missouri Janet had a mishap, she fell out of bed with Kristi by her side. Kristi was age eight and maturely called Beanie and Tom, Janet's brother came over to assist and get Janet back into the bed. Next day Kristi flew into the Tallahassee airport and was the first child back in Thomasville. Upon Kristi getting off of the jet she turned to me and said, "Daddy, last night mommy fell on the floor and couldn't get up. I had to call grandpa Beanie and he sent Uncle Tommy." Since they had just returned from a long trip it really didn't surprise me after my experiences with Janet and simply said, "Let's just hope Janet/Mommy is OK" We had a few of Kristi's friends come to our house to simply welcome her back. Shortly after Kristi's return while playing with her friends, Beanie called. "Gary, 'with a great pause' this is Beanie. I hate to tell you this as Janet has just passed away." I immediately told Beanie that I know Janet is with the Lord and I am not looking forward to telling Kristi but I will. Thank you Beanie and God's blessing. Beanie went on to say. Due to the circumstances I don't think it would be best for you and Kristi to come to Janet's funeral. I hesitated and simply said,"OK. And goodbye" Unfortunately I summoned Susan to take all of the children back home. I explained to their parents of Janet's death. I then had to sit down with Kristi and tell her that which I didn't want to say...ever.

*Sometimes one's air of life runs out. But her balloon has departed full blown...*

"Kristi you know that I love you and so does Mom." 'Yes Daddy" "You know that your Mommy Janet has been a very sick person, don't you?" Yes Daddy, she was very sick last night." I stated that she was correct. I hugged Kristi as close to me as I possibly could and said very softly, "I am very sorry that your mother died a few minutes ago and she is in heaven." Immediately Kristi started crying as I was in tears as well. Kristi left to go into the other room and somehow work out in her mind as to what I had said. I let her and simply mentioned I'm here in the other room while I brought Susan up to date. Kristi came out a few minutes later hugged me and then went to Susan and hugged her as one of the sweetest miracles I could ever witness occurred. Susan didn't tell Kristi how her father was killed when she was just seven years old. Regardless Kristi had someone who empathized and understood her pain well. It wasn't much longer that we put Kristi and Amy to bed. The next morning Kristi seemed fine and seemed to want to simply...move on. There is always light in the morning, a new day. We will never forget Janet and wish her Godspeed. Shortly thereafter, I assured Kristi that she would continue to visit her grandparents and other relatives in St Joseph. She was pleased. In hindsight it was nice to know at least in all of our minds who knew and cared for Janet. Janet will be forever young...

Melissa and Scott were flying in the next day. The family was once again united and we once again were all together. I think everybody was glad to be back and Scott said, "I have two great dads!" Once again we didn't and never will knock the ex-spouse, it hurts the children. Church attendance and family bible study was about to start as the summer was turning into autumn. Scott and Melissa both found out about Kristi's mother's passing, they each expressed their condolences in their own respectful way. Life is good.

Once again promoting fairness; we decided to let each child have 'THEIR DAY' which simply meant 1) The special child will be served first at dinner 2) Choice of seats in the automobile 3) First to be excused from dinner, etc. THEIR DAY became a really neat thing for each of them consistently. Until baby Amy decided she wanted in on THEIR DAY. Initially the older kids didn't like it until they started making deals with Amy giving minor favors and such. Fairness and competition reigned once again. It pretty much died down after too many 'their days' were burned out for everyone involved; which led directly into 'Bug' back in the late eighties and early nineties we all saw a lot of slightly used Volkswagen bug automobiles almost around every corner of the roadways.

The game the family liked to play was BUG. The rules were simple, 1) If you could point out a Volkswagen Bug first you would receive one point. That was pretty much it until further into the game. The initial rules made it so who ever had the most bug points won. Of course until Scott and Kristi decided to start saying BUG/ Herbie by faith. In other words they started guessing that most likely a bug would be around a certain corner based upon a certain average of bugs seen philosophy. Often times the bug did show up and points were given. But often times the bug did not show up. So I had to amend the ruling, if you said BUG and no bug showed up after the first corner you lost a point. Scott and Kristi often had zero or minus points after the change. It seems that the bugs- Volkswagen beetles just quit coming our way in South Georgia, time to move on.

I really enjoyed 'imagination radio games'. I would dial a certain slow playing radio song like Bach, Mozart, Haydn and such. Give an example of what situation the particular song reminded me of and verbally express what I saw in my mind's vision so to speak. It was fun to do, there was no right or wrong answer and as a result the expression of art in a verbal sense was given as we simply imagined and expressed it accordingly. We generally did these type

of activities on long trips before a break and such. Sometimes the kids would come up with some great and interesting concepts and nobody won or lost, they just participated.

In the meantime Baby Amy was getting bigger, while her siblings challenged her...often in very good ways.

# GOAL AND DREAM PLANNING

To us the grades didn't matter as much as what our children's individual goals were. As parents we knew if they individually had a really good goal the result... grades would increase automatically due to their personal incentive pointing towards their imagined and conceived prize. At ages 10-12 years of age I would sit down with each child and let them brainstorm regarding their individual futures which would help them reflect especially before they approached the hormone enraged teenager stage. I kept a file on each child and I believed they tried very hard to imagine 'faithfully' what their individual purpose in this earth might be. Melissa, the oldest just loved animals especially dogs and horses. She initially stated that she wanted to be a veterinarian until her last year in high school. She was accepted at the US Air Force. Scott was very specific and consistent as he wanted to be a Army man. He said he could make his army men play and march around the bathtub edge. I just wrote down what they said, I wasn't there to judge it had to be their individual hopes and dreams as best they could. Kristine was very consistent; she wanted to be a mother. Amy being the youngest started of course later and after seeing what happened with Melissa wanted to be a United States Air Force Academy graduate. Every year I recorded updates, changes, edits and had them sign the various documents. They all knew the scripture in proverbs 'Plan ahead for the future' I wasn't about to laugh at their goals like my father did me. I just wanted to direct them accordingly.

The planning sessions really helped them all in each of their high school teenage years. Simply because they all took 'their plans' into account when the course of teenage life was needed in times of clarity when other temptations/directions may beckon oftentimes for a temporary high risk event such as (alcohol, drugs, lustful sex) or feelings of wantonness. *We all need something to hang on and our dreams and goals really do matter. By the way, goal planning will always increase your grade point because it allows one to often see beyond the cloudy presence of academia.* We all remember how insignificant it seems especially with mundane subjects in school that seemingly and appears to have absolutely no purpose whatsoever. Yet when one has a goal that goes beyond this type of thinking he or she will go much farther than the throwing in the towel mentality; all because he or she has a plan. And who knows, that mundane stuff might somehow fit into their personal plans and eventual work plans. Life has many dreams and disappointments...Let's dream.

In addition to her plan note the picture below turning a barn into a house. The children were going to be gone soon. We had a beautiful 60 acre farm. The barn had 'good bones' so to speak. 'In my mind, this was my adventure it would be a great and challenging project for the future!'The trailer was a temporary dwelling fixture until the end of the project. My objective was to show our children how other people survive. We all had some great times in that trailer. Simplicity sometimes beats complexity. I personally like both. I had us the last two at home live with us in a small 2 bedroom mobile home until we got the converted barn ready for occupancy. <u>Once again I wanted everyone to know good people also live in mobile homes.</u> We all have choices 'aim high'!

'Above' <u>The family picture</u> when everyone was still in elementary to high school

'Below picture' <u>Our beautiful daughters 'just before careers and marriage'!</u>

Thank GOD Scott's Back...Celebration from 7.5 months in Iraq with 2 weeks off and 7.5 months to go.....All the children and families showed up for a wonderful weekend in Newport News 1-10 thru 1-13-08

The remake...Melissa, Kristi and Amy .. beautiful sisters...

As I helped develop my children's plans this also caused me to pursue my plans as to where I was with planning time as well. From the beginning, Susan's and my relationship and our family 'children's individual plans' I felt we needed some planning because the US economy was starting to show signs of recession and downturns. Jimmy Carter was the President when we all became a family. Initially I thought Jimmy being a resident of a nearby county would in fact cause the south Georgia economy to spring forward. Unfortunately for me and many others there was simply no 'spring' as interest rates went sky high, gas prices were inflated and the Carter administration manipulated the ASCS (agricultural stabilization and conservation service) which managed several agri-loan functions but the one I noticed really made a difference. THE FARM LOAN DEPARTMENT! Most of my grain bin deals were financed through the ASCS in addition to farm equipment (tractor, plows, hopper, rakes, etc.). The Carter administration decided to stop the low interest rate loans which farmers and farm related firms had some access to. This caused the common farmer from the North to the South find themselves in a financial quandary beyond anything they could have imagined. A huge number were thrown into bankruptcy. Instead of applauding our President they were huge signs on Georgia interstate 75 that condemned the President for turning his back on the farmers and apologizing that he was from Georgia.

I knew this was not good for me. I had even put up Jimmy Carter's farm bins through one of my millwrights 'bin installers' while these bins were being installed President Jimmy Carter with Anwar Sadat the 'soon to be assassinated' President of Egypt in 1981 inspected the Plains Georgia site. Not to mention scores of individual farm bins and my biggest site The Seminole Sugar Plantation where we installed an entire commercial 120 foot bin systems which included in bin stirrers, huge drying fans and 120 MPH rebars for bin strength due to hurricane possibilities which was going to be used for storing rice as they would flood the sugar cane fields to prevent disease plus earning rice dollars. This site was in Belle Glade, Florida one hour north of Miami and the only way other than drive 'a very long drive from any direction' was to fly my small Piper Tri Pacer aircraft onto the highly elevated eight foot wide asphalt roads with swamps on each side. They would put bulldozers on each far side to stop the drug smugglers from using their roads. I would have to call ahead for the Seminole Sugar Plantation clearance which was managed in some part by the Federal Drug Enforcement personnel. This was definitely my most exciting site and great fun for me to have arranged such a transaction which was easily allowed for millions of dollars with my company.

The ASCS debacle grew and I told my wife, "With this downturn my firm would not continue much longer. Now is now my time to plan." This was an especially important time due to the fact that Susan was pregnant with our youngest child Amy and we needed stability in this unstable time. We prayed and planned accordingly. I knew the southeastern part of the USA was in upcoming financial troubles. I started planning to switch from mixing concrete to mixing various donut designs with supervision per Dunkin Donuts-Tallahassee of course.

I got ahold of this close Dunkin Donuts franchise and made a deal to sell Dunkin Donuts in south Georgia. The towns of Thomasville and Cairo Georgia were selected by myself and I immediately went to work while going through the motions with my agricultural concerns. The deal was simple. Dunkin of Tallahassee would ship 20 cartons of various fresh donuts to Thomasville and I would distribute wherever needed including Cairo Georgia as well. I secured two sites and put in very realistic Dunkin Donuts type counters and donut cases in each site. The Cairo site was even more special because I secured game slot machines which brought in thousands of dollars each week.

As I planned and plodded through the USA farm economic observations the Modern Farm Systems of Iowa including the President and Vice president flew into Tallahassee to meet with me. I knew this meeting was inevitable and was reasonably prepared. They simply told me what I already knew concerning the farm economy and yet they did something that I did not expect. The President gave me his regret for the times which we could not control but stated," We would like to offer you a position west of the Mississippi river…" Upon hearing this I simply stated, "I appreciate the offer but I just bought a large house in Thomasville GA and I doubt it could be sold anytime soon. I have enjoyed working with MFS and wish you both continued success with the company through these difficult times." We parted and wished each other success and just as the jet departed. I stopped by the Dunkin Donuts shop in Tallahassee and plotted the furtherance of my existing business venture. By the way MFS gave me a three month severance, concerning the times; I thought it to be fair. After all I had a plan.

*Thomasville's largest firm was the Flowers Baking Company. I really didn't think specialty donuts would ruffle their feathers much. I was wrong. Flowers put out a bulletin/rumor that any Flowers employee found in my facility would be fired. As a result, the employees didn't come in just the stock owner's children.*

I have encountered various rumors and troubles with misled verbal statements before. This was not going to stop me. We had a great grand opening; I even dressed one of my delivery boys up in a rented gorilla suit. His name was Adrian and he was a show stopper in the gorilla outfit! Thomasville was not used to anything quite like this. Massive crowds came and there was almost several car wrecks as 'Adrian the gorilla' was now on the roof. Adrian really took his job seriously. All of this made for a lot of fun and we even ran totally out of product. I had three employees and we offered our services from 6:00am until 6:00pm except on weekends when we closed at 10:00pm. In Cairo, we even stayed open longer due to extreme demand. The teenagers and middle teens all loved the games so in addition to donuts and coffee we added Ice cream as well. Thomasville was good but Cairo was much better. By the end of the year; whatever Thomasville lost Cairo gained. The whole operation was not a loss or gain, just even on paper. This is where the principal of monetary gain must be perceived. I found this to be the most frustrating weighing this decision.

Economically speaking the average business takes approximately 3 years to make an income. I had to be patient and if I couldn't stand it I would sell out. As a fairly young man I had a problem with this principle. But I had to acknowledge the quitting concept as well. The second year I started paying myself a moderate salary as I worked. I also had to fire a young woman in Cairo for stealing. So I found myself filling in where needed. Fortunately, a man in Cairo was very interested in my business. He eventually talked me into paying ½ and financing the other ½ with payments. I thought about it and gave him the opportunity. The second principle was simple as well. It's not good to let someone pay ½ because he could cost you the original front ½ by not paying taxes, supply bills and such. As time marched on that is exactly what the debtor did. He had Dunkin Donuts short $1,000 and taxes weren't paid. I took over the concern. At this point game machines for homes were at present booming, accordingly the business dropped by ½ in Cairo. Once again I found myself in a minus position in year two. That was it!

I closed shop put all the equipment into a warehouse I had purchased when I sold my first rental house in Tallahassee. The warehouse was located in Boston Georgia. I did not have a plan. For the first time in my life, <u>I was without a plan of action except to pay on a bad business debt.</u>

What were I and my family to do? I believe many families have had this same question. Our budget got so tight that Susan and I got on our knees at the edge of bed and prayed to God that he do some type of miracle or action accordingly. After the prayer we had a mutual peace and somehow felt much better. We simply had to walk by faith.

I called my State Farm agent and told him I couldn't pay the insurance. I called my banker and told him I could only pay interest. I suspended and cut almost all my debt but I did not go bankrupt. I had several good pieces of property and my dreams needed an upgrade and were simply on a temporary hold.

In steps, my State Farm agent Hugh Rockett contacted me from time to time as we all went to First Baptist church together. He said, "Gary let's go shooting on the river bank." I said, "Let's go, I don't have anything else to do" At the river's edge Hugh proceeded to tell me that "You could do well as an insurance agent here in Thomasville." I said, "Hugh I don't know anybody very well in this town" He assured me that what I said "Wouldn't matter"

Hugh was right. I went to the Gulf Life Insurance Company and applied that day. Next week I was hired with a small salary-commission deal. To make a slightly long story short "I sold 3 million dollars of insurance in my second year when Gulf Life was overtaken by American General Life Insurance Company." My old Northwestern Mutual background served me well." I wound up being the keynote speaker at the National Convention at the MGM

GRAND Hotel in Las Vegas. Before I was set to speak I was having severe lung problems. My Doctor told me," You might live 3 years, maybe" My lungs were shutting down and I was on steroids to survive. I was so exhausted that I overslept and barely got into the convention room as the couriers were sent to find me. Upon arriving the huge conference room was packed all the way to the back. I threw my speech into the trash. I said, "I have learned the debit business in the south. I learned the ordinary life business in the North with the Northwestern Mutual. I'm telling you the truth. Accordingly when the American General came on board with interest sensitive life I could convert strong debit accounts to ordinary insurance and we all won. The American General and me! I would be amiss to not give thanks to God himself for giving me this opportunity and I truly hope God will bless you all in your insurance endeavors". This was truly one of my shortest speeches ever but it caused a positive stir.

Immediately I received District Agency offers in two different regions the biggest was "The Lookout Mountain Tennessee American General Agency" I did not take this opportunity as the company sent all of its leaders 'including me' to France for two weeks. I really wanted to remain in Thomasville and I greatly appreciated... the all expenses paid trip. After all of the pomp and circumstance of doing very well with the insurance concerns one thought/gut feeling would not leave me. "I did not like selling insurance but I really loved the people, I simply had to adjust so my life would be as fulfilled as possible in assisting people". Therefore I had to plan over the next year on eventually leaving the insurance industry.

About this time the psychiatrist Maslow started re-dealing with me.

# MASLOW's HIERARCHY of NEEDS................

(See the Chart below)

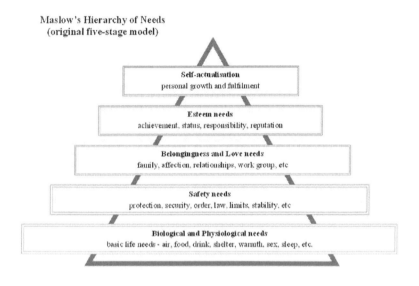

I believe each one of us wants the best for our friends, families and all the people we come in contact with. Especially when some of our personal goals are met. This is why Maslow is so important. He put the icing on my cake of my life so to speak….from the bottom up.

5) Biological and Psychiatric Needs- The basics food, drink, sex, sleep, etc.

These are the basic things that I want but does not completely satisfy...

4) Safety Needs- We are need protection, security, order, law, fairness.

Except in war we expect this from our Country, State, County...

3) Belonginess and Love Needs- Who doesn't want these

Family, affection, relationships, works groups, etc. I NEED THIS!

2) ESTEEM NEEDS- I really want to feel good about myself. I demand this of Me.

Achievement, Status, Responsibility <u>Feeling good about Oneself!</u>

1) Self Actualization-Feeling good about yourself. With personal growth,

Fulfillment, <u>In other words doing exactly what one wants to do!</u>

- *Some of us demand this 'the above' of ourselves. Some just get by 'not seeing one inch above #3' and some fail horribly and often tell of when they were young and if they would have done this or that everything would have been different. I always think of my ninth grade football coach," Excuses do not go on the scoreboard" This is the first day of the rest of your lives. Plan on making a change, it will take everything you've got faith, courage, strength, financing you might even fail but at least you really tried to make a difference while finding your Maslow 4th and 5th Hierarchy. Don't forget personal growth almost always is 'journey oriented'. Don't forget WW11 General Patton," Victory is Fleeting" Let's fight on.....continue to challenge yourself!*

So here I was not getting much past # 3 myself and I had to rechallenge myself and others to achieve my dedicated new found goal. Enter 'Real Estate'! Statistically I remember how Real Estate helped me in the beginning and now I was ready to really take advantage of the possibilities in the present. I already had the basics, a few pieces of property. I knew I couldn't accomplish this task with my own personal finances. I needed at least three people. Once again, it's very hard for a 3 strand rope to break especially if the certain people are individuals of integrity. I talked with Susan my wife about my goals and as usual she was wonderfully behind me. She knew my dreams and I was determined to accomplish them.

The CHURCH BUS....After a while I developed a personal spiritual goal, hopefully to get closer to God. Our family had just recently transferred membership to New Covenant Church from First Baptist. Maybe I could find these individuals in this church especially with all of the exciting and joyful spiritual dimensions. In fact I thought this task really would be very easy. I was wrong.

The first item I want to assure you is true. We did not leave First Baptist out of anger or strife. There were so many lovely warm hearted folks there. We left because we felt possibly we might learn for ourselves and our children what it is to be spiritually filled as opposed to just heart filled. Of course it's best to be both but in that time it wasn't happening. I wanted the best spiritual outcome in our family's Christian environment.

Over the next few months and after the adjustment of changing churches was met. I felt possibly this would be a good time to find 'interested brothers' in developing possibly a better way to make money with real estate investing. We had a speaker from a Birmingham preacher who shared with our church and invited us to attend and assist their church in Birmingham, Alabama. Great this is my opportunity, a bus trip with men, all in a bus. "Behold how good and how pleasant it is for brethren to dwell together in unity" Proverbs.

The trip from Thomasville north to Birmingham Alabama was 5-8 hours as I remember. After our initial prayer we all conversed and laughed along the way. As I best sensed my simple declaration to be delivered came unto pass I thought I would have to take numbers. I was wrong. I preached the potential of wealth through strength and testified to all members of the van about the benefits and strength of a 3 strand rope, the fact that 7 out 10 millionaires in the USA made their millions in real estate. I told them how I made a lot of money in this endeavor as well. Immediate results... No takers, some good conversations but no takers. I found myself asking myself, "Have I lost my sales touch?" or maybe none of them have faith! I gave my best shot and gave a few of them my business card. After all we had a great trip regardless, there and back home. I found 'results came later'.

With an entire bus load of 18+ people. One person named John Turrentine called me 2 days later regarding 'my challenges', our discussion and real estate possibilities. We met and within a few days we had another man named David Jones who was a banker become interested; as I had hoped and prayed for with my positive discussion with what I truly considered to be great investments...real estate. It started coming into fruition. Within the month John, David and I were not talking real estate but plotted a corporation we called and named the 'Vector Investment Corporation'. This would be our investment vehicle. The trip did workout, it oftentimes takes more than time. The people affected need to 'think about it'. With me at times 'impulsive behavior' has to remain at bay, especially with such an endeavor.

# VECTOR INVESTMENT CORPORATION

I was elected President and the others followed accordingly. We started out 'All for One and One for All'. We would behave this way for the next 5 years or so. We went from a few houses and expanded to 120+ houses and 2 apartment buildings within this period of time. As President I wouldn't allow anyone taking any money out of the firm until the time we sold or bought each other out. I kept my promise of strong asset growth.

Our company acquired an 8 plex multi family unit from a local Colonel who wanted us to take over payments of his high rent commercial apartment building. As a former member of Archbold Mental Health Counsel I thought it would be wise to take in some state funded mental health patients in hopes of funding the units. Whenever one is a member of a mental health program you often visit mental health facilities within the hospitals realm of operations. One Friday evening I got a call from one of our units mental health clients. She said, "Mr. Cooper there is water coming out of my electrical plugins." Being a member of the mental health counsel, I thought she was hallucinating due to my so-called expert 'wanna be' a somewhat better psychiatric advisor and responded, "If water starts coming out of the ceiling please call me back." We hung up. A few minutes later she called again;"Mr. Cooper there is water coming out of the ceiling lights." I said, "I'll be right over." When I arrived and entered her apartment it looked like a Disney theme water park. Water was everywhere and she remained in her bed clearly on a schedule during the entire group actions of water removal experts, insurance adjusters and mental health staff members. I went upstairs to check out the water source and the second apartment's bathroom toilet had blown off the top of the water closet and was shooting water 8 feet high. The entire 8 unit structure had to be evacuated; we lost thousands of dollars- no rental income! He did have insurance which paid over one hundred thousand dollars for reconstruction efforts without any renters and we allowed the Colonel to regain his apartment building again. There are many choices in real estate purchases this proposition looked good but in reality this purchase was not good for our company we used a wise time limited waiting period prior to an official takeover. One doesn't always win but to not try at all is to never gain! The greatest baseball hitters do great at a 35% hitting percentage. A basketball player hit 50% does very well.

Over time the next 5 years the net worth of our firm was quickly thrust into the million dollar plus range. I was slowly getting out of the insurance business 'when I was no longer motivated by this fine industry, it is often best to find that which one truly needs for the proper balance' I was now waiting for God to 'show me' and with 'HIS' direction preparing to go into the bail bond business as David had left banking and was doing something he liked with medical contracts. John had become an employee of our firm and directed various carpenters, electricians, plumbers, painters accordingly. We all planned John's work program. Agreed and let our fellow partner work for our firm. This took a full time position to coordinate the various activities. The rental income was about $19,000+ per month most of the time. Every month paying the various property mortgages down meant that our asset values were increasing with every payment.

*Please make note of this, "With each monthly payment of the various mortgages we were increasing the company's net worth by thousands!" Our society often allow certain firms that advertise with a seemingly clear economic message can often cause an individual thought manipulation which causes one to think that your loan is somewhat evil, thereby ebbing away at your perception of debt attitude. The result is devastating. First you miss a payment, then the late charge is too high, then you hear or see a way out! Which often leads to bankruptcy and/or repossession; We all know the rest of the story- bad credit. We all have losses but if we persist in a defeatist attitude this does not help over a long time of personal or business economic recovery. Let's get our head right. Accordingly, I will not buy anything unless in lines up in value and affordability with the peace of mind that follows. Don't let your losses beat your gain! Play Ball!*

This also allowed us to pay off several smaller rental units to increase cash flow. We all had given a good bit of sweat equity 'personal effort for the firm' over this period of time as well. We had used the method of buying houses at as good a price as we could. With ten houses you could generally pay off 1 or 2 in short period of time. This would give us incentive and increasingly good credit to continue in this fashion. As long as no extra monies were taken out the firm was destined to simply continue on. When we reached 100 units we all decided to sell. The firm with good property services could easily achieve $30,000 per month at this point. They all knew the way I worked, the asset building and paying the bills on time. But we all had developed our separate goals for our personal greater good as well. This was in my opinion 'normal' we want the best for our associates. We all came to the point of 'selling the entire firm', not many people could do this, at least not in a fair and equitable method. We thought it best to sell the firm to one of ourselves. One of us would buy the firm and pay off the other 2 investors with bank funds from our huge bank credit lines provided with our solvent firm.

We all agreed as to sell the firm for $150,000 total to the selling investors. I told the group the best way to accomplish this as Christians was to 'roll the dice'. The bible talks of God knowing which way the 'dice would roll'. Before we rolled we all agreed anyone of us who won, would immediately payoff the other two; Very fair to all concerned investors and almost never done in our present secular business society. To the very last day of my life; this economic and spiritually discerned business mannerism allows me to look at this 'sale of firm' with honor and virtue. In other words 'nobody got beat'.

I lost the first roll. It came to David and John and 'John won the company' and therefore had to pay us off. David knew exactly what he was going to do with his $75,000 and I knew what I was going to do with mine as well. I contracted to buy my second airplane the following month. 'Mooney C Trophy 211' (high performance/complex) aircraft. I soon found out by using this plane as a business expense gave me the greatest IRS write-offs you could ever imagine. I also bought my next rental house in Indiana. My goal was to shoot for family and business visits together. Who says family and business don't mix, it's only the character of the individual's ethical values which make up and decides the eventual outcome. It worked great for me.

Top: Gary's Airplane Below: Grandpa Cooper, Susan, Amy and me the Pilot.

The picture 'above' is from Medieval Times Dinner Show in Orlando.

Our purpose in Orlando was attendance at a southeastern economic/ business group event. In the past we heard some good ideas. Unfortunately those type events slowed over the years. We were like three strands of rope/strong and grew exceptionally well. John Turrentine (middle) was our manager/investor while David Jones (left) banker/etc. Gary Cooper (right) President/ Bail Bondsman. Clearly this firm made us all stronger in brotherhood and financially as well.

John took over the company and we both wished him well. He was given just by the 'roll of the dice' a great opportunity! It was now his show. To gain, sell or persist was his option. Not one of us walked away in shame or insult and this was my best sellout ever! I couldn't wait to transition from the insurance business to the bail bond business.

*If I ever find two to three other investors that believe in delayed gratification let me know. Opportunities always are often available. We are only limited by our minds and concepts. The numbers always work!*

# EXPRESS BOND and Collection

Before I ever entered the bail bond business I had to wait upon God to show me this was the right move for me. From my Maslow indicator I felt and sensed this might be the business for me. So I asked God to show me."Should I attempt to get into the bail business and can I be your witness? I won't act accordingly, in other words, not on my accord. I patiently waited to advance until I knew without a doubt. Not my will but God's will was my preference. So I continued at present as an insurance man. I felt as though I was a 'tentmaker' as the apostle Paul called himself, just another way to get along; Just a job. I was not personally prepared to 'just get along'. I wanted my life to count for something more. I was not satisfied regardless of the possibilities without a 'sense of' or possibly a touch from God! I needed a substantial confirmation! I was now waiting patiently on God. In the meantime..

An orphan client called my insurance company and requested service. I was sent out to handle some minor paperwork. Being an 'orphan client' simply meant that for whatever reason an agent wasn't assigned to the client's cause. I was going to service the older couple accordingly. I went by their residence presented the service paperwork they asked for. We signed it and were sent out. The paperwork came back to the office completed and I was going to stop by and deliver their insurance papers mostly dealing with life insurance proceeds. This was the same period of time when our four children would get out of bed, come down to the breakfast table and we all would read one chapter of Proverbs per day 'there were 31 chapters' so it was fairly easy for us all to read or hear the great wisdom of Solomon before he eventually lost his sanity. This was mandatory for each child at 6:30am on the school day mornings. This particular morning the proverbs spoke of 'when someone approaches you with a loud voice, speak softly and it will turn away wrath'. I was trying to touch each of their lives while this particular proverb was about to 'save my life'.

After reading and prayers, Susan and I prepared the children and ourselves to go to their schools and her school-special education and my insurance work. Susan and I previously discussed, "Who was that Sculley boy who shot the Brinson boy over a card game- apparently heated with misunderstandings generally about the money or lack thereof." this was the top news in our local newspaper. We didn't know them and went to work. Upon entering the insurance facility I was handed the paperwork for the Scully's. They were both in their late seventies and not in very good condition as I recalled. I thought to myself on the way to their house, 'could these folks be any relationship to that Brinson/Scully shooting?' With this question the answer would be given over the next few minutes. I would have the answer and it would change my life as well.

I approached the Sculley residence with my paperwork in hand, normal insurance procedure. I knocked on the door and Mrs. Scully asked me to 'enter'. I entered. As I walked past the kitchen area into the dining room Mr. Scully was in a rotating chair facing away from me. There was at least a twelve foot table between us. So I gave the paperwork to Mrs. Scully and then it happened!

Mr. Scully swung around in his rotating recliner, lifting up a handgun cocking the hammer pointing it directly at me and said," I'm going to kill you just like my son killed the Brinson boy!" Instantly my curiosity was answered and I thought there is 'no life in his tongue', this guy means it and 'why'? I then thought of that proverb of 'speaking softly' so I did. While I was gently talking my mind was wildly racing, 'If he kills me what will the family think. If he wounds me I might have a chance'. I said, "Sir what did I do to you…? (Very softly)"

Mr. Scully said, "You robbed me the last time you were here." I softly said," Sir, I didn't rob you maybe someone else did it?" He said, "Our housekeeper never would take our money!" I thought to myself 'oh yeah!' but remained in quiet mode. I wanted to work on him with soft words and started telling him about my family devotion and I mentioned his son. I also told him about how

'Proverbs gave us wisdom' as to how the men treated each other which might not have led anyone to hurt on either side. I was talking sincere forgiveness and love...

During my talk his hand and gun started shaking vigorously 'that was good' and his wife who apparently wanted him to shoot me got somehow convicted by God's words and started walking toward me from the left apparently convinced that 'I didn't do it.' The stealing of the money. When her body came within the shooting perimeter 'especially in front of my left chest and heart' I 'shot like a rocket' out of the room so fast that <u>my shoes never left the floor! I'm sure I set a 'adelinan based 'track record of getting to my car on the street. I finally ran that elusive football days 4.3 forty yard dash!</u> Where's a stopwatch when you need it?

As I approached my car relatively far from the house, I was surprised my socks were the only items on my feet. I knew he couldn't get to me on the street and he came out of the house and said 'while carrying my shoes', approaching my car. "Don't worry I left the gun inside (I made him turn around to check for a hidden gun) but if I were a younger man I would have beaten your butt" I just looked at him, took the shoes and drove away without comment. I wasn't going to waste anymore words on that maniac. I instantly drove to the office filed a police report and they simply stated, "A man cannot be held for pointing a gun in his residence. WOW! I drove off thinking about what just happened. And found out about a new domestic law I didn't know. Interesting…....

This event was my main thrust and decision making stimulus for getting into the bail bond and fugitive recovery business. Number 1 'Don't ever let anybody get the jump on you!' Number 2 'Get as much information as you possibly can with anyone and everyone you write a bond on.' Number 3 'Collateralize everybody you get out of jail.' 'How can I stand for you if your family won't'? More importantly my bail agents and I would ask each person before they got bonded out of jail these three questions prior for them to hopefully and prayerfully comprehend. 1) Did you pray to God before you got in here/jail? 2) Did you read your bible before you got in the jail? 3) Would you be in jail if you had gone to church? I hoped to convict these bail bond clients about the spiritual aspects of their lives in spite of their surroundings.

I was now ready to meet with the local Sheriff 'In Thomas County. A Georgia Sheriff is the only one that can appoint bail agents' regarding my position as a Bail Bondsman. Carlton was slightly older than me and graying at an early age. He was very likable a I told him that 'I wanted to share the gospel with various bail bond client's.' He said, "Gary, I'll give you a shot at this but you will have to pay the bond if the people cannot or will not submit accordingly. This business of dealing with these people could surprise you if you don't really pay attention." I said, "Sheriff I've got two children presently in the military and I want to do something as exciting and dangerous on a local level." He said, "OK, Best of luck and go to every school you can find on bail bond and fugitive recovery matters." I agreed and left Very happy. Yeah! Thank you Lord! In the meantime my attorney told me that Georgia Sheriffs are legally called 'High Sheriff' which means almost nothing is higher. That's who you are dealing with.

Being the businessman I am. One who overlaps opportunities rather than the other way? I continued in the insurance business for 3 months until I realized I could make it in the Bail Bond Business. I then did two immediate things.

1) I bought a totally rebuilt Mooney M20C Trophy 211 from Dr. William Hogan a plastic surgeon who was leaving town. He had really super customized this plane to make it the fastest Mooney of its type anywhere. The plane had a new bored out engine, wing nuts on the fuselage were turned inward for less drag, a great radio system and I was ready to get 'typed' to fly this plane over the next several months. Typed means taught the entire ways of this 'high performance, complex aircraft' it took more time to learn almost all of this aircraft's ways than originally the time to get my initial aircraft license. All of this was under the watchful eye of Irv Nesmith our local Aircraft Instructor. In the meantime, the bail bond business was starting to really boom as I had just bought the property beside the justice center and was renting a building with 'Express Bond and Collection' signs all over it. <u>The name 'Express' implies fast and willing to quickly get to the Justice Center and get</u>

the client out! and the collection meant that I would collect receivables 'rental incomes' for various real estate investors that couldn't or wouldn't want to collect on their own rents. I was collecting fee based in the daytime while bonding occurred mostly in the evening. The weekends became very hectic at times. I stayed the course and for several months and I never missed a forfeiture payment due to the *families personal guarantee* 'if the fugitive could not be found in the state or city court limits' when required by the City/County government 'bond call event' it was simply time to pay. For the most part most bondee's were collateralized individuals from 'working relatives' who could pay the bond if their relative went missing or ran. We would charge a lesser fee for apprehending him or her and bringing them into custody for missing court. A few months after getting my feet wet regarding the bail bond business I went to my first school 'How to Catch the Fugitive' with Bob Burton, he was well trained and well known coming from the big time older bounty hunters of the recent past.

Bob showed us a lot of tricks of the trade. He had an associate bring in a bean bag gun that shot a wrapped shot 'encased with little pieces of shot in the bag' it shot the bag 30 feet in ¼ of a second and would blow a hole through a cooler while being propelled with a simple compressed air C02 gas insert. This is what he said would get us out of legal trouble instead of using a lethal weapon in a fugitive pickup with nothing more than a C02 element. It looked like a short sawed off 10 gauge shotgun without the stock. Bob also endorsed some really effective 'pepper spray' units. Most of the students were relatively new in the bail bonding business as we bought the handcuffs and ankle cuffs. Later in the day he showed us 'how to apprehend a fugitive and how to wrap a rope around his cuffs and have you sit on the back end of the rope under and around the driver's seat so he couldn't grab you without pushback.' He also told us the philosophy of fugitives. 'Out of 10 people the fugitive has 3 people that like him and 3 that say they like him but do not and 4 that simply don't care either way' Bob said, "If you find an ex lover or ex wife, you will know everything you need to know within seconds." He also said, "Ninety percent of all fugitive apprehensions are done on a telephone." This was a very rich meeting for new bail agents like me. I stayed in touch with Bob from time to time... A Great man with loads of bail wisdom.

The Sheriff clearly told me to attend as many schools as possible but didn't seem to care after I showed or told him about the school's agenda and backgrounds. I really wondered if he thought I would make it in the bail business. I didn't just make it in the Bail Bond business, I thrived! Within 6 months I was responsible for at least 65% of the local Bail business. I had put my office right beside the new City/County Sheriff's office and jail. We were the naturally convenient place and choice.

Time moved along until my first National Association of Bail Agents of the United States via Washington DC meeting in Las Vegas Nevada for the members and prospective members 'like me' regarding their annual meeting. It was very well put together and I got to meet and discuss bail with individuals from all over the country. I also found out that Georgia was only one of a few states that appointed bail agents by the Sheriff. Many of the other states agents referred to a Sheriff appointing agents would lead to real problems as opposed to being contracted by the insurance dept of the various states and using surety companies to guarantee forfeiture and losses occurred while acting as bail agents. The other states agents had to write bail under surety companies only. They made me truly wonder and was somewhat troubled about Georgia Bail rules.

Although as a bail agent in Georgia, if the Sheriff appointed you; you can underwrite and pay your own bonds by saving a percentage of bail income (usually 15%) thus saving it in trust accounts for the rainey days of forfeiture.

As I added bail agents from the very beginning of their contracts, they would be required to have an account held in their name by Express Bail Bond to enforce and guarantee monies owed the court system, in the event of forfeiture. Clearly, everyone in the business would sooner or later lose money simply because you couldn't find the perp in the allotted amount of time given by the courts. Each agent had to have a required confidential survey that listed past residencies, at least 3 friends and telephone numbers, present and former work histories, various court information and required court dates. This required paperwork gave the bail agent; secretary and me the best possibility of finding the whereabouts and exact location of hundreds of fugitives over time. We became very good at skip-tracing almost every bondee that we had as they went on the 'lamb' or run. Over the next few years we would add 5 more bail bond counties trained, approved and contracted bail agents by Express Bond & Collection.

We couldn't have grown so quickly had we not joined the National Associations and State Associations as in most cases the information kept us up to date on laws and procedures. The Thomas County original Sheriff's office required that my company submit financial statements each year as to acknowledge funds set aside for forfeitures. At the onset of my bail career the Sheriff's Captain did not like me at all. When I approached the Sheriff's office in the beginning the Captain was generally the one you visited with. I had unknowingly gone to the wrong guy in the beginning...The Sheriff according to Captain Geer. Captain Geer felt slighted. He never seemed to forget it and always made it difficult for us to accomplish most menial tasks. I really think the Captain was behind my first huge problem with Bail Bonding. The bible clearly says, "Boast not of today for we do not know what tomorrow may bring" Proverbs.

# MY ARREST WHY?

I had the mindset that I would never get arrested maybe because of my great high school and college experiences. Maybe because all I ever got charged with was running a stop sign which produced a ticket, maybe because of my lack of confidence or foolish pride. Could it be that 'in my mindset' I just couldn't conceive me being arrested! I was a Christian! Put all of this together and here I am! ME, MYSELF and I just did not see myself as a criminal 'maybe as a child but never as an adult' After this disturbing story, I believe 'my empathy for my clients' will definitely be increased. In the meantime hundreds of bail bond contracts had been written from our company.

I had bonded out an oil-rigger from Louisiana who took off and fled He was charged with 'aggravated assault-felony' regarding his abused girlfriend in Thomasville Georgia while working for a lumberman named Buck. Buck had called me, guaranteed his bond, and I got him out of jail and that was that. I had a typically professionally secured bond and if he hit the road-took off. Buck was told he would pay. This was the normal procedure for all of our bondee's. The bondee from Louisiana took off and didn't come back. We traced him to a 3 month stay on an oil rig in the middle of the Gulf. A Forfeiture notice was given to our company. I called the lumberman and he said 'Linda is going to drop charges. So, I went to the Justice Center in order to discuss the case with the Sheriff, 'It was one of the only times I ever went to see the Sheriff regarding any case'. I asked the Sheriff, 'If I could see the person-witness who had been beaten and told him the lumberman's name who had guaranteed the bond. ' The Sheriff said, "OK, go ahead." So I called her house and set a time to meet.

I went to a bail bond convention and returned the following week. I thought I would be better able to understand how the 'drop charges works'. I was wrong.

When I returned, the next business day; I received a telephone call from Linda's mother. She said,'Mr. Cooper I want to meet you and pay the 'drop the charges fee'. I told her that I had no authority to drop charges at all. You need to see the judge who presided over the case. She said, "could I meet you at the justice center?' I said, 'OK and set a time' I simply wanted to lead her to a judge who might answer her questions. She drove up beside my car in the parking lot of the justice center.

She got out and we started talking. She said, "I want to pay you." I said," I cannot take the money" I started walking towards the Magistrate Judges office. "I'll go in and tell the Magistrate judge, please wait here." I knew something was very wrong; none of this seemed to make sense. I cautiously approached Judge Garland who was the Magistrate Judge and told her 'the lady out there wants to pay me for dropping the charges and I don't know what to do?' The Judge was extremely nervous and fidgety she told me, 'do not take the money'. "I can't advise in this situation" I said, "Thanks" and left. I re-approached the mother of the victim and told her I would only hold the money until the Judge at Superior Court could see her. So I started to write a hold the money contract for Superior Court results regarding the various names. While I was writing the contract on the hood of the car outside the facility she suddenly put $500.00 on the paperwork. She had obviously been coached. During almost the same second I was arrested '1 GBI agent and 1 Sheriff's deputy were hiding behind a car nearby' as they were rushing me into the jail, was taken into custody and read my rites. Seated, I couldn't talk my throat was so dry. I was given some water and asked, "What am I charged with?"

The arresting officer said, "Influencing a Witness" 'I responded, "What is influencing a witness?" The officer said, "A mafia type charge with 1-20 years in prison." I found out later that I was charged with 'attempted murder' Mafia Style! 'Influencing a Witness' they the local law enforcement must have equated me with the Mafia up north 'there is a mindset (mostly from backwood rednecks) here that Northerners bring money 'that's good' but here they don't want you to make any money in their area therefore taking from their economy. They just want you to spend the money. This mindset plays directly with what Hitler did with the Jews-ethnocentrism. This type group behavior is the cause of most wars and conflicts simply thinking that one group's mindset are better or more deserving than other groups, countries, etc. What an irony as I had never written a bail bond for such a charge...only me! I never thought of myself as so incredibly threatening. 'Attempted murder...really!' Then they led me into the Magistrate's court for bail. I was initially numb and was starting to get somewhat excited to fight or plead my case. I had no intent? when it came to me, in the courtroom for my bail hearing. The Judge was now much calmer and said, "Gary, You will show up for court won't you?" I said, "Your honor I wouldn't miss this for the world" She slammed her gavel and said, 'Mr. Cooper is released on his own recogni-nish -' in other words' 'on my own!" She knew my intent, Innocent! I immediately left the area. By the way, my arrest was one of the biggest stings ever at the justice center" They about 75 personnel and Police, GBI etc. were all watching this thru the sun screened dark windows. I think they enjoyed this attempted 'witness murder Influencer' go down. I sure wasn't happy about it.

The next few nights after the arrest; I believe Satan himself was buffeting and condemning me all through the night. In my subconscious sleepful mind it was dark, horrid and depressing. I finally came to my wakeful senses and I shouted out, "I am a Christian and I do not have to take your lies and the bible says in Philippians 4:6-7 'Be careful for nothing with but with everything by prayer and supplication with thanksgiving, let your requests made be known unto God. ....'it goes on to say. And the peace of God, which passes all understanding, shall keep your hearts and mind through Christ Jesus". From that point on my misery ended 100%. In fact I started praising God each morning and thanking him for this opportunity that he is greater even in court. "I even started telling my good friends that maybe I'm supposed to be in the prison ministry from the inside" My attitude would eventually become magnificent even in the court's position of doom, prison or the slick methods of probation.

This same day, the very first person I told was my wife. She was calm as usual and said, "You probably need an attorney." I immediately went to Andy my attorney on various real estate needs and told him my story. I told Andy and then it was found that when I mentioned Buck the lumberman to the Sheriff his eyes sparkled, for a reason."This lumberman was the one who was formerly charged with growing marijuana 'this occurred in 1980 one year before our young family's arrival in Thomasville, Georgia' and his attorney named Ronny Cohen and got him off with 'NO Charges' therefore truly embarrassing the Sheriff's Dept. with the charges being dropped. I think the Sheriff was also getting somewhat of a hassle from a longtime bonding company who had lost a lot of business because of my smart location like buying up the real estate beside the Sheriff's office. Possible good old boy connections with exchange of money and goods...all in secret of course; I didn't bribe anybody this wasn't my way. I knew the Captain of the department didn't like me. It could be a large combination of things but the one that got me the most was the callous way "<u>The Sheriff denied that I had ever talked to Gary Cooper regarding this particular witness!</u>" My attorney told me that I should have had him sign off regarding my intentions with the witness. *My friends trust me. Keep records and get 'sign offs' it could prevent you from facing this type embarrassment, cost and potential jail time involved, if convicted.*

I felt this is the week 'The lights went out in Georgia on me'. It seemed like everybody in the justice system was against me and were even lying! 'Sounds somewhat like Jesus, doesn't it' I'm dead to myself or so I thought! My attorney told me he was going present a huge number of folks who knew me and my kids in the military were planning on testifying also. In the meantime Harold Herman my wife's uncle had previously acted as a bail bondsman for me. Now I couldn't write bail due to pending felony charges. So I did nothing except bail enforcement (picking up fugitives or court fees) until my court someday. Felony court takes months and months….Time... Limbo...always remained in the back of one's mind, especially mine. I became convinced that so often '<u>nobody really feels your pain, whether real or imagined</u>.' This is the typical social emotional response from most people including me. We can't read other persons minds or feelings, this is a fact! But thanks to God 'HE knows what's going on,. This really influenced me. One of my personal goals is to be 'more sensitive' but often our society tells us to 'just be tougher.' Where's the balance? Truly a question of the ages...I could only answer in part.

In the meantime, Lon Shadrick, a lumber company owner 'I had purchased many supplies in the past from Lon and he knew my plight with the Sheriff's Dept.' He asked me to put in a check point security system with guards at his wholesale-retail site. I managed the system and hired various security checkpoint guards to check receipts and quantity of purchases for stopping and slowing thefts in general. This went on for several weeks while I was reviewing some case files. Lon said," Gary, do you do investigations?" I said, "Yes, mostly pertaining to bail enforcement not general investigations." He said, "My wife is running around on me, she is a professional accountant in the major leagues and I need to know what is going on." I said,"I could offer some minor bail investigation procedures for this type of situation. I need a picture of her and I need to inspect her trash can. Is it full?" I proceeded for several weeks, on the side only without the typical investigative grouping of pictures and occasional long waits with a newspaper at my side. <u>We found what we needed most in the trash can...the phone bill.</u>

During this period of time, enter Harold Herman. Harold was better known as 'Uncle Harold' my wife Susan's uncle, he was in his middle seventies, required almost no sleep and drove like a Wildman to get to the jail as each bond call came through. <u>Harold was solely responsible for keeping the company going as I could not write bail while being under suspicion for this felony.</u> Although I did adviseHarold for most situations he administered accordingly. Harold was not only my wife's uncle he was also a genuine New Yorker, with accent included.

Several months earlier I had developed a severe lung disorder. Due to pollen, molds and spores in the air my lungs had started responding in a really bad way. My lungs were operating even less than 10% of the three major lung functions. My doctor told me 'I had less than 3 years to live without taking serious action with medications'. I was immediately given prednisone which helped me feel and breathe better but the side effects was massive weight gain. I went from 210 lbs to 245 lbs overnight! In addition I couldn't sleep. This problem started while I was previously in the insurance business and I sold 3 million dollars of volume in that year. I spoke at various conventions, particularly The MGM Grand in Las Vegas, until I eventually realized that euphoria due to cortisone caused this incredible sales effect. In the bail bond business I had to stop using cortisone or possibly die of early onset cardiovascular lung & heart disease, due to long term use and side effects.

In the meantime, ironically my wife brought home a workout tape that stressed hard and healthful breathing techniques for losing weight. I didn't care much about losing weight but I sensed the workout lady was on to something. I just wanted a more natural way to exercise and expand my lungs. As a result I started deep breathing with hot steamy air at the YMCA sauna room. This helped a lot and the Thomasville YMCA has a great steam room. My breathing procedures became very developed and are very effective when used properly. In addition I have helped many men overcome allergic responses and increase lung development somewhat. At this point my lungs were slightly better as a result of this type of action. Although I still had a very serious lung problem.

Enter the 'infamous Jimmy Keller', Uncle Harold's wife's nephew from Louisiana. I had heard about Jimmy K. and his chelation exploits with many well known movie stars on the west coast. Chelation was a huge mystery to me and it was originally used in the coal mining days to take the bad minerals out of the miner's blood. It was a vein drip method type of treatment. Jimmy found the tremendous level of benefits through working closely with an elderly physician who formerly had helped coal miners and others clean their blood supply. Jimmy developed cancer and the chelation made him a real believer as his cancer went into remission. As a result, Jimmy was now on a mission! Overtime many people became aware of the tremendous appearance benefits as the very sick cancer patients and movie stars also became his clients. After the very helpful and courageous physician died, Jimmy was forced to move the clinic to Mexico. Mexico didn't have the medical license requirements, constraints and check-offs which often causes slow results of potentially helpful cures, mostly due to the MDA and FDA administration's huge political machines. When they learned of Jimmy's activities in Mexico they petitioned covert actions as the Feds went into Suarez Mexico and kidnapped Jimmy. Jimmy was also sent to prison and awaited trial by jury after the Mexican apprehension. During his trial Jimmy's one attorney pointed these covert actions were federally motivated through the MDA attorneys and their expertise.

Fact: Jimmy saved over 17 documented lives-people from cancer and other various diseases. The Feds had 15 attorneys battling against Jimmy's one attorney and he almost won the case. The American Medical Association was furious, as one of the biggest and richest lobby in the country they yielded a huge sword and did affect Jimmy receiving the charge of giving medical treatment without a physician's license. Jimmy served approximately 3 years in jail and while there wound up treating a large part of the prison staff. Clearly chelation works. It makes your cells stronger and with his USA, European/Mexican treatment meds he really could make a difference. So you may ask, why am I telling you this?

Unbeknownst to me Aunt Lou called her nephew Jimmy Keller 'above' and kindly told him about me. He also wanted to see Uncle Harold and Aunt Lou and Jimmy came with the plan of chelating me! I was the type of guy that asked my wife when we got married, "Are you sure you want to do this?" Just before the needle got put in my arm, I was clearly not a natural for this vein oriented procedure. By the grace of God Susan's cousin who is a very well known and respected builder in New York, whom I respected, was visiting his parents and getting chelated by Jimmy as I looked in the slightly opened door room and somewhat observed. He completed Kenny the builder's procedure and Jimmy looked up at me and said, "Gary, you're next. Aunt Lou told me about your lungs and you are going to see a difference." He gave me the most positive and confident statement as I cautiously submitted my arm as I sat down. OK!

I couldn't believe all of the big and little colored bottles. They were from 'Europe and Mexico' all in his bag that he was 'injecting' in me! My face became brighter, slightly pink, and the next day, week, month and years I joyfully did not have any major lung problems anymore! I continue to this day to do my deep breathing routine as well! It's been 20 years and so far so good. I haven't been able to find another chelator like Jimmy. His visit surely helped me. Jimmy Keller died shortly thereafter from simply not taking care of himself plus the various anxieties and stress associated with his career. Auto mechanics often don't take care of their cars the way the way they take care of other people's automobiles. Jimmy was somewhat like that and clearly on a mission being very dedicated to righting his wrongs. Thanks, Jimmy K. you saved me!

Also during this same period of time, I had called a co-signor regarding a recent city incident we held a bond for (simple battery-misdemeanor) violation. I still couldn't write bail bonds but they didn't stop me from bringing in cases -forfeitures that haven't appeared in court. This action was simply arranged to save us money. As I looked through his file it stated he originated from New York and it was a small bond of $360.00 simple battery. It was due so I called her again. I told her how she promised to pay the total amount if he didn't appear in city court. *That's when everything got strange.* Upon inquiring she said, "If I tell you where he works will you promise not to tell him? If he finds out he will kill me!" 'She meant this and responded in the most scared impactful voice ever', especially concerning this little city bond where the clerks just wanted the bond/fine monies. I just wondered if this guy had a big time criminal history considering the way she acted. So I called the Chief of Police. I said, "Chief this particular subject who needs to be picked up on a city charge seems somewhat dangerous and we may need city backup." The Chief quickly responded 'He knew about my influencing a witness charge - it was still awaiting trial and it all happened on his side of the justice center.' "You wrote the damn bond you go get it! pause, Or call the Asst. Chief." I called the Asst. Chief and he said," What did the Chief say?" I told him and he said," I stand with the Chief." 'OK', we hung up, I then called '911 Emergency Services' and clearly stated, "I'm on my way to pick up a city fugitive and 'gave the bondee's name' and stated the Thomasville City Police Department refused to assist."

I drove to the security guard shack at the former pork and meat packers plant while aware of his description, he came out. <u>I was thinking, how can I get the jump on him?</u> He was black, very short and very muscular. I was wearing a bulletproof vest, had handcuffs in one hand, and a vicious looking non-lethal bean bag gun in the other hand, a pistol on my hip. He looked very athletic so I acted instantly throwing the cuffs at him and he caught them just like a good football or baseball player would. Within the same instant I held the bag gun on him while he placed the cuffs on himself. I then called his supervisor while I put ankle cuffs around his ankles. I handed his supervisor his guard shirt and put him in my car. I put a rope under the seat attached to the cuffs to keep him in a position that would prohibit any actions toward my side of the vehicle. I proceeded to put him beside me in my auto. We were about ready to go.

All of a sudden, 4 Sheriff's Dept, 2 GBI agents cars, 1 FBI auto... all pulled in and one of the deputies rushed up to my car and quietly said, "Gary, you've got a three time serial killer in your car!" I said, "Good I got him and I'm taking him in!" I was still pissed off with the way my good ole past buddies treated me with the witness scam. So off we went, 2 cars in front and 5 cars to the rear. Flashing lights with no sirens were blazing everywhere on every police car as I had full authority of the Thomasville road for this moment while traversing all the way to the Justice Center. When I got to the Justice Center intake overhang, I pulled under the intake ramp, I walked him in, went through the steel doors, put him up with gentle but firm force facing the waist high shelf, facing the intake officers while uncuffing him and said, " You've got a live one, watch out" as I turned and left the area through the unlocked steel doors. There are still rumors and many wonder as to 'How did Cooper get that guy all by himself?" As a result the Sheriff got so mad at the Chief he threatened his office. The Chief resigned a short while later. This fugitive apprehension gave me added status from the jail justice rulers of the South Georgia legal groups that maybe this bail agent is someone that might be a little more formidable than expected. I reminded myself of Coach Chiarotti, "If you want to play you better make me play you!" Time and court slowly marched on.

After a while...The Lon Shadrick situation with his wife needed some more in depth information after my fairly intense investigation. I found viewing trashed telephone bills that Lons' wife had been making telephone calls to this special telephone number very consistently in state and out of state over the last several months. This would be our suspect/ culprit in my opinion. I told Lon to call the number instead of me. I did not want to get charged by acting as an investigator.

I was shocked when Lon told me who our culprit was. It was one of our highest ranking officials in South Georgia. I made a copy of the records 'one in our personal vault plus a special file for Susan, my wife' pertaining to all those telephone calls while at his law office.

With several records I decided that I needed to approach this person in the hope of leveling the playing field regarding my case. I also prepared for the worst; my imminent death by some strange occurrence could easily take place as well. Just ask the relatives and friends pertaining as many strange deaths took place concerning my friends Don Massey, Scotty Evans, Dr Bill, and Billy Wilder.

At some point in time, I read of Billy Wilder being sentenced to prison for 10 or so years. I knew of Billy as a fairly nice guy who got caught up on an illegal drug opportunity and was sentenced accordingly. Upon his return from prison, Billy got a job, reunited to his wife and seemed to have served his jail time and was simply ready to move on. A few months after Billy's return, while walking down the road with his wife hand in hand, Billy was run over by a lady from out of town. Ironically the lady stated, "Just hit the man because I lost control of my car and regained the car's control somewhat afterward." Notice the lady was from out of town was in an unusual place to be driving in the first place. We all wondered what Billy was about to do? Tell on his fellow traffickers and/or officers who were investing the drug business? Enter The Georgia Mafia?

Don Massey had been married to a lady who's daddy was very prominent in his businesses. Don also was fairly prominent with his personal and competing business as he later remarried. There was bad blood between the daddy and his former son-in-law Don as Don stayed in the fuel business and started a gas station/convenience store on Hwy 19 in Thomas County. Don's nature was cocky, somewhat wild and fairly arrogant, yet somewhat friendly also. I was shocked when Don approached me at our rented aircraft hanger stalls at our local Thomasville airport. Our private airplanes were parked beside each other. One day after exchanging normally brief hello's he came right over and spoke with me. Don said, "Gary I need you to be a witness. The Sheriff's Dept and my former father-in-law are trying to kill me. They have put bombs in my car that didn't go off because of their negligence. I believe they are out to kill me. I want you to make a record and call the GBI/FBI because if I get killed, it will definitely be foul play." I questioned Don regarding the bomb and told him to call the ATF immediately. Boy could I empathize with Don and I promised to be a witness. Such an ironic word for me to say as I had been charged with 'Influencing a witness.' A few weeks after our airport meeting Don was gunned down on his porch by a supposed 'in/out of towner' who stated that 'Don was running with his girlfriend!' The person was a Thomasville City worker ex-con who most likely had nothing to lose with a payoff. But it was rumored that Don was in fact running with this guy's wife. Always remember that the Georgia Mafia seems to use 'out of towners' and ex-cons for their dirty work. In response to my standing as a witness I called the GBI to make a complaint referring to Don's comments and resulting death. The Agent simply told me, "This case is closed as we found the killer." Like I said, "Sometimes if you want something done...an ex- con and 'out of towner' works very well." *Marg, Don's wife and Dana, Don's 26 year employee, both initially thought they knew what really happened to Don. Dana couldn't believe the investigators didn't ever call him regarding Don's death. Life clearly wasn't fair with Don and his wife Marg.* <u>*This still may need to be reinvestigated. I promised to be his witness and if possible, reopen this case.*</u>

Although, this could also be a case where in his mind someone was supposed to put Don away (kill him), but he may in fact have complicated his personal matters with a jealous man's wife thus nullifying his earlier claims to me and totally unbeknownst to Don himself and causing his demise. Initially, I was mentally prepared for the later result. I'll be questioning his response to me for some time, only God really knows. I find all of this very disturbing.

Scotty Evans was a former Bondee who worked for my friend Lon Shadrick. Scotty was a 'good ole boy' and we liked each other. He did some farm work for me as well. Scotty had told me about his heart condition and family history of early death. Yet he ate carbs and greasy stuff like it didn't matter. Like Don, Scotty came to see me at my office. He said, "I know where the Sheriff plays cards and I'm gonna get more information." I didn't ask for any of this from Scotty... he simply must have thought it meant something to me. All I know is Scotty died and I never got any more information either. Maybe Scotty got whacked or he just died due to family's cardiac problems. Goodbye Scotty.

I thought about these deceased individuals as I pondered my actions pertaining to my possible felony conviction. Who did they upset, what did they know or maybe it was just coincidence which at times I found very hard to believe. I had in my possession 'telephone records', a possible case breaker. I had to believe that it was handed to me to save Lon's marriage possibly but to save me as well. As I prepared the multiple copies of the telephone records, I also prepared my heart and mind to say the right thing at the right time. This was the same week I had just been indicted by the grand jury which is simply saying, 'Case on'. Believe me over the last several years concerning my clients a felony charge is often like flipping dice. With certain juries there is no telling what the outcome will be until the last jury's vote. I didn't want my case to stand in a jury's hand, if I could help it. Remember I'm just a damn Yankee in many of their eyes, although several white and most of the black folks seemed to really like me.

I also knew the considerable efforts the investigators and D.A. had 'for the sting'. It cost them thousands, to recover and 'tap' my telephone calls and it took considerable effort. I knew this because at bail bond conventions I seriously looked into setting up phone taps for some of my 'jumps'. I must have over performed as a bail agent- after all I believe in righting wrongs and helping people recover big cosigner debt, like the $3,000 that Buck, the forester, might have to pay.

I gave my profession my best efforts. But one wrong move, I would be out of business, with a continuing sense of conviction, lastly the publicity I got locally probably scared the powers that be. Rumors seemed to fill the air. Maybe I might run for the office of Sheriff, of which I had no inclination to do, generally I personally would never want to be in law enforcement. In the meantime the investigators were pursuing with all systems on go, while developing my case and they 'the detectives' seemed to have what they needed especially the way some of them acted with attitudes implying, 'We got you!' I could hardly believe they had a case but when I told the witness, 'The person who beat her could attempt some type of retribution" I'm sure they were going to use that conversation against me. Actually all I was trying to do was get the consignors money from being spent and after all I thought I had 'permission from the top law officer' So much for assumptions.

The day arrived! I was armed with a telephone record notepad. It was a pretty day and not too hot. I walked in by myself into the Sheriff's office. I couldn't help but feel I was in the den of thieves but I'm sure everybody who's almost convicted feels the same way. I asked the same secretary who somehow couldn't remember me the last time I went to see the Sheriff. Gee I wonder why? As I asked to see this particular official she would surely remember this time.

As I entered his office it was fairly relaxed. He was obviously in control and my days were like many numbered. He said, 'Gary what can I do for you." I said, "Sir, I'm not here to waste your time but I thought you might like to see these telephone records." He picked them up and 'gasped '. "I don't want to condemn you and I don't want to be condemned as well. The bible says, "When you find a speck in your brother's eye watch out you might find a log in your eye. I figured 'this might be your log.' "I immediately walked out without saying another word. I told no one what had been done. It was now in 'God's hands' as far as I was concerned.

The next day, my attorney called me. "Gary, I believe the D.A. and the Sheriff must want to make a deal, they called me for an appointment tomorrow at 10:00 a.m. I want you to know when they remove a case they generally try to make you feel horrible and they will cut you down but just keep your calm and let's make it through this." I said,"OK"

The next day we entered the Sheriff's office I had a much greater confidence than my attorney had. I knew what was really going on and I was quite willing to play any game they wanted to play. The next thing the Justice officials said was amazing, " Gary, you have a great family with 3 serving in the military, your wife does a wonderful job in the county school system, and you have run a very good business as a bail bondsman. As a result we have decided to 'Nolle Pross' your case. This Nolle Pross simply means if, you do anything like this again. You will be re indicted." Immediately I responded, "I have no intentions of ever talking with a witness again." I signed the form and my attorney witnessed the signatures of all involved. It was over and I first thanked God in my heart and proceeded to walk out of the Justice Center. Outside of the building I asked my counselor, "What do you think of that?" He said, "Gary, you just have one good attorney." 'I guess so…..Thank you.' We departed.

In conclusion, I was truly amazed the newspaper never caught wind of my case. At no point did any adverse publicity hit any one of us. I never planned on entering the Sheriff's office again for a long time. I wanted to do our bail bonding services and get out. We hit the road again, bail bonding with at least 10 or more bonds per week.

There was some great interest from various attorneys. They wanted to know… 'How in the hell did you get out of that?' I simply told them, "I know some folks in very high places". I left it at that most of the time. I was just glad I had another chance to bail bond! The system never forgets and we know they will continue to try to get anyone who challenges them. It's their nature!

# OIL - WATER & RACISM

When I was a child I vividly remember a type of prejudice because I was not doing well in school. When I would go to my relatives 'mostly from Kentucky' they talked of niggers. They referred to them as 'far less important as the rest of us'? As I got older I was shocked by the race riots of the 60's and such. When I first moved from Tallahassee, Florida to Thomasville, Georgia in 1981 I was asked by several people, 'Are you kin to anybody here and where are you from?' I also heard many comments like, 'red birds and blue birds never mate' or 'There is only one good Yankee, the one who moves here and spends his money'. "We don't like the Yankees who moves here and takes our money. We call them Damn Yankees." We have all seen the bias of racism which leads to anger for just being different. Then the newest form of prejudice became one of sexual choices and when the disease Aids was becoming a problem the Gay Lifestyle's got most of the blame. Currently in our Defensive Driver School we currently find that drivers view other drivers as somewhat less, based upon driving skills, and the appearance of various autos cause a type of bias. Prejudice has permeated our lives since biblical days right up to the present.

I was never so directly affected with a racial stance until one night at a church meeting when our pastor Leon said, "I need to meet with the deacons right away after church." This statement somewhat got my attention because he looked so serious until the next day when my wife got a call from the New York Times. The lady said, "They had heard that a black baby was to exhumed from our church's cemetery." It was Monday evening and Susan didn't expect a call like this. The reporter then asked Susan "what is your take concerning this action?" Susan said, "All I know is that *God is a respecter of no persons.*" The lady then asked," Is your husband Gary Cooper, the Sunday School Teacher?" Susan responded, "Yes" and hung up the telephone and directly contacted me.

You can imagine my take on all of this. I questioned my wife very carefully because I knew the news was going to go wild and explode with a shocking story like this. It so happened that Lila Wireman, a member of our Sunday school class, was 'the grandmother of the mixed race couple who had lost a baby due to a brain disease, which had eaten her brain tissue'. Leon Vanlandingham, also in my class, was our pastor and good friend. Logan Lewis, a friend, class member, and well known community leader, was all involved in this without our churches foreknowledge. Prior to all of this shocking news I did understand that Mrs. Wireman's grandchild was to be buried in our cemetery. With grace our church would give a cemetery plot at no cost to the Wireman's due to their lack of funds. The entire situation was very sad as we, the church body, didn't know any of the rest of the family. The funeral was now on schedule for the baby's family. Apparently, after the funeral was officiated, Leon became very concerned because they had never had a black person buried in the church's graveyard. I wasn't aware of this, the church members for the most weren't aware, and I believe the action was clearly worked out 'under the table' so to speak as to not let anyone else be made aware.

The under the table action was quelled immediately when the mother in Tallahassee heard of exhuming the baby and a burial elsewhere. She called the news and the story was in full swing. What else could we do? What is our member's liability if the family sues the entire church for wrongdoing? Would we be able to meet in this church again? Why would these leaders even consider such an action? My mind was racing.

I called an unofficial impromptu prayer time, due to my Sunday School Class involvement, and was pleased that many members showed up in a large circle inside of the church. The prayers were varied and very sincere while nobody condemned the child outside, buried in our cemetery. There were many prayers that God would allow the baby's body to remain. There were prayers that somehow our church could continue. I also remember prayers regarding that 'God is no respecter of persons' and that our Pastor and Deacons will do the 'right things regarding the proposed actions'.

Once again, I was the Sunday School teacher for most of the accused individuals. I also prepared myself to 'become a spokesman for the church as a whole and give good news as often as possible.' I had no idea what was going to happen the next day. I was also asking myself why am I involved in this at all. What would be the cost? God, what can I do but expect to use His direct words.

I arrived at my office the next day to find at least 30 yelling reporters with cameras flashing while sticking microphones into my face. Immediately one said, "What do you think of a document since the 1830's and how it affected your pastor and deacons decisions?" I told them 'I wasn't aware of such a document but it should be changed immediately!' They then asked, 'Are you going to stay in this kind of church?' I said, "Only if they change the document regarding racial and prejudicial language." They also asked 'How long have you been in this type of church?' I responded, "About 3 years." What do you think of the President of the Georgia Baptists stating, "This situation at Barnetts Baptist Church is reprehensible!" I said, "Impulsively, I would have to agree but I know a lot of fellow church goers who simply don't think like this." I closed the event as I was entering my office with this set of simple declarations, "God is a respecter of no persons, Man looks on the outside while God looks on the inside."

They all left to go directly to the church and then to the home of the Wireman's whose family started the breaking news and subsequent church actions. Mrs. Wireman had previously told me that 'her grandchildren were rebel rousers.' Her daughter in Tallahassee had made most of the complaints thus far. I only saw Mrs. Wireman a few times after this fiasco. The immediate demand found the parents, a young multiracial couple, were so impoverished they couldn't afford the fuel to put in a car when it ran out along the way to give a television interview. This resulted in a loss of time and a resulting cancellation while on the way to Tallahassee in order to fly to New York and tell their story on The Today Show. Otherwise this story would have been even bigger with this proposed news story.

I'm attaching the Associated Press and part of the New York Times articles. Racism is alive and well in the United States. We still see it in all parts of our society. Sports, Schools, Politics, Jobs, Police, Military,etc. Attitudes of being greater or better than another, even in churches that preach love, grace and hope. We have to get better or we will get bitter. I decided that even though I didn't plan these horrible events I was still there and somewhat guilty by association. Since these trying times our church has had several black visitors and even black members. But none of this would have happened if our Pastor and Deacon hadn't gone to the Wireman home and asked them to forgive them which they did. Case closed.

The press just can't handle forgiveness. I had a real excited 'hair on fire' Disc Jockey out in California covering the story. He couldn't wait to put me on with any news of these atrocities. He was shocked that I didn't have a southern drawl. I had to explain that I was originally from Indiana. I told them I love the south, the people, and the beautiful area where we live. I stated, "I used to see the same kind of racism in parts of the north as well, just not as pronounced." The length of this shocking story would last one and ½ weeks, thus far. Although, I had a breaking story for him and his station and radio audience.

It went something like this, "Folks,, I have Gary Cooper the Sunday School teacher at Barnetts Creek Baptist Church who had several of his senior members practice racism in the cemetery! They were planning on digging up a black baby and replanting it elsewhere. Yes, this is in Thomasville Georgia! What's the news, Coop?" "Its really big news and I'm not sure you can handle it!" He then said, "We can handle it, this is California! What is it?" "OK, they have all just gotten together and forgiven each other!" THE LINE IMMEDIATELY WENT DEAD! I never heard from the station again. They really couldn't handle it!

**The New York Times**

U.S.

# Anger Over Effort to Disinter An Infant of Mixed Race

By KEVIN SACK  MARCH 29, 1996

Southern Baptist officials today denounced efforts by leaders of a small south Georgia church to disinter the body of a mixed-race baby who was buried last week in the church's all-white cemetery.

But officials with the state and national Baptist conventions, which have recently taken stands against racism, said they were prohibited from expelling or otherwise sanctioning the church, which abandoned its effort this week under criticism. The officials said strict rules protect the autonomy of the country's 40,000 Southern Baptist congregations.

On Monday night, three days after the burial of Whitney Elaine Johnson, who died 19 hours after birth, a deacon of the Barnetts Creek Baptist Church in Thomasville, Ga., apparently told the infant's family that church leaders wanted the tiny coffin moved to another cemetary.

"He said they don't allow half-breeds in their cemetery," Sylvia K. Leverett, the baby's maternal grandmother, said she was told by a deacon of her church, Logan Lewis. "He said, 'That's a 100 percent white cemetery.'"

1800s has barred minorities from the cemetery.

The decision to remove the remains has divided Wireman's family and the church. The burial lot is owned by Wireman's grandmother, Lila Wireman, an active church member who sided with the deacons' initial decision.

Wireman, who has attended the church only occasionally, said she was shocked at the proposed exhumation because VanLandingham has regularly preached against racism and hatred.

"They just didn't seem like that," she said. "Maybe that's why God took her from me, to let people know what's going on now."

Johnson said, "You don't bury nobody and then dig 'em up. That's not right."

Thomasville is known for its barbecue stands, its annual rose festival and its high school football programs, which have produced several professional players as well as former Heisman Trophy winner Charlie Ward, now with basketball's New York Knicks. Nearly 40 percent of the city's 19,000 residents are black.

Gary Cooper, a bail bondsman who teaches Sunday school at the church, said church members had no idea what was going on.

"I can assure you on behalf of the congregation that the whole church didn't know about this situation," he said Wednesday. "God is no respecter of persons. Man looks on the outside but God looks on the inside."

PUBLISHED: MARCH 28, 1996, MIDNIGHT
Tags: discrimination

Click here to comment on this story »

## More like this

SUNDAY, JAN. 15, 1995
'I Think God Wants Us To Come Together' Reunion Of Faith Ministers Bring Spokane's Southern Baptists Together In Observance Of Martin Luther King Jr. Day
SATURDAY, MAY 26, 2001, 8:04 P.M.
Fairview Cemetery's unofficial historian

I hoped this type of action would simply stop. After similar types of these actions/news articles have taken place. But racism continues to raise its head. So let's be vigilant to require our leaders, friends and fellow man to look at a person's character and one's knowledge rather than color tone of his or her skin. After this proposed race action failed the Black churches of Thomas County condoned it but went on to say, "We often like similar people, like ourselves, due to greater interests within our race as well to attend our churches." The black leaders remained 'cool' and did not impulsively throw out comments like the Georgia Baptists did. We need wisdom with understanding in dealing with racism. Not soundbites of condemnation and division. May God bless our country.

In my life I couldn't help but believe that blessings were possibly going to come my way because I stood up for not only what was right but actually righteous persons rose up concerning these matters during these times as well. I could have never expected what was next to come.

A spark can cause a fire

A bullet can take a life

A ride might be your last

A bill may cause you strife

Our world may shock us so

We've been taught to not let go

Faith often has an answer as

God acts only within His time

But the chance of a certain letter may alter one's life…almost forever

**American Movie Classics**

February 5, 1999

Gary Cooper
Cooper-147
301 Cooper Lane
Thomasville, GA 31792
**Reference Number: Cooper-147**

Dear Gary:

**Congratulations!**

**American Movie Classics** (AMC) has selected you to be one of our "ambassadors" for the *From Coast to Coast Hollywood's Leading Men* promotion. As an ambassador for AMC, you and one guest will experience VIP treatment Wednesday, March 3rd through Sunday, March 7th in New York City to help celebrate Hollywood's Leading Men movies on AMC in March.

Your VIP Experience will include:

* Round-trip airline tickets for you and one guest to New York City
* Accommodations for two people in one room at the exquisite [hotel]
* Participation in a scheduled NBC TODAY show segment featuring all 5 AMC Hollywood Leading Men on Thursday, March 4th.
* Two tickets to the Tony award-winning Broadway show "Chicago"
* A "double-decker" tour of New York City attractions and landmarks
* A VIP Celebrity Luncheon, hosted by American Movie Classics
* $700 in cash to be used for incidental expenses, etc.
* Luxury ground transportation to and from the airport in New York City
* Limousine transportation to select events

On Saturday, February 13, you will receive [via FedEx] a check for $700, your airline tickets, and a detailed itinerary of events in New York City. Due to the value of the contents of the package, FedEx will require a signature for the package. The package will be sent "AM Priority" for a early morning delivery time.

In addition to the VIP experience and media opportunities in New York City, your local media may have an interest in speaking with you about your experiences as an American Movie Classics Ambassador. I will keep you updated on any local media opportunities to determine a mutually convenient time for an interview.

Again, congratulations on being selected. I hope you enjoy your experience as a Hollywood Leading Man. I look forward to seeing you in New York!

Regards,

*Pamela Aniello*

Pamela Aniello
Promotion Director
GREAT!
131 Killington Way
Orlando, FL 32835-6809
Direct Line: (407) 532-9482 (please call me collect)
Pager: 800-204-4938

# The American Movie Classics

I had just arrived home. Checked the mail and saw a letter from Great Promotions. I opened it and read the comments while noticing an enticing statement. 'We have found 6,000+ Gary Coopers'. At the ending I noticed questions which required my responses. I threw the letter in the trash. I thought junk mail wanting information and my signature. While sitting in my chair sipping iced tea it occurred to me *reread the letter s*itting at the top in the trash. I took it out and noticed something very different. <u>The return letter had a real stamp attached to it.</u> They asked, "What 5 actions in your life reminds you of the Movie Star Gary Cooper." I quickly wrote the 5 comments below. They liked #1 and #5:

1) Brought in a three time serial killer- Result: *winner/AMC*
2) Wrestled a bear and won
3) Married a girl from New York
4) Flew my airplane thru a hurricane
5) Saved a boy from drowning- Result: *winner/AMC*

I sent in the letter in the self addressed envelope. 4 days later what happened next for me was unbelievable; the promo company asked if I had teeth. My wife was the only one at home. She stated, "Gary definitely has teeth and why do you ask?' <u>'You and your husband are most likely going to get a packet from the American Movie Classics and they are going to treat you both like movie stars!'</u> They wanted to confirm and approve what I had submitted.

She said, " Did Gary really save a boy from drowning 'yes'. Did Gary really bring in a serial killer 'yes'." That's all we need to know because those two items are what the real *Gary Cooper the movie star would have done in the movies*. You're going to like the AMC packet and tickets. We received the packet and found that I would be teamed with Clark Gable, Elvis Presley, Paul Newman, etc. all people with 'Famous Names'. Shortly after that American

Movie Classics sent out nationwide press releases. I had relatives from Missouri call me, not to mention people from all over the country. The big event finally was about to happen. They sent us to the Tallahassee Airport.

We flew to New York. While waiting we each had individual limousines with our drivers looking for Gary Cooper and the other famous names. The limo drivers were holding up signs with our names. It was amazingly funny as the people were trying to figure out where the real movie stars were. Truly we didn't look the part. I just kept quiet with my wife Susan while she enjoyed the interest. Eventually we were all picked up and landed at some really swank restaurant called 'W' whre we were offered an unbelievable selection of meals and menus with no price listings. Apparently movie stars didn't look at prices. I ordered lamb and they brought me a half rack which I couldn't attempt to eat. The AMC people were all there. They welcomed us and told us we were really in good fortune as you all are going to be movie stars for at least this week. They called us by name and we stood. Gary Cooper, Paul Newman, Peter Sellars, Marilyn Monroe, Elvis, John Wayne, etc. all of us were introduced and all had a great time, laughing as the names and faces didn't jive. The dinner meeting had just about ended when they gave us an itinerary and AMC badges for identification. The next day we appeared on the TODAY SHOW and took a tour of New York in a double seater open top bus.

The most interesting item for me at the end of the Today Show was Jane Pauley as I remembered her being on the local news in Indianapolis. She was particularly beautiful back then and I mentioned her co anchor Chet Coppet. She said, "We need to stop talking you're taking me too far back". We both laughed and discussed our previous Indiana hometowns and our respective colleges. During the double seater bus we toured the twin towers. 9-11 would change everything. Although it was chilly I think Susan liked the bus tour the best, and the Broadway Show we all went to.

The last full day all of the Famous Names including myself got to 'Ring the Bell' to 'open the stock market'. The American Stock Exchange was so packed with brokers that they truly looked like they were falling out of the ceiling. The floor was packed so tight with brokers I couldn't help but notice that in all cases the brokers seemed far more stressed than happy. That evening we all got to appear on Entertainment Tonight and that's where we all met and talked with Shirley Jones. She was in the Thomasville area, *my home* quite often and said she always had a good time there. It might have been Ted Turner in Capps, Florida, just 20 miles away. Or her former college roommate in Monticello, Florida. I wrote and recited some Shirley Jones movie facts with prose and got a kiss from Shirley on my balding head. We all had a great time and were each given a couple of thousand dollars to spend. I bought a solid brass Lady of Justice. It looked pretty good in my office. I had no idea what the power of press releases would do for me. I also believed that Mom used the 'power of the tongue' as I somehow knew this AMC event was going to happen. She confessed it my entire first eighteen years of my life.....'Gary Cooper the Movie Star' and it actually happened for a week. I fervently resisted all that time and it still came to pass! This is an example of how we think or talk. I find these events hard to imagine. So be careful what you say, plus or minus, positive or negative! It just might happen...but hardly the way one thinks. That is God's way which is always higher and better. Check out these pictures and documents.

- The Limousines will be on stand-by to take our Hollywood Leading Men back to the "W-New York" hotel following the appearance on the TODAY show.
- The group will arrive back to the hotel by 9:30 AM, at the latest.

and their guests in the Raven Room of the "W- New York" hotel.
- A surprise celebrity guest will be in attendance and "Entertainment Tonight" plans on covering the event!
- We have hired a professional photographer to take pictures at the luncheon. We will send you copies of select shots following the trip. You may want to bring your camera for spontaneous photo opportunities.
- Hot and cold hours d'oeuvres, wine and mineral water will be served butler style beginning at Noon.
- The seated luncheon will be served immediately following the reception beginning at 12:30 PM.
- By using simple, whole ingredients, executive chef Michel Nischan will prepare a luncheon that will entice your taste buds. The luncheon includes:

• A celebrity luncheon on Friday with a special star host at the Forest Room of the W-New York hotel. "Entertainment Tonight" is scheduled to cover this event.

In closing we all had a great time. Who wouldn't! We were truly treated like stars except none of us had to work for it. We just kind of lived movie parts or movie actions in our normal lives. Many try but only a few are selected like Jane Pauley and Shirley Jones. I now understand first hand why they call them the beautiful people....because they are! All of the movie star participants all slept well the next week, including me, but I had no idea what was to happen next.

# 'PETE THE PYTHON'

# The secret revealed...

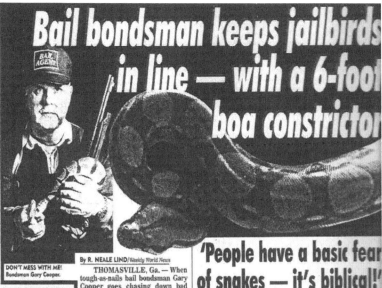

# Bail bondsman keeps jailbirds in line — with a 6-foot boa constrictor

**DON'T MESS WITH ME!** Bondsman Gary Cooper.

'People have a basic fear of snakes — it's biblical!'

By R. NEALE LIND/Weekly World News

THOMASVILLE, Ga. — When tough-as-nails bail bondsman Gary Cooper goes chasing down bad guys, he takes along a partner who's even more intimidating than he is — a 6-foot-long boa constrictor!

"I'm the first guy since Moses to use a snake effectively in my work," says the burly Cooper, who teaches Sunday school when he's not bringing in bail jumpers.

"People have a basic fear of snakes. It's biblical. In Genesis 3, God says snakes and people will be natural enemies."

And Cooper, who owns and operates Express Bond and Collection Agency, plays on that fear by taking his buddy "Pete" with him when he goes out to bring in criminals.

"If the guy resists my request to come along peacefully, I just threaten to reach into the pillow case and take Pete out," Cooper says.

"Pete tends to make rebellious people fearful. I've seen mean Miami drug dealers melt at the sight of him."

But surprisingly, Cooper says the greatest danger in his job doesn't come from the fugitives themselves.

"It's the friends and family you've got to watch. It's the half-drunk cousin or the wild-eyed girlfriend or the 70-year-old grandmother standing there in the kitchen with a carving knife — these people who think I'm picking on the poor innocent guy — who's usually about as innocent as the driven mud.

"But all of them keep their distance when I threaten to introduce them to Pete."

Cooper, who was named after the strong-but-silent 1950s screen actor, says he only uses Pete in dangerous situations where the likelihood of violence is high.

Most of the time he doesn't have to take Pete out of his pillow case.

Boa constrictors eat small rodents, killing them by squeezing them to death in their coils. But they're nonpoisonous and a boa the size of Pete is no real threat to people.

"It's the idea that works," Cooper says, "not the reality.

"Once I went to a house where a fugitive was holed out. The guy's mother answered the door.

"I said 'Ma'am, please don't make me pull out my viper.'"

The guy gave up without a fight.

## Dead man leaves grave, goes home!

ALMATY, Kazakhstan — A man who was electrocuted and buried shocked his friends and family by showing up at his own funeral feast.

The man had apparently died while trying to steal power cables in eastern Kazakhstan, reported local media.

The man was wrapped in a cloth shroud according to Muslim tradition and buried in a shallow grave.

But two days later, he regained consciousness and rose naked from the ground, Express K Daily said.

The paper said he had difficulty flagging down a vehicle to take him home.

## MALE MENOPAUSE IS FOR REAL, SAY DOCS

MEXICO CITY — If you're a middle-aged man experiencing irritability, anxiety or depression, you may be suffering from male menopause!

By BARRY DUTTER
Weekly World News

At one time, the idea of men going through menopause — which is traditionally a condition associated with females — would have been ludicrous.

But now scientists with the Mexican Health Institute have identified a decline in testosterone in middle-aged men, which is similar to the decrease in estrogen that women face when they experience menopause.

Researchers are calling this new condition ADAM — androgen deficiency in aging men.

It involves a temporary pause in the production of testosterone. Symptoms include concentration problems, weight gain, hair loss, sleep disturbances, low sex drive and difficulty maintaining an erection.

If you think you might be undergoing male menopause, see a health care professional to find out if you might require testosterone supplements.

An herbal treatment that may work to try is Mexican wild yams. Herbalists report it is effective in treating many of the symptoms of this condition.

WEEKLY WORLD NEWS
January 23, 2001   $1.43 U.S.   $1.99 CANADA

A few months prior to the AMC happening and events I wanted to see if I could apprehend a fugitive with the *idea of a snake*. There happened to be a small animal shop next door but it didn't stay in business very long. I purchased a small 'ball python' from the owner in order to prevent office break-ins. Was this a waste of my money? I couldn't help but really ponder what I could do with it. Then I remembered what the bible says in Genesis 'God put enmity between women and snakes and she would bruise the snake's head and teach her kindred to hate snakes.' This curse came after Adam and Eve were evicted out of the Garden of Eden. Obviously since I had a python this fugitive apprehension idea might be perfect for 'Pete the Python' which I placed in a soft airy pillow case. Clearly I didn't want to scare anybody to death or present the snake out of the bag causing intense shock to all concerned. I only wanted to present the 'idea of the snake' in order to change or confound the fugitive's mindset. Clearly the snake must be kept in the pillowcase without exception. With a snake held or placed on the ground 'especially in the daylight', again it might cause way too much chaos and someone could possibly get hurt.

During the AMC event I wouldn't dare mention *Pete the Python as* it was experimental and was not fully developed at that time. After the AMC event I would give it the proper conceptual testing, probably more like a 'scary movie' prior to the 'shocking real time exposure of the monster, etc.'

One of my female bail agents in Mitchell County had written a bail bond contract in her same county. The bondee took off and relocated in Thomas County in the hope that his knife yielding mother would scare us away. He was now a fugitive and needed to get apprehended. Learning more regarding the mother were these basic facts: She was very large and would always keep a knife on the kitchen counter. I did not want to get anywhere near that woman with the knife. This was a job for Pete the Python. The Mitchell County agent's name was Dana Jeffcoat and she seemed to think it might just work. Let's try!

We approached and quickly entered the residence. With my guns, badges, bulletproof vests, and cuffs I told the mother who I was and clearly stated her son needs to be apprehended. *As expected I* noticed the knife on the counter and her glances and subtle movement towards the weapon of protection and aggression. It was time for the test."Ma'am, I need to see your son. I know he's here". She denied he was there and was moving toward us and the knife! *It was time to respond!* "Ma'am I sure wouldn't want to let this Viper out of the bag". She looked at my pillowcase with the snake gently wiggling and she zoomed out of the trailer as similar to a launched guided missile as I've ever seen. I think she even left a vapor trail. Poof she was gone!

I went to the first room...no one. 2nd room as I opened the door...he was by the bed with his arms and legs fully spread on the wall. I quickly cuffed him and he was back in jail. On the way to the jail I told Dana, "I can't believe it, it works!" Pete was now officially a fellow bounty hunter! With quite an edge...

I made it very clear to all of our bail agents and bail enforcement agents that the snake was for specific instances when encountering certain obstacles and clearly rebellious people. We found that when we used the snake as an enforcement tool it generally caused a unique distraction and made apprehensions much easier. Once again, the idea of the snake was only for specific use instances otherwise business as normal.

Our short term motto:

*Just remember once the word viper/snake is out there, there is little need to scream and shout as we keep him in the bag.*

*We would prefer to see you choose to put out your hands and spread your legs as we intend to take you in.*

*We truly don't want to make a fuss and we will not cause you to want to cuss. We will treat you better than the police, always my friend.*

At this point we were writing bail bonds at an average of 1,176 persons per year with an average size bond of $1500 with the total amount at $1,174,000. The bail jumpers averaged 6% which put our annual risk at $105,840 and the forfeited (paid to court-not found) amount averaged $23,500 per year.

With 5 agents in 5 counties bail underwriting with proper collateralization became essential. Initially the local Georgia Justice folks were not quite up to date with our required bi-annual schooling in Georgia and Las Vegas. We became experts at securing the smallest to biggest bonds. With great ease all my bail agents would simply say to the clients friends and family," I can't stand for him/her if you won't stand for them" In other words, if you really want this person out of jail you must be willing to guarantee their bail bond total amount. The average bond was $1500 so at 12% the bail bond fee would be $180.00 in Georgia. All of my agents signed an agent's trust account for each bail bond commission and I would take 10% from each bond. At the $1500 averagethe bail fee would be $18.00. If the agents underwrote their bonds properly after a short period of time, they would have thousands of dollars in their respective funds. This procedure was essential for protection against forfeitures and a reward for good underwriting at the bail agent's termination of service.

This all means if an agent had a forfeiture of his bonds totaling $1000 the agent would have $500 taken from his fund and my company would pay the remaining $500 providing the bail bond was properly underwritten. Express Bail Bond and Collection remained prompt and with this system never came up short on any bond in any year. The future looked good but the effect of the American Movie Classics started showing up. Unbeknownst to me, Georgia Sheriff's at times become threatened by their Deputies or bail appointees getting publicity. This was just the beginning! High Sheriffs/local Kings are jealous.

Earlier a small Florida newspaper named the Sun Times of Florida called me up. They wanted to know 'how did I bring in a 3 time serial killer'. I explained and was ready to hang up when the newsagent asked if I used any other technique. I simply said, "Upon special occasions I use a snake in a bag for psychological reasons." I never saw the article except I had a former bail client come up to me and say,"The Sun Times did quite an article on you with a snake." I said,"Ok, 'that's what it is." I left not making much ado regarding the article. I didn't even attempt to find the article or read it. Who reads the Sun Times? I was really wrong!

*As a former Stock and Baird equities broker I could only dream of being in the Wall Street Journal. Because of my unique 'Economic skill level' there I was listed as a WINNER!*

**Winners**

▲ **Fugitive Squeezers:** Bail bondsman Gary Cooper of Thomasville, Ga., credits success in rounding up bail jumpers to Pete, a 6-foot long python that he carries along in a pillow case.

▲ **Fido:** The Cape Fear, N.C., chapter of American Red Cross begins teaching Pet First Aid, a three-hour course that includes CPR for dogs and cats.

▲ **Voters:** The Mobile, Ala., public bus system agrees to offer a free ride on Election Day, Nov. 7, to anyone with proof of voter registration.

**Losers**

▼ **Road Trips:** University of Georgia suspended classes last Thursday and Friday so students could travel to an away football game against the University of Florida, but the Bulldogs lost, 34-23.

▼ **Pass Play:** Doctors say the Duke University football team passed food poisoning to its opponents in a 1998 game, the first known transmission of a virus by pigskin.

▼ **Seniors:** Students in Milledgeville, Ga., will have to retake their high-school graduation exam after a box of unscored tests disappears from the local school board office.

# A&E Wild Justice

## HE SCARES BAD GUYS SILLY WITH THIS 6-FT. SNAKE

**HE ALWAYS GETS HIS MAN:** Bail bondsman Gary Cooper shows off his python Pete, who gives fugitives the shivers.

BAIL BONDSMAN Gary Cooper packs an unusual weapon — a 6-foot python that's helped him round up some nasty snakes!

"It's pretty doggone weird — a bail bondsman bringing in fugitives with the aid of a snake," he told THE ENQUIRER with a chuckle.

Gary Cooper — yup, that's his honest-to-goodness name — has been in the business for years. Five years ago he came up with the idea of using a snake to nail fugitives after he noticed how much people feared his pet python.

Cooper, 49, of Thomasville, Ga., has used python Pete to help him nab 15 fugitives including a three time killer, rapists and a drug dealer.

"I use Pete for only the most dangerous guys," said Cooper — who enlists the snake to petrify tough guys who aren't fazed by artillery.

"These are guys who are used to violence and guns. They're not used to a guy coming at them with a snake."

On the job, the married father of four carries Pete hidden inside an old bag next to his waist.

"When I confront the fugitive I say: Look, you have a choice. I've got a viper in my bag. You can either come with me peacefully or I'm going to pull my viper out and we'll see what happens."

"I never say it's a python — just 'viper.' That way they can use their imagination. They start thinking — is it a rattler? A copperhead? Or some other terribly venomous snake? And their eyes start getting bigger and bigger.

"When you look at him outside the bag, Pete doesn't seem to be that big for a python, but when he's coiled up inside my bag he looks a lot bigger, and they start thinking, 'My God, what is that thing in that bag?'

"Then I reach into the bag and they start having visions of me flinging this huge poisonous snake around their neck. Their eyes look like they're about to pop right out of their head!

"They are so distracted I just walk up to them and cuff them. The snake works like a charm every time. And the amazing thing is I've never yet had to get him out of the bag."

One time, Cooper went after a fugitive called "Junior" wanted for assaulting his wife.

"I found Junior at home, and he had his mama with him. Now Junior wasn't about to give himself up and I could see big mean ol' mama wasn't going to let him go without a fight.

"All I said was: 'Ma'am, I have come to apprehend Junior. I want you to know I've got a viper in my bag. I don't want any hassle from you, because if you do I'm going to pull the viper out of my bag.' Then I went to reach my hand in my bag.

"Well, mama took off like she had roller skates with rockets on either side of them — and Junior whipped around and put his hands on the wall with his feet spread apart. He didn't say a word. He was scared stuff.

"It was hilarious. I had to fight not to burst out laughing."

### DOC'S TIP

MEMORY works best at age 25, but after that, it's all downhill. Yet you can easily avoid senility and keep your memory strong by using common sense. Read, do puzzles, solve problems, eat properly, exercise regularly. Those and other methods give your mind a workout.
— James McGaugh, Ph.D., Center for the Neurobiology of Learning and Memory, University of California, Irvine

"Will you shut that thing off? The man is trying to putt!"

I was called by a field agent with A&E. He stated "We want to do a story on the 'how and why' you use a snake." They said they would send a video crew and the next week they will be at my office. You couldn't believe what a 'can of worms' was going to be opened. And they were my worms!

I figured that Bill Curtis was going to just make a slight mention of us as his show ended. But instead they called the series 'Wild Justice' which compared me to a New York City big time bail agent. In my office and out in the field I was relieved that he said, *"Mr. Cooper seemed to act more like a concerned parent than a mean old fugitive recovery agent"*. I also got to explain the effect of my snake named 'Pete' which I never took out of the bag. I went on say that since 'Adam and Eve' because of their sin a curse arose between women, their kindred (children), and snakes.

Man would step on the snake's head and the snake would bite at the ankles. This battle has been going on since the beginning of time. I was using the psychological effect created from this biblical experience. I knew that if I brought the snake out of the bag, I would create a certain kind of chaos. One which I could not control that would surely have consequences in a legal way.

I knew that if I kept the snake in the bag I would have the same control of number 1) distraction- take one's mind off the present. 2) Just like scary movie we are fixed by the 'not knowing what is behind the veil or bag', this creates anxiety. When we used step 1&2 on the right kind of Fugitive we never failed. This action put us in the most favorable position due to this special effect.

By the time this program aired I was blitzed by every angle of news media agents. I was now a mini 'rock star'. I had people coming through town hoping to get my autograph and see 'Pete' who was generally asleep in a motorcycle helmet inside his glass 6 foot cage.

I was very pleased to hear a famous older newscaster claim that my idea could revolutionize fugitive apprehensions. His name was Paul Harvey although I didn't get to talk with him. He aired my story on his radio show.

During this time period I was asked to go to Tallahassee Florida and appear with a teleprompter and spend a half an hour with Nancy Grace, a crime reporter. I was placed on her show called 'Pro's and Con's' and oddly enough Nancy and I got along very nicely, much to my surprise. If I was to rename this show I would have called it 'Nancy Grace Unhinged'. I expected a very mean and demeaning type personality. She was delightfully the opposite. She smiled a lot and seemed to completely understand my plight and purposes. So when the audience voted me down 45% against compared to 37% for….Nancy said," Folks, I'm bunking it, I'm voting..YES". It's true Nancy Grace voted for me and also voted for the concept of Pete! I was very pleased to say the least.

Next was the Kathy Krier Show. She had a very similar introduction as Nancy Grace but had an animal activist in her shadows. I gave the concept as I did with Nancy and others but the activist screamed that I was ruining this snake's life. I just listened and my only response was "After all you know how everybody just loves snakes." The show ended and I was glad. I did not like her show as much as Nancy Grace. We didn't vote.

Next came the German and the Japanese press. This was amazing. I did informational shows for both nations and their press corps. I never got to see any of it. It occurred to me after a while that I created a concept that extends around the globe. No telling where this will lead.

I believe the Sheriffs of Georgia's blood was starting to reach the boiling point. Once again the Georgia High Sheriffs were very upset. Could it be that they were upset due to the fact that they didn't find this? Or were they jealous, not getting enough attention. I wasn't about to give them any credit based upon the way most acted. I even had one Sheriff call and ask if I could get him on A&E! I told him straight up that I had very little to do with all that except it was an idea that has pretty much gone the course. I was wrong about this also.

# Snake helps round up fugitives

By Elliott Minor
Associated Press Writer

THOMASVILLE, Ga. — Bail bondsman Gary Cooper speaks softly and carries a big snake.

If someone Cooper posts bond for doesn't show up for trial, he goes looking for the bail jumper armed with Pete, a 6-foot boa constrictor.

Cooper rarely has to pull out the snake. Just the sight of the huge serpent writhing in a pillowcase Cooper carries is enough to make most fugitives submit.

"There are two kinds of people I deal with: fearful people and rebellious people," said Cooper, whose mother named him after the Hollywood movie legend.

"The snake makes rebellious people fearful people. I have seen mean drug dealers from Miami melt at the thought."

Cooper owns Express Bond and Collection Agency in Thomasville. Surrounded by plantations, Thomasville's streets are lined with mossy oaks and Victorian homes built in the early part of the century when the town was a winter vacation spot for Northern industrialists.

Pete's mansion is a 4-by-2-foot aquarium in a back room of Cooper's office. The snake likes to sleep coiled beneath a black motorcycle helmet.

When Cooper takes Pete out, the serpent coils around his arm, peers around the room through beady, black eyes and flicks his forked tongue.

Boa constrictors are nonpoisonous snakes from the jungles of Central and South America. They kill their prey by squeezing it to death and then swallowing it whole. Most adults are between 6 to 10 feet long.

"I give him everything he needs," said Cooper, 49. "I'm his daddy image. I give him a rat once a month."

Daphna Nachminovitch, a manager with People for the Ethical Treatment of Animals,

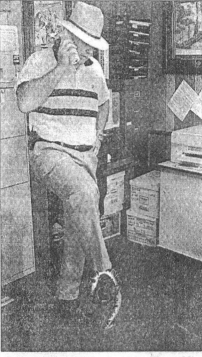

*AP Photo*
**Pete, a six-foot boa constrictor, coils around the ankle of bail bondsman Gary Cooper in Thomasville**

which opposes the removal of exotic animals from their natural environment, said she thought Cooper should consider kick boxing or karate as a more humane way to bring in fugitives.

"What, heaven forbid, if he was in danger?" she said. "He'd . . . have one hand occupied by a pillowcase."

Cooper, a Sunday school teacher, said the idea of partnering with a serpent came t him while praying. Hoping t avoid the use of guns, peppe spray and violence, he said h asked God to help him find a wa to nab fugitives "nonlethall without abuse and trauma."

"I got to thinking about tw words: rebellion and fear," h said. "This poor viper has bee cursed and has had to crawl o its belly since Adam and Eve. It i the base root of absolute fear."

He purchased Pete in 1993 at pet shop.

"I only use Pete in high-risk sit uations, where a person is ver dangerous and has a violen background," Cooper said.

Bondsmen can go anywhere i the country to capture a fugitive Unlike law-enforcement officer they can bring fugitives acros state lines without the extradi tion process.

To travel quickly, Cooper flie his own plane. In his spare time he writes poetry and shows Pet at schools and nursing homes.

When Cooper goes after a fug tive, he carries Pete in the pillow case. For backup, he packs pistol and a beanbag gun, a nor lethal, carbon-dioxide powere weapon that packs the punch of heavyweight boxer.

"I've never had to take out m snake," he said. "It's the idea tha works. Rebellion turns into fear.

Cooper said he went to on house where he knew a fugitiv was holed up and was met at th door by the man's mother.

"I said, 'Ma'am, I don't want t pull out my viper,' " he recalled.

When he entered the house, th fugitive was already waiting fo him, standing spread eagle an propped against a wall.

"This is just another way to di tract people enough to get ther back in the criminal justic system," he said. "We're desens tized to pepper spray and gun We know guns will hurt us, bu for some reason people don't seer to know because they shoot eac other all the time."

# WE WANT YOU TO BE SNAKE?

My mother wanted me to be a movie star. I seemed to be in most cases very fortunate. I cared more about my wife and family than about anything else. I really did want to make a difference. My priorities had to be right.

Telephone rings......."Is this Mr. Gary Cooper of Express Bail Bonds?" "Yes, this is Gary." "I am the program Director with A&E and we want to do a 'Reality Series' called, 'SNAKE THE BOUNTY HUNTER'. You will be featured several hours each day and you will become World Famous!" Sounded to me like Satan tempting Jesus while perched upon a high place. I could have been everything most would jump for but my heart could not allow this action. Fame isn't everything. Look at the lives and early death of the so called 'Stars'. Most insurance companies will not insure 'Movie Stars' due to exceptionally high early mortality experience.

My mind was speeding 'faster than fast'. All I could think of was 'I can gain the entire world and yet lose my soul'! I said, "Sir, I want to thank you for this unbelievable opportunity but I'm afraid it's simply not for me." He said, "Thank You for Your time." and hung up. I was proud of myself and realized that I have just dodged a bullet that would possibly ruin my family, my wife, and me.

It didn't take but a day or two and DOG the Bounty Hunter was introduced. To this day you can ask DOG and he will tell you,"Gary Cooper gave it to me!" From what I understand DOG makes millions. Go DOG! I've got my own 'Golden Streets' all lined up! Just ask MY KING JESUS! The beat had to restart and most of the publicity was winding down. It was back to business as usual. But, my Sheriff never forgot. Too much publicity? Name was too well known?

# THE DAY 'OUR TIME' STOOD STILL..........

I was walking into the local Carroll Hill BP service station to pay for fuel and the group standing around said, "Hey Gary, you're a pilot aren't you?" I said, 'Yes, what's going on?" They all were quietly standing around looking at the small television on the wall. They asked me the 'How's and Why's' regarding flying a plane into the World Trade Center. None of my responses were any good until the 2nd plane hit and then everyone knew our country the U.S.A. was under attack. We were all now watching with intensity regarding which plane was flying where and did they know if anyone was in the towers until more breaking news! The Pentagon has been attacked!' Instantly it occurred to me that our daughter and son-in-law was at the Pentagon! I told the bewildered group, "2 of our kids are in the Pentagon and I better go see my wife!" and left.

Susan was an evaluator for the special education program. I went directly to her office and told her not to worry. I gave her the news of our kids. I told her, "I had a dream last night and God told me to 'pray for our children' at 2:00am in the morning. So I prayed for all of our children and went to sleep" We felt clearly emotionally upset but not without faith that our children were in fact alive'! It was almost lunchtime and I assured Susan that I believed everybody is going to be alright. I proceeded to convince her and restated my dream. We waited all day and didn't hear from Melissa for 8 hours. Fred, her husband, was frantically looking through the scores of body bags because the plane hit directly beside her offices. Melissa wasn't around! It killed every one of the Navy officers next door to her office building. Ironically the commander of the Naval unit was in the back of the jet that sadly slammed the building. Fortunately for Melissa it threw her across and up against a wall. She was able to get out without major injury or physical harm. Her mental state like most everyone was in question. Later we found that our other children could also be in harm's way as we had 2 more military children: 1) Amy Coope,r cadet- Air Force Academy, and 2) Scott Davidson-Army Officer and his family in Mannheim, Germany. We had no idea of the scope of this attack at that time. The attached article tells the rest of this dramatic story for we knew our children were all quickly involved in the future war and Middle Eastern conflicts. I told a newscaster that 'A family that doesn't stand for something will fall for anything.' and I meant it. May God bless America!

I will not say the 'where they are stationed and where they all live' I don't want to give terror minded people any extra chances. Except to say that they all were a blessing to our country. Please pray for them and their families and we will also. Please remember when your child joins any of our military forces. They are no longer your children. They are controlled and owned by our country in just about every way. So please pray for us also, we need it. This is the reason most families skip joining these services. Every other generation it gives the middle generation time to forget or not know of the immediate family sacrifices. With the next generation in my opinion there is a type of 'longing to make a difference'. Which in many situations military service works very well for most. What a sobering time. May God once again, bless our children. HE did after multiple tours: Iraq, Kuwait, Saudi Arabia, USA, etc. They served in Flying, Communication, Transport and Missiles.

Years later, once again while serving at the Pentagon, our oldest, Major Melissa, took us on a tour and told us the sad Naval story. The aircraft directly hit the Naval section. Everyone in that area next door died instantly. Ironically the Commander of the Navy area was in the plane that smashed into the Pentagon. His entire immediate family was with him as well. This time Melissa was very specific. It's very hard to comprehend the results of this attack. We will not forget!

# THE JUMPERS

Most of our apprehensions were fairly typical and 'Pete the Python' was used sparingly. I had an older lady call me and tell me that her house was going to be repossessed due to her grandson's courtroom neglect. She had apparently exercised her bond property rights or 'put up a property bond' for collateral. He jumped bail, better known to us as a 'jumper'. She offered me $1500 to go to Ft Myers, Florida, and pick him up.

I found everything I could find about this man. I asked myself,"What kind of man would do this to his grandmother?" I really wanted to get this person. So I contacted somebody who could stay all night on this pickup, none other than an old friend named A.J. Jeffcoat. He was trustworthy, enjoyed the fellowship, and he of course wanted money as well. His wife Dana was our Mitchell county agent.

Off we go! I had pictures, descriptions, addresses, habits, etc. all in Ft Myers, Florida. I drove a 1 year old Cadillac loaded to the gill with shotguns, AK 47's, 45 caliber handguns, bean bag guns, pepper spray, ropes and whips, leg and hand cuffs, and 'Pete'! I had the traditional outfitting. 'I planned for the worst and prayed for the best' and we got a little of both.

We left right before supper. The trip was 7 hours and we clipped along with warrants and fugitive bullet proof vests. We planned on arriving at 12:00 midnight and we did. When we pulled into this part of Ft Myers it was nothing like the beach area. His address was a tall 8 story high project building. As we pulled up to the single road entrance we came upon two policemen standing at the main entrance. I showed my arrest warrants and as we were approaching their car the officer said, "You got more than that, don't you?" I was showing only my handguns on my hip. He continued to say ,"We've had two policemen killed here this year!". I proceeded directly to the trunk of my auto and pulled out an AK47 and a military shotgun. They both said, "That'll do." We proceeded on with them behind in close pursuit. They wanted to make a deal. I was shocked. They said,"We need to get a subject and we want you to point your rifles towards the rooftop of that building." As we did we stood and hid behind concrete pillars and observed what seemed like a small armed group on the roof. They were peering down. We stood strong with the 'beads of our rifles' directly on them. While we were protecting the cops our subject (I recognized him) ran behind us into his car and took off! As the officers loaded their subject-man they said, "Don't worry we've radioed ahead, he'll be pulled over." I thought, great! We all hustled out of there and followed them to another car. I presented my warrants and had to make some adjustments. This guy wore a size 16 shoe and had wrists bigger than my legs. So the only cuffs that would fit were leg cuffs on his wrists. I tied his feet together. But we had an advantage. Pete! I could sense that this person was a possible jump out of the car and run type. In order to prevent this type of incident it was time to implement the secret weapon that this guy would never expect, Pete!

You should have seen the face of this 'jump the bond' and 'leave Grandma hanging' person as I placed the infamous bag between us. He looked very serious as I placed the bag and said, "Don't worry if you don't touch the edge of the bag he won't bite." He said, "What's in the bag?" I simply said, "Just a Burmese Viper, they have extra long fangs."

The entire ride back was a classic. The wayward grandson hugged the side door 'like he had glue holding him the entire way back' and was somewhat exhausted as a result. We had picked him up, loaded him in the car and delivered him into custody at the Thomas County Justice Center and Grandma's forfeit was ended. We (Allen and I) only had one problem left at this point....we were completely exhausted. I think I was more exhausted due to the drive after the pickup. The adrenaline level was higher than most apprehensions due to the almost military type shooting from the group on top of the building, with assisting police officers in their pickup, plus the excitement of apprehending the jumper. I was so tired that I literally could not drive the 7 miles to go home. I had to stop at the Day's Inn a ½ mile away and get a room. Allen was tired but not nearly as much I was. As fugitive recovery agents we slept about 3 hours and we were ready to go. Obviously we both slept better in our own beds the next evening and it was surely nice informing the Grandmother,' all is well with her former obligation.' Happy was she!

\*\*\*

My top bail agent and fugitive recovery agent in Thomasville was Mike Oliver. Mike had a jump and needed my assistance. We set a time and left for a country setting. The Georgia/Florida Drug Task Force had called us in regards to our jumpers. They wanted them for questioning regarding additional drug witness cases. They told us right where to catch the perps. Apparently they didn't tell us that the house was a duplex as we each started at opposite ends in our search. As I was trying to get into one end of the house one of the task force people ran up and yelled at me, "Go to the other side!" So I ran down to the other side just in time. One of the men in the room had a large glass goldfish tank held high up in the air and was planning on throwing and crashing it on Mike's head as he wrestled and held the fugitive on the side of the couch. I almost dove through the door and pulled my pistol and threatened the man, "If you want to live you had better lower that tank!" He knew that I was very serious and had full intentions if he hadn't complied. We brought our fugitive in and the Task force intervened. Just another day in our line of work.

\*\*\*

Sometimes appearance wins the day. We had a bail jumper who worked at a lumber yard in Perry, Florida, miss court. Mike and I went to get him and it just so happened I was driving a brand new Cadillac that I had just picked up. The jumper was not only very compliant in his apprehension but he couldn't wait to get into the new car for the short trip. I believe the car made the difference that day. He was very happy to be delivered in a Cadillac. We picked this man up at 12:00 noon! I guess you could call this the 'HIGH NOON' pickup just like the real Gary Cooper except 'my horse had wheels.'

\*\*\*

Uncle Harold, one of my other Bail Agents, didn't quite do the proper paperwork for the 'drive the car into the pond 'client. Tammy was formerly a nurse from Ohio and somehow she came down south. She had gotten drunk several times and at least twice driven her car into a local apartment's pond. They would trace the car to her apartment. It made colorful prints in the local newspaper. She got caught a third time and skipped town because the same boyfriend who got her out in the past had finally given up on Tammy due to her activity level while drinking. Harold believed her lie 'they were still dating' without his validation of the relationship. He got her out only to find that the co-signer boyfriend was no longer with her. Harold made the wrong assumption and he was due the entire bond 100% due to poor underwriting. I had to pull all of the files that she had and review and give copies for Harold to go into Waycross, Georgia, asking anybody and everybody where this Tammy had gone.

We were shocked to find in Waycross that she had taken off with an ex-con and was living near Atlanta then a local probation officer told Harold that he thought that he had seen Tammy on Music City Lights in Nashville, Tennessee, a television show. As I looked in her file it stated that she loved to sing. This made sense. Harold also got the name of the ex-con who she left Waycross with and ex-cons cannot give false names or they will get sent back to prison instantly with additional charges. After checking telephone and work histories of the ex-con I found him in South Atlanta in a tough side of town. When I got her medical histories I was shocked that she had: 1} Stomach cancer 2) Hepatitis C 3) at least three personalities. I told my wife Susan that I planned on being there at 10:00pm because we had notes that Tammy 'stayed up and read until 10:00pm'. I had now tied her with the ex-con and I knew she was personally ill and in serious trouble.

As I pulled into Lake Park, Georgia, (south Atlanta), I went directly to the Lake Park Police Dept. I met with a Command Lieutenant and gave him my bench warrant, additional medical information, and the address. Almost immediately, they put me with seven officers. They told me that an officer was killed in the same neighborhood that past month. I told them of her medical conditions and we all put on long rubber arm protections against possible infection.

I was dressed, armed and full bulletproof vest with 'Fugitive Recovery Agent' written on both sides. We all pulled into the trailer park with two policemen in front and three police cars with multiple officers as well. The two officers drew weapons and led me to the front door. A muscular man with no shirt came and opened the door. I said, "Where's Tammy." The man said, "I don't know her!" I said, "Officers wait right here." I went to the side upper window of the trailer and jumped up, there she was, in bed and said, "Hi Tammy!" She said,"Hi Gary, just give me a minute" OK! And I returned to the door. Tammy appeared and I cuffed her hands and legs. The man in the door said, "What will it take to get her out?" I said almost in jest,"Oh, about $10,000 or so" He said, "I'll see you tomorrow!" I thought 'Yeah, Sure' and hustled and secured Tammy into the car. By this time people were everywhere and one said referring to me 'He's with the DEA, the other said, 'He's with the FBI, another said, 'He's a Marshall!' As the crowd grew...

Meanwhile the Lake Park Police said, "Mr. Cooper, please drive out of this circle in this trailer park at the highest speed you can achieve, these cats are dangerous!" I said, "Thanks and O.K!" I drove like an Indy Car driver through the park! I even drove 100 MPH down the first two exits of I-75! Boy, I felt very fortunate to get farther down the interstate highway! Then it was fairly smooth sailing as we entered South Georgia. I asked Tammy a few questions but the biggest ones were never answered. Sometimes people get in so much trouble that there is little to say. I suppose that's where Tammy was. It was late as I put her back in jail.

The next morning at the office I was truly surprised to see the man without the shirt from the night before, dressed decently, before me and handing me $10,0000 in cash! I gave him a receipt and told him to sit down and wait until I can contact a judge. I called an attorney who I knew fairly well. I told Steve my situation. And Steve said let me call the judge. The judge wanted $5000, I gave attorney Steve $2500 and I kept $2500 for my efforts.

That night in a 'special hearing' just for Tammy the judge banished her from Georgia forever. He let the $5000 pay for all her fines and wished her well.

Poof! Tammy was gone! I did find the answer to the 'how did you come up with $10,000'. The man with no shirt was a roofer and had lost his finger while doing a roofing job. The payout with his dismemberment insurance program provided that in case of dismemberment of a finger the recipient would receive up to $10,000 per action of loss. Of course 'how else could anyone from Lake Park come up with that kind of money?' He seemed to really like Tammy and said, "We're going south and I don't mean Florida, we are going to Mexico!" "Have a great trip" is all I could figure to say. Bye Tammy. Money Talks...

\*\*\*

We had never had anyone skip court and dare us to come and get them. This was a military incident with one of our jumps who happened to be in the military. He gave us his residence and was in the Navy stationed on base in Norfolk Virginia. This gentleman didn't realize who he was tempting. I am a pilot and I do well with officers as I have several officers in my immediate family myself.

I contacted the co-signer and he couldn't believe that 'his friend wouldn't show up for court'. He was very determined to bring him back and not have to pay his bond fee. I made him a temporary bail transport agent. As owner of our firm I had that authority. I then told him to drive up to the Naval Station and present paperwork while I talked with the military officials regarding Naval bail bond jumps. The Officers were not very happy with this fairly new recruit who was now in hot water with us and the Navy. They presented me with the man and an escort who drove us to the main gate as the temporary bail agent was pulling up.

The jumper couldn't figure out how quickly we got there. He didn't know I was a pilot and that his friend was on an emotionally charged mission of apprehension. They dropped me off at the local airport and we secured the subject very well as his friend at least for awhile longer, then delivered him to the Thomas County Justice Center after a 13+ hour trip. Later, his friend 'my temp bail enforcement transport driver' said that 'he was heavily roped-cuffed and I made him starve.' I believed him.

***

We had a Miami based drug dealer get put in jail with a $10,000 bond. His friends from Miami came up in their big Cadillac with chrome reverse tires and axle pumps that raised and lowered the vehicle. They appeared very obvious as if saying, 'Look at me!' Regardless, without any sign of emotion I told them "$10,000 hold money plus $1500 bond fee." They paid, got a receipt, and said, "We'll be back at the end of court!" "OK" is all I said and they were gone.

Several months had passed and he was released and here comes the big pink Cadillac! They walked into the office and said boldly, "We want our $10,000!" I came around the corner and said, "I want proof." They handed me the court documents.......Then it happened!

The Leader/toughest guy of the gang breathlessly gasped ......, "He's the one!" 'Nervously shaking while his men looked at him like he was crazy'. "He's the one who has that viper and he gets people with it. He's all over the TV!" Then I heard one say, "Oh, Yeah!".

After all that they acted like little totally compliant children as they finally departed as I appeared with the money. My secretary said, "You scared those boys half to death!" I simply said, 'It works.'

****

Leon Vanlandingham was my pastor and then later on retired and became the Grady County bail agent for my company. I really liked Leon and gave him some leverage in dealing with hiring agents and fugitive recovery agents or both. I will never forget one of Leon's female black friends who absolutely did not want to go to court. I really didn't want to get involved because of the obvious petty problems. But Leon said, "I need you." "OK". I was immediately on the scene and off we went to her house. She opened the door and said, "I will not go to that court!" I didn't hesitate and grabbed her as we sat on her couch waiting for her to comply while she was handcuffed by me. We had to sit on the couch Leon on the front/left side; she was in the middle and me on her right side. We sat and sat and finally she said,"OK, I'll go!" Whew. It took at least 2 hours of baby-bail sitting.

Enter Marty Harrell, Marty seemed like an excellent prospect. He was 6'4'' tall and weighed 350+ pounds and in addition he appeared to be a fairly prosperous farmer in the Mitchell County area. I told Leon 'he had recruited someone that I could have never found'. After a few weeks and paperwork Marty was a bail bondsman for Mitchell County and the City of Camilla, Georgia. All seemed well with Leon and Marty in the Mitchell County area.

Marty's first bond was a lady who got a DUI and lived in Tallahassee, Florida. He turned in the paperwork with some additional bonds. The money was correct and allocated properly per his turn in. I told him as well as anyone else who bonded for us, "You are at risk for any and all bonds that you write. Remember to stay in touch mostly by telephone unless a co-signer is stating that the bondee is going to jump bail. Then we may need to start premature bail enforcement procedures. Leave this up to me and your District Manager Leon Vanlandingham." Somehow Marty never heard or comprehended what I said and gave to him in writing. I got a call from Leon my manager and the lady that Marty bonded out from Tallahassee said that Marty was stalking her. I immediately called the lady and said, "If Marty does this again please call the police and remove him from the area. We will back you up." Marty showed up again the next night and I removed Marty from any and all bond agent listings throughout all of our counties. Thank goodness we distanced ourselves from Marty Harrell.

Approximately 6 months later we read in the local and state news that Marty Harrell and his father had killed a Hispanic person that didn't pay them back, or their actions had something to do with a money transaction that occurred between Marty, his Dad and the

Hispanic....somehow. Who would have figured...this Marty had an attractive wife and 4 beautiful children when I first met him. He and his Dad are both now in prison.

\*\*\*

Baseball City while on the lam. We wrote a bail bond on a female that disappeared. We couldn't find hardly any information at all. She apparently had a mental problem and took off. *None of her relatives and a friend or two didn't have a clue and did not seem to really care about her.* I thought this to be odd. After an exhaustive search for contacts we got word from an insider at Thomas County Mental Health that she had a boyfriend from Moultrie, Georgia. We now had a name; he was a diesel mechanic and no longer lived in the South Georgia area. We finally traced him to Baseball City, Florida; it was a major/minor league town in central south Florida. I felt uncertain as to who or what we would find down there so I asked my wife, Susan, to go. She was listed as a bail enforcement agent but was hardly ever used. I needed a woman to witness the apprehension and return for legal and ethical reasons. I told Susan we would make a weekend out of it. So we moseyed down there and staked out where we thought they might live. The residence had a man that was working on a diesel truck with the engine on a rack. The house was moderate and without any noticeable movement on the inside.

We went out for a nice meal and toured Baseball City, if you like baseball you need to visit this place. We checked in to a local hotel. The next morning around 9:00am we would approach the dwelling. I always prepare for the worst and pray for the best. I decided the best approach would be to contact the mechanic who seemed very busy fixing diesel engines.

We parked and I walked directly towards the man and said, "My name is Gary Cooper and we have a warrant for the person from Georgia in this house." He said, "You can have her and I'm tired of her anyway." "OK". I proceeded into the house with Susan observing from the car close by. She answered and I whipped her over a couch, cuffed her arms and feet and marched her out to the car. She didn't say a word the entire time traveling back and she wouldn't eat either. It was obvious she wouldn't be in jail long, she was definitely mentally sick. Before we took her out of the car at the Thomas County Justice Center, we prayed for her and she seemed somewhat relieved.

\*\*\*

John Turrentine, one of my bail agents, was sincerely interested in helping the Hispanic persons who were incarcerated thus we searched for an easier way to achieve bail on their behalf but it didn't start out easy.

John had bonded out a Hispanic male who lived in the city. Cosigners were somewhat hard to find due to language interpretation problems. So John felt pretty good due to the fact that he lived fairly close to our office. He jumped bail. I assisted John with the apprehension and we pulled up to the residence. We asked a young Hispanic male while he was working on a car tire, showed him a picture, and asked if the person was inside to the best of his knowledge. We entered the room and there were 12 almost identical men sitting on the long couch watching television in Spanish. We showed pictures all around the room with his written names and one of them pointed towards the door. It so happened the first person 'we saw and showed his picture to him by the car' was our bail jumper. I guess you might say 'they all looked the same!' This statement works for all of us at various times. Now our jump was on the run. Most are terrified of all aspects of the law due to horrific treatment in South America. The next day we showed up at his work on one of the 93 working plantations in our county. We pulled up to one of the big houses. We saw the roof and about 15 Hispanic roofers on the roof as the eaves (edge of the roof) were about 20' feet high. We called out his name and the next second we couldn't believe what we saw. Our jump was literally a jumper. *He at a running pace ran full blast off the roof while still running in mid air as he connected with the ground he didn't even flinch as he ran through the adjoining woods!* We then went directly to the plantation manager and he said, "I'll take him in." He did and we never chased a Hispanic again. I wrote the new procedure for bonding out internationals.

Upon further investigation we found that most Hispanics have seven different specially sewn pockets in their pants leg. This keeps their monies on them at all times. We found in the jail that the jailers would say, "They don't have any money." A minute later we found they not only had paid the bail fee but the entire bond fee as well. We developed a Spanish titled form that allowed us to hold the entire cash bond fee or fine up to court date when we would show up and pay the courts his or her fine. Occasionally we would get a call from a court official when they needed the money for certain court rendered occasions. This rolled along at a good pace and we suddenly became known by the Hispanics that 'these guys hold your fine fee and pay it on demand!' OLAH!

\*\*\*

# Cooper appeals order

**By Patti Dozier**
patti.dozier@gaflnews.com

THOMASVILLE — A bond company ordered to pay Thomas County more than $350,000 will appeal the ruling in the Georgia Court of Appeals.

Two notices of appeal were filed Tuesday in Thomas County Superior Court on behalf of Express Bonding.

Two orders filled in late August by Superior Court Judge Richard M. Cowart call for Express Bonding to pay $360,000 due when two defendants did not appear in court in 2003.

COOPER

The notices of appeal were filed by Valdosta lawyer Converse Bright.

The defendant court no-shows are Jian Ming Huang and Qiang Lin, who remain at large. They were charged in December 2002 with multiple charges of theft by deception and credit card fraud in connection with a flimflam.

Express Bonding posted bonds of $180,000 each on the suspects.

Bright, at a January hearing, contended the suspects were not properly notified about the court date.

The state, represented by Jim Prine, Thomasville-based Southern Judicial Circuit assistant district attorney, cited Georgia law contrary to Bright's contentions.

On Wednesday, Jim Hardy, Thomasville-based chief assistant district attorney, said his office had no comment on the appeal notices.

Thomas County Sheriff Carlton Powell said last week he would place a levy on property to satisfy the lien against bond company owner Gary Cooper.

The office of the Thomas County clerk of court has issued a writ of fieri facia, or fifa, to allow the sheriff to levy and seize property owned by Express Bonding.

Express Bonding apparently is out of business. Its former Smith Avenue housing is occupied by another bond company.

The sheriff said Wednesday he would consult County Attorney Bruce Warren to determine the next procedure.

---

**TUESDAY, SEPTEMB**

## COMING WEDNESDAY

### LOCAL

Bond company owner Gary Cooper discusses his decision to appeal a judge's call for him to pay $360,000 due when two defendants did not appear in court in 2003.

---

### Is it legal?

"Is it legal for someone who owes the government mega-bucks to run for a public office?"

Over the thirteen year period I was in the bail bond business we wrote over 15,552 bonds and picked up over 1500+ fugitives. I never had to shoot anybody and I didn't even have one fight. I believe I was more than fortunate which I was but I believe 'I simply was blessed' in this regard.

When you are an owner in one of the biggest bail bond operations in South Georgia you tend to take advantage of other pursuits. These were my pursuits:

YMCA- I played lunchtime basketball MWF at lunch every week possible. I loved this and we had very good comradely most of the time.

Church- We knew our source, attended regularly 'our goal was to make Jesus real'. I believe this is what our family tick!

Aviation- As our children grew Susan, Amy 'our youngest' and myself flew to various destinations. Indiana in 3.5, Key West in 1.5, hours,etc.

English as a second language- Susan, many others and myself got very involved in teaching English to Chinese and Spanish persons. We loved this.

Commercial Real Estate- Sold off except when it could be used for my business pursuits. The Smith Avenue properties proved very valuable for rents.

Commercial Businesses- such as water systems-EPA, Express Bail Bond Service and Political pursuits- Kiwanis-helping children, Republican and Democrat attendances.

I was forced out of bail bonding by our local Sheriff who just happened to be in charge of the 'Georgia Sheriffs Association' that year. Politically, he was very strong and could easily get other Sheriff's to' buy into' or follow his suggestions. I was going to be suggested for all the wrong reasons. This year 2013 would be my end with bail bonding. I was forced to pay $200,000 for a couple of bonds that would normally be $3500 bonds except that the local powers convinced a very sickly magistrate Judge 'who died shortly thereafter' to put $180,000 bonds on two Chinese boys that hailed from New York. The Sheriff told her the two boys were 'thought to be terrorists'. Nothing could be further from the truth! They were simply buying low and selling higher up north, with misdemeanors efforts at best. They had bought 7 cartons of cigarettes from a local convenience store. They bought the items with 1- 3 bad credit cards. This was their crime. A $3500 bond at most.

I had just come from an ESL 'English as a second language' state meeting where we reported making major headway 'great language improvement' with our 3 female Chinese young ladies who were all involved in the Chinese restaurant business. Susan and I had just been invited to one of our favorite student's wedding in New York. This bond was presented to me by Mike Oliver, bail agent. Over my 13 years with over 1500+ bonds written 'no felony bonds were ever called due by the courts'....But I was in the D.A's and Sheriff's radar! They were willing to change the law or procedure with me and my company! Because they could in our small legal jurisdiction. I was very unimpressed with the proceedings.

I couldn't believe the prejudicial acts concerning our local courts adjusting these bonds to these horrific amounts. I couldn't help but think what would happen if one of my south Georgia residents went to New York and accidently used a bad credit card with a few items and then got $180,000 bonds by a local Magistrate. I had one of my former employees in the court system call me and state, "Gary, they are going after you with these bonds!" I immediately got on a plane and went to New York.

Gary Cooper, left, shows his $200,000 settlement check to John Holt in the office of the Thomas County clerk of court Wednesday afternoon.

I visited the vast Chinese Market Offices. I saw over 3,000 white vans exactly like the ones my clients were driving. I was overwhelmed by this huge operation; I had never seen anything like it. As I approached their head offices that sat directly in the middle of this vast marketing network I saw that the operational aspects of this Chinese operation was guarded by many men all armed with machine guns. It appeared that it would be futile and dangerous just to ask a few questions to this group. I clearly needed a different approach.

So I went to the two addresses given by my bail agent back in Georgia. I found the consignor and he claimed, 'he didn't have any money!' He was beyond terrified that I came to his meager house. After I talked with the New York PD, I would catch a glimmer of this man's terror. I was now going to find the most amazing event of this entire trip would simply be very basic yet incredible at the New York P.D. Investigations Dept.

I was somewhat in awe as I proceeded to the very large investigative division of the New York Police Dept. I met and presented my bonds, the Investigators saw their pictures and ID'ed the race, the bonds, and commented $180,000 each 'big bonds' and then assumed the charges. The two internal Directors sat with me in their office and said,"How many people did these two kill?" I said,"None, they had seven cartons of cigarette boxes and many bad credit cards." They both started laughing and said, "These two are definitely in the south river and you'll never find them and let me guess where you're from. …..GEORGIA right? Don't worry in the next 100 years they'll figure the legal system out. Just ask for the mercy of the court, they might lower this farce. We have to go." I shook their hands and thanked them for the time and left.

*Years later I would go to 'Forensic and Law school' at Indiana University. This was another eye opening experience. One of our speakers was a high standing attorney from New Jersey. After his presentation I asked him about my $360,000 case. He said, "Small municipalities often make their own rules. The only way to expose them is in Superior Courts who usually will throw out or greatly reduce such bonds." Surely I should have taken this to State Superior Court. This farce might have been righted.*

At this point, I found myself thinking about Billy Graham's comments concerning money,"If you lose your money, that's nothing. If you lose your health, that's something. But if you lose your character, you've lost everything! Don't lose your character!" This phrase would be with me throughout the entire legal process and beyond. I received a Georgia Forfeiture letter the following week. It simply acknowledged the present legal happenings. It was time to get an attorney so I called Andy.

The Sheriff and the District Attorney was really planning on making me pay the entire amount. $360,000! So the court date was set and my attorney seemed like it could be reduced somewhat. Meanwhile the Sheriff had a reporter that he had a very good relationship with, a certain news reporter. In other words 'in his back pocket'.

Every week a new article appeared regarding these bonds (see news articles last few pages above). $180,000 each 'huge bonds' without ever telling what crime they really did. She used phrases like 'The clock's ticking' 'His Time is Running Out'. They would show pictures of the jumpers and say, "Cooper Must Pay!" This went on for months. In my mind this was time to run for politics. Any time someone gets so much positive and negative publicity statistically speaking according to most political pundits is 'a great time to run for office'. But I privately had another reason to run for politics. I knew I could get whacked (killed) like possibly Don and Billy had been assassinated. These court debacles would eventually stop.

I wanted people looking my way. I was now in politics and continued teaching Sunday School. Dad's dementia was getting worse as the court date arrived.

The courtroom was full and the Judge called all parties into his chambers. He said, "How can you justify this amounts for these charges?" The Sheriff and DA said, "Because we can." I don't know what my attorney said, but that's what he told me <u>just before he left</u>.

That's right, just when it became time for my attorney to make his opening statement he turned to me and said, "I'm running for a court position and I can't do this!" I said, "What do I do?" He said, "You can do it, just ask them questions." He left....Suddenly I thought 'I really don't know what to do! I haven't planned for this- ever!' I've got the two most powerful local officials I know ready to testify and I'm the one questioning and presenting arguments! God help me! The Judge was made aware of the change and looked towards me. I nodded, OK. As I implied....That was it! I almost asked for recess, but I didn't know how to ask!

Yes, I proceeded after conferring with the Judge. I questioned the sitting Sheriff and DA Jim Hardy each at different times. 'Do you think calling a felony bond without warning is fair?' 'Is this the way you like to treat bail bondsmen in these type situations?' 'Did you influence Judge Garland wrongly regarding this matter?' ' Do you think this bond amount is fair?' They both answered the same questions in complacent ways. Yes, No , maybe, I'm not sure…..Don't ever volunteer as an attorney unless you really like arguing...I'm positive they were humored at this impotent Yankee without counsel asking unprepared questions.

I couldn't help but feel, '<u>This could be my 'rainiest night in "Georgia'</u> event. 'They're going after me again, this time my money!'

No local attorney would take my case so I went to a semi-famous attorney, Converse Bright of Valdosta, Georgia, who wasn't concerned or affected by distanced Sheriff's or DA's. $35,000 was required and I put it up for my defense installment.

Felony Court actions take months and even years. Converse extended the case 6 months. Bright told me, "They couldn't put you away criminally so they clearly want to get your money. When you questioned the Sheriff and DA in the court, 'That shackled me as your attorney because I now have little room for an appeal. *The initial court dealings is where all appeals come from.* All he said he could really do was 'delay'. In other words I had no chance for much of an appeal in this case. Due to my first unplanned futile attempt at being an attorney. I was bleak! Unprepared and destined to go down.

I told Converse, "Is this really fair? Being left to handle my own case without some leverage?" He said, "You do remember when they tried to put you away 'prison', don't you? I said," Who could forget!" He then implied, 'they have legal power and want you bad' 'prison or money'. This time it's just money.

I had two choices 1) Worry and get sick maybe die, 2) Do something positive, something technical, that won't take much time. So...

With my free time I became a certified clinical Hypnotherapist after just 6 months. A hypnotherapist gave my first wife Janet some information that made her last days somewhat better. I also opened a Title Loan Company and became a Pepsi Distributor as well.

I wasn't going down without a fight or purpose as I came down here in 1977 with $3,000 and I was now worth millions. 'Billy Graham's saying' was only a breath away.'Keep the 'character!' Just like the challenges with sports, my first wife and various other life challenges. This was no time to relax and play a fiddle! 'Quitters never win and winners never quit' I'm still a Winner!

Six months passed and Converse upset several of the D.A's legal plights. Converse found that they couldn't 'ID' one of the Chinese guys. The DA was arresting Chinese men everywhere in the USA as the various accused Chinamen would call me screaming 'I never have been in Thomasville Georgia I didn't do this!' while speaking broken English with Chinese accents.

Accordingly my forfeiture amount went from $360,000 to $180,000! After a few more months I made a settlement offer, presented with a loyal friend of mine, Logan Lewis, who knew Sheriff Powell fairly well. My intentions were strong, "I'll sweeten the pot and pay $20,000 more, totaling $200,000 and settle this case". The Sheriff accepted. My attorney approved. The State Solicitor met me at the Courthouse and I produced a money order in the amount of $200,000! I had just paid the highest bond in the history of Thomas County! Another record! Perspective is everything! Move on...

One week later...I lost my bid for State Representative at 41% of the vote! My secret mission (other than survival) was to change the title 'High Sheriff' to just 'Sheriff' if I had won. That's just politics.

But I was Alive! Therefore, I won! In the meantime the Sheriff sent a deputy to inform me that I could no longer bond in Thomas County. But the Sheriff said, "Lowndes County may be good for me." I set up an office over there for one year without writing one bond. Another setup... I had the Brooks County Sheriff Richard Chafin steal my $20,000 Thomas County Federal trust fund in addition to various other thefts as the Feds took him to prison for other deceptive various High Sheriff crimes. Mitchell County and Grady County all sent me instant forfeitures which I had to pay and disallowed any bail therewith for me as well. Georgia allowed for the most famous bail agent to get terminated. The Georgia High Sheriff's has spoken... I suppose I could have taken the A&E contract. Being untouchable from the local's and due to the A&E Snake the Bounty Hunter status or maybe God just wants to prune my tree. I really don't know. My 'Change Curve' was now in play and I was entering the valley of despair. I truly did not want to lose my attitude.

*They can take my money, the position, but they can't take my memories and subsequent victories with 8 Life changing salvations confirmed! Which was my original goal for entering the bail business in the first place. That was the most important mission of all... Accomplished!*

The State of Georgia paid a lot of attention as to the 'how and why' I and others had to pay such outrageous bail bond forfeitures. As a result all new legislation in Georgia bail bonding procedures was drastically changed. Every bail bond written must be guaranteed as all Georgia Bail Agents now have to keep their total bond revenues with the Sheriff's Dept as they hold the surety with documentation as they process out each month on a certain day of the month with the various bail bond agencies. I'm glad this law was changed, I'm just sorry it was written on my back. Most sacrificial lambs get slain. All I had to do was pay.

*I could only laugh and think what would have happened, if I had truly jumped on board with A&E 'Snake the Bounty hunter' which would have been a fate worse than death. It was time for me to 'dust my feet off' and move on...In the morning comes a new day!*

My wife was beautifully 'still my girlfriend' and working at the highest pay rate in her career so this really helped me. I was back, almost at the beginning, with no present career except I had a lot of stuff-possessions. Most women might have hit the road. Our 3 military children were advancing beyond belief and my civilian daughter Kristine would meet the man of her life and settle in with great hopes and benefits. He happens to be the Public Defender on the Georgia east coast and likes me! Besides all of this we have 11 grandchildren with three in the oven! Three pregnant daughters! *#14!* We have a great future… Now it's all about perspective.

# The 'Middle 50's' Stuck in the South Georgia Mud

I'm not a negative person but I had to be honest with myself. I had planned on retiring someday as a Bail Bondsman. When that was ripped out from under me…

*I had to take a certain period of time to reflect, overcome and rebuild in some manner that would allow me to 'enjoy life again'. Without the curse of looking back so much one can't go forward. I had to keep going...*

Afterward I started a vending company and it grew to be a fairly good income earner after 3 full days of vending services. While I was delivering a Pepsi machine by myself at night guess who shows up. Yes, Sheriff Powell and he physically helped me move that machine on rollers - I was impressed. We had to forgive each other in the past and we did forgive each other. Regardless of what anyone has done to you, you also must forgive. *Sometimes it hurts so bad, you don't feel the forgiveness. But if you confess with your mouth and believe in your heart this is what happens...* Yes, I even wave at the Sheriff and wish him the best. Remember above all else 'if you can't forgive you can't really restart!' When I look in the Bible, particularly referring to King David, the King had an affair, then to disguise his lover's pregnancy he had to kill her husband and protect his reputation by putting him on the front lines in battle to die. The story goes on but God forgave King David for the affair and murder. What have I to complain about! Besides all this... God had called King David a man after his own heart! All because David asked God to forgive him. I have a future and only God knows what it is but I'm now clean and the new start is within view.

Mostly because I'm still a businessman. I also started a loan company and was told if 'I got 400 clients that was the key'. I got 400 clients and still didn't like that business. I simply closed the company, it's just not me! God knows I tried but I want his will for my life. I had a painter/ preacher combination use his position to swindle, yes, he stole a lot of money but I had to forgive him also.

With one of our previous homes we had a so called Architect-Preacher take a $160,000 check to repair a house we financed with him, he bagged the house with a huge plastic sheeting so it looked like it was under repair but it wasn't. Then he took off with the money. After our attorney won the court case in 'The Georgia appeals court' our attorney was killed in an accident. We couldn't financially proceed with another attorney's large take over fees. So once again, we had to forgive and go on with our lives. *Whether it's lost funds or lost relationships we must forgive or God will not forgive us!* In addition to being a Pepsi distributor I still had my water company and several pieces of good 'commercial properties' and not so good areas in residential real estate. I had to put one foot in front of the other foot, move on...If you noticed reconciliation (getting back at my enemies ) is not my part, I leave that only to GOD.

*At times I would remember a crazy show from the 60's and 70's called 'Hee Haw'. The Network would get these washed up looking guys to sing 'Gloom despair and agony on me. Deep dark depression excessive misery. If I had no bad luck I'd had no luck at all. Gloom despair and agony on me.' I would think of this song even in church. I think everyone goes through a type of depression and re-evaluation when these type events occur. Although nothing I did excited me yet like the bail bond business. I had to leave my attitude to God.*

I hated to feel this way so in addition to my various businesses I became a substitute teacher in our local school system. I liked the kids and did pretty well holding their attention. I have a lot of stories. I knew that I didn't want to be a teacher, but the 'the schools' kept asking and I kept teaching. I think the reason they liked me was I demanded the children's attention and kept the classes on 'course with their absent teachers requests' Over the next

2 years I was getting close, but I just wasn't there yet...I kept thinking about one of the minor or little said biblical 'fruit of the spirit traits- <u>long suffering</u>' and mine was minimal as compared to the finality-end of life that others have with long term illness and disabilities. The Bible also says 'rejoice in your tribulation it worketh patience' OK, I'll just try patience. 'I felt like I was Bear Wrestling in slow motion' During this period of time we also had two to three of our children in and around Middle Eastern war zones. My prayer life almost hit rock bottom. I refused to 'wear blinders' and tried my best to keep on keeping on.

When I attended a Lt Governor's event with my Kiwanis Club I had a revelation of sorts. <u>I participated in a simple color test and found that I was a 100% lover of fellow man!</u> Impulsively, I thought to myself *after going through all this crap* how could I be a 'lover of fellow man'! In addition to Maslow's Hierarchy of Needs, Christian teachings of love, mercy and grace, I now have found that I really do love people! I immediately started asking God if I was supposed to be an evangelist. HE never responded over the next few years. Accordingly, I have now resigned myself to the likes of being a tentmaker. The apostle Paul was a tentmaker. Just making a living I suppose. I simply did not want to be a tentmaker. Over the next 7 years I would live my life with a purpose that didn't behoove me but humbled me. It wasn't all bad or good. Regardless life goes on! And I really do love people!

<u>Celebrating a 40th High School reunion causes these types of pictures. My daughter Kristi with my granddaughter Emily! Buddies from High School John Keach, Gaynell Smith, David Andress, Randy Kirts, and Randy Nentrup and Dad. Randy convinced me to ride a motorcycle! From N.C. to Indiana! It was great except I had my legs and back cramped up due to extended bike riding near Jeffersonville Indiana and Randy had to massage my legs. We really looked like two fruitcake motorcycle riders! Nevertheless we still made it to the reunion. We even got to sing a song....</u>

I got to visit our children and grandchildren a little more. The money was less and I didn't like that. I really enjoy being generous. I then found something else while substituting in schools. The Junior high kids really seemed to like me. I would tell them stories of bear wrestling, bringing in serial killers, flying through hurricanes or the one they really liked was 'how to be more than you can imagine'. I got a class that due to schedules had a twenty minute time period where I could test this concept. The kids liked it so much they all stood up and clapped. Maybe I was on to something. After all I have had some incredible experiences. I still had a degree in economics and I enjoyed planning with a dream procedure based upon my hypnotic's background. The Bible says, "Seek and you shall find" My hunt was on for my new purpose. I hope to finally re-wrestle that bear, this time he will not get me down. I intend to keep going and just reflect a bit. Nowhere in my Bible does it mention retirement. Moses climbed a mountain at his age 120+ and then died. No quitting till it's really over! Carry on my friends...

Out in Colorado: top right- Scott's family, Amy in the middle, Fred and Melissa on right

Bottom right- Scott's Family, Amy in middle, Susan/ myself- Grandpa Cooper-standing, Fred & Melissa

Bottom left-Dorothy Pitts, Amy in uniform, Susan and Grandpa Cooper (it was cold)

Top left- Amy standing by a monument

# The Heavenly Touch on me!

I was driving my truck on our hill near the house. We were going to have some type of a small New Year's party. I think it was a few friends and that was good. I wasn't thinking about anything in particular. Just another day... Of course that's when God always seems to act! When you aren't expecting anything anymore. I guess you could say that I was 'dead' to myself then... BOOM! 'HE SHOWS UP!'

As I was driving up the hill near our farmhouse I was enveloped in an incredibly sweet aroma laden fog all around me in my truck. It was fantastic as I was amazed and scared at the same time. I wondered if this scent was from the angel of death. It had an awesome power in it as well. I had my truck windows down as the air temperature was in the middle 60's and 'in the natural'. I couldn't see any flowers or plants when I viewed the surrounding landscape that could make this kind of mist and unbelievable scent. Afterwards *I immediately went into the house to make sure I was really alive as I talked with Susan. To me, this event was clearly God! Yea! HE touched me again! Subsequently, God was dealing with me in 2 ways. I found myself encompassed with anticipation and peace fullness. I just knew something good was going to happen. But what?* Over the next few weeks 2/3rds of my vending accounts dried up from 3 full days to just one day's worth of vending (my attitude-no problem!) I was enjoying almost everything: I've been touched! Pepsi and Coke did an 'Institutional Takeover' with 3 of my largest accounts in the school systems. This didn't bother me in the least bit because when God touches me!

'Especially if you don't die.' Although due to the fact I'm a Christian I was humbled and thrilled at the same time. Especially with God because he is so awesome and omnipotent (all powerful)! I just knew HE's got something really neat planned, way above my thoughts! I went in the house directly afterward this incredible event. Susan agreed after hearing of my incredible miracle and we decided to simply wait on God. We didn't do anything different; we were just waiting with a strong calm expectancy and warm faith. God is never an Indian giver! We quietly waited...I decided to not tell anyone. If I told it would be another crazy Christian. 'World attitude', just another delusional Christian.

Kristine, my daughter, had recently married Reid Zeh. We were so happy to see our entire immediate family 'from Oklahoma, Washington DC, Indiana, Florida, and Georgia' plus a lot of our extended family and friends were there also. Everybody had a great time. A few months later we returned to see them just before they bought a breathtakingly beautiful house on St Simons Island. I spent some time talking with Reid as Susan talked with Kristine while the children were playing. Reid is a huge Jacksonville Jaguars fan and of course I'm always pushing for the FSU Seminoles. The Jags were starting to draft from FSU and that made us both somewhat happy.

Near the latter part of the day prior to supper, Reid made a simplistic type of observation about me. "Gary, I just figured out who you remind me of?" *People are all the time confusing me with other 'balding people' - maybe we all look alike.* I said "Who?" He said, <u>*"You remind me of a DUI Instructor.*"</u> At that moment Reid clearly did not seem to realize the impact of what he had just said! <u>But, I sure did!</u> I heard Reid make a very simple and kind observation, but Reid did not know how I quietly and to myself compared his response to Simon Peter when Jesus asked him who he thought Jesus was. Simon Peter said 'You are the Christ' then Jesus said, "Only my father in heaven could have revealed this to you." I believe God himself spoke to me through one of my initial meetings with my new son-in-law and HE prepared me to respond accordingly. No one was more surprised by 'all of this' than me. I told him, "I think I'll check this out, you never know." My mind was racing with a great anticipation but my actions outwardly showed almost no emotion as we finished our visit and had a great time and left to go home. Now it was time to investigate - 'seek and we shall find'.

The next week Susan and I explored the internet and found that 2 years of public school teaching allows one to become a DUI Instructor. I had substituted for two years exactly to supplement our income. College transcripts were also required-no problem. We were also encouraged as we found that we could also become Defensive Driver Instructors- once again great! Later on we found 'Alive at 25' School to help ages 15-25 wake up and drive instead of distracting themselves with each other. In the process of proceeding with the State of Georgia's lengthy and time consuming certification requirements, we planned and became certified as Owners, Directors and Instructors! One course after another and sometimes two courses in the same week. *All of this before we had any classes whatsoever.* It didn't matter... We were motivated! We had a fantastic vision! Thank God!

After we got our multiple state certifications we also had to certify our facilities. We hustled, promoted, and had a belief that we were being led accordingly.

It was truly beautiful to me how Susan simply trusted and followed my lead. What a privilege after 36 years of a loving beautiful, trustworthy relationship and marriage while actively pursuing these types of spirit led endeavors. She never seriously questioned me as we faithfully staffed the office and took 8 months until we had our first class. This happened because we believed and had faith in what we were doing. We had many disappointments but we never gave up. Our patience would eventually flow into joy!

It became obvious that 'Gods peace helps us rise above our circumstances'

This is our approved 'logo' for our schools. The crooked line is embedded in our motto and is called the <u>Change Curve.</u> The change curve shows a line coming from the left. 'In this logo' this represents current lifestyle. The 'V' shape represents the 'valley of despair', this occurs with various human trials we all go through; when you hit bottom one has to go up. Notice with life lessons learned on the way up you ascend to a higher level. Obviously posted is the name of our school. The saying below the Valley of Despair symbol are the words 'POSITIVE CHANGE' - this is what we want for each single student. The stars represent current grandchildren at time of logo. Then we had nine, now we are expecting 14. <u>I suppose I will have to change my 'Change Curve Logo' someday!</u>

Schools: 1) COOPER-ZEH DUI and Risk Reduction School (20 hour) mandated

2) Safe Way Defensive Drivers School (6 hour) mandated

3) 'Alive at 25' School (4 hour) mandated by individual plus groups

The top two schools are State Mandated which mean specific place/school and approved curriculum. The 'Alive at 25' can be taught anywhere via the National Safety Council. We are in several locations and have multiple Instructors. People need us! We truly need people! Making us some of the happiest people in the world! And business is gradually picking up! Thank God the bail bond business is finally like a fading cloud as compared to helping people at times allowing themselves to overcome at various degrees. We call this a Positive Change!

# "AM I SUPERMAN'S COUSIN?"

2012: 4-5 years ago I hurt my hip playing basketball at the YMCA. I was tripped accidentally and fell on my right hip, it hurt and I paused for a few minutes. I figured I had a hip pointer- it hurt but didn't appear to be much of a problem or any great consequence and I assumed 'it would get better' and continued as if nothing much had happened, play ball! In the past, I would do my own therapy with occasional sprains, inner leg muscles and most of the time I simply recovered.

A few years ago prior to my 'hip accident' our lunchtime basketball gang was playing 'our favorite game' when a well meaning woman named Sally entered the gym and was clearly prepared to make a comment. We 'all the basketball players' completely stopped playing 'while holding the ball' standing quietly while listening to Sally who was the wife of a formerly injured lunchtime basketball player' who couldn't play anymore due to ankle injuries from playing basketball. While stopping our game she proclaimed her viewpoints of our athletic passion regarding basketball as a type of reproach to the humanity of all men's health. She proceeded to simply tell us to 'grow up and quit playing this child's game'. After she was done talking she walked out. No longer in sight we all paused after a slight reflective thought, then one of the men said, "What are we doing?" Responding, immediately another player yelled, "Play Ball!" It was my Pastor Milton Gardner, our oldest player at the time, who was in his late sixties! Discussion was over except for "who won?' We all took winning seriously. Last game winner until possibly the next week. Maybe Sally was right.

Over the years we had various people imply that basketball was truly bad for our health in a variety of ways and reasons. We found that the people who made these statements often had a much higher rate of medical problems due to their inactivity. We thought of ourselves as moderate. While attempting moderation in all things hopefully mind, body and spirit.

In the past during times of injuries I would get in the YMCA pool and work on my shoulders after getting my arm pulled too far back or soaking my groin muscle in the hot tub. We often used ice with ankles for the lesser injuries. In these recent times it all really worked and I was back attending the routine at the YMCA and enjoying life in general.

It was now two years after my hip injury that I found myself slightly limping without any pain. I couldn't figure out 'why?' So I continued in my athletic endeavors and did my usual routines of basketball, while implementing Zumba because it was safer than basketball and provided good bodily movement, conditioning and great Hispanic songs. Months later I had increasing pain and exclusively used the pool for some water aerobics. My limp turned into even more pain while getting progressively worse. At this point in time I had finally arrived at age 65 which meant in theory that Medicare with a supplement is all I needed for medical care. WRONG. That is, not so in these recent days. The hospitals, clinics, medical centers, etc. all have several thousand dollars of additional costs projected, as my condition worsened.

Due to my steadily declining medical condition I was now forced to walk with a cane and clearly needed additional help. For the next two months I enrolled in rehabilitation at the Hughston Clinic in Thomasville. This clinic is well known and has facilities all over 3 southern states. In the beginning the attending physician gave me cortisone shots directly in my hip. Neither shot in two separate sessions worked. The pain simply did not subside although I always react with euphoric 'energies' which offer zero sleep. The cortisone shot reaction always makes me want to attempt to try and sell somebody something-I had the extreme temporary energy like my insurance selling days...but the shots once again this time did not work, only 1 day of less pain on the first shot and 2 days of lessened pain on the second shot. My next area of medical direction was pointed towards the physical therapists and chiropractors which I tried for the next 2 months. Regardless of the many methods and well intentioned efforts they ever so slightly helped ...my hip remaining continually stiff and hurtful. I had to decide what I had to do and therefore get a referral for surgery with MRI and xrays which we scheduled in Tallahassee, Florida. Some type of surgery for me was increasingly becoming an option.

My uncertainty increased as I had only one former operation in my medical history and that was for tonsils at age 5. So I started inquiring about some doctors in the Thomasville, Georgia, area. I found a few that had a history with hip replacement surgery in the recent past. I mentioned one of the doctors I was thinking about using to my Sunday School group which met once a month for lunch as we ate in our special room and talked. I was shocked with the many people mostly older than me and their comments pro and con. They really seemed to care about my circumstance. I really appreciated that because I was not well informed regarding doctors and hip surgery. 'They knew their stuff regarding' our local Doctors...good and bad. After their valuable responses I decided to look elsewhere. I thought to myself, how caring these friends truly are. Their various convictions regarding physicians were far more bolder than I ever expected. I decided to discuss another choice elsewhere.

*I then mentioned the Hughston Clinic and 'they' seemed to not have any problems with them due to their history of excellence in many medical areas of orthopedic expertise with well qualified physicians.*

It occurred to me that as the Bible states, 'there is wisdom in a multitude of counselors'. Boy did they come through for me. Not just in their prayers but leadership where I was pretty much devoid of current medical knowledge. As a senior Sunday School class teacher one gets a lot of medically experienced persons and real life comments. I transferred my files to the Hughston Clinic and off we went. My wife Susan was very involved as well. She was expecting a several month time of rehabilitation for me according to most of the medical reviews she had read. I was truly a rookie at this and I was very uncertain in many areas as to 'how this would benefit me?' Would the pain leave? Would I be destined to limp permanently? How would this alter my life?

I met my Valdosta physician at the local Hughston Clinic. He took my X-Rays very differently from a sideways manner as compared to straight ahead X-rays and showed me that I had a large jagged bone growth on my hip probably from my fall which protruded way out and greatly irritated my entire hip area. He said, "Complete hip replacement surgery is imminent."

I was now facing a major operation with a certain feeling of hopelessness. I wasn't used to turning my life over to any person let alone this fine doctor. As he interviewed me he asked my concerns. "I'm concerned about 'staph infections'." He said, "If you are a clean person and haven't had any stapf in the past you are fairly unlikely to get staph now but I will give you a 'anti- staph cleanser' before the procedure." For the 'preoperative' time with doctor and hospital the physician asked, "Which way would you like to be operated on 'inside leg or outside leg'." I asked him which one he preferred and he said, "Outside leg is easier and just as successful." I said, "Outside it is and I want to be number three on your surgery date list so you will have lots of practice with the other two." We both laughed and the schedule was made.

As of June 14, 2016, I was admitted to the Valdosta/Lowndes County Hospital. After $2300.00 and a few extra hours at midday my surgery took place. Right before I was called to surgery I had one preacher and one wife with two deacons seated waiting for the news per her husband's operation. I wouldn't ask anybody to pray for me prior to the surgery. I wanted God to do it. So He did it! Without me asking an unknown man asked if they could pray for me. 'This group of 4 Hahira Baptist people laid hands on me and prayed! Now my faith was beautifully full.' As I was wheeled into the operation room, I wanted to boldly look at the equipment, bones, and blood but they 'knocked me out so fast I couldn't hardly see anything' via a very sneaky Anesthesiologist. I didn't see or remember anything after that. Until 5+ hours later! Afterwards, I was unconsciously wheeled into a small room with a bed. I woke up in a world of major uncomfortability! I squirmed like never before in about every possible positions while absurd statements spouted from my drug induced hallucinations! Nothing seemed to help until they put morphine into my vein tube. Boom I went completely out, again! I awoke while still finding myself almost totally out of my mind. My mind and body was simply not used to the heavy duty drugs and it spaced me out for the entire two days. The physician came and checked in and talked with Susan. He said, "Gary is in very good physical shape compared to the other two before him - they were fat. I did you know Gary has a deformed hip. I couldn't find the normal bone for the hip socket screw attachment so we had to make Gary a specially designed hip socket attachment location." Susan responded, 'Gary has always been different anyway so this doesn't surprise me." Everyone, the nurses, the PA's all thought that I had Alzheimer's disease, I was really bad. Without any personal awareness of bothering nurses whatsoever I constantly bothered the nurses. Accordingly, they put me on constant watch patient status. I walked 300 feet my first day with a walker, IV bottle and drip lines all attached, with Susan, two nurses and me happily walking and 600+ feet my second day plus I climbed some stairs. As a result, the nursing staff had to take off all my tubes because the doctor said those wonderful words, "Dismiss this man!" This really excited the nurses, 'He's leaving, yea!' Just that fast I was gone. I had 30 needle packets for one month of 'stop the blood clots' shots, a 4 wheel walker, bedpans, pain pills and the promise of physical therapists coming to the house, if needed. At this point I didn't need hardly any of these things except the shots, a few pain pills and the walker. I used the walker approximately 5 days. The pain pills I took very cautiously ½ prescriptions of oxycontin for less than 1 week and shots for 30 days. I injected into my own stomach folds which would apparently prevent 'blood clots'.

Success! I taught a 'Defensive Driver' class the next week with a cane. I went to the YMCA everyday and did the exact same exercises I was taught before surgery at physical therapy. I became somewhat stronger each day for four weeks until I saw the physical therapists at the Hughston Clinic. At this point I did not have a clue as to my progress or lack thereof.

I walked into the clinic and later to the Physical Therapy unit. As I somewhat normally walked in the back corridor area the 'older therapist' said, "What do we have here! Hip replacement. I'd say 3-5 months right?" I said, "No five weeks!" He said, "No way!" and left to check my medical files. *He returned while watching me walk and run and stated, "I haven't seen a recovery like this in 45 years!"*

*This statement made me feel like...Superman's Cousin! A few months prior my sister called me, "Gary your high school mile relay team held the record for 45 years. It was broken last week." 45 years suddenly had a time on me that I never wanted or expected and yet I am so glad this all happened!* Once again. Who says, "I am old!" Just remember a healthy Moses climbed a mountain to die and was over 120 years of age and when he died, 'his eyes were not weak or his strength gone!' It's amazing this extended life and with HIS promises.

# The Miracle of the Ones who never give up...

I have been a Sunday school teacher in the senior ministry for over 20 years. I've seen 96 year olds ride motorcycles and fly in small aircraft for fun. They weren't always in control but nevertheless they always tried. Many told me at these later ages when in reasonable health they felt about '35 years old'. They often worked more for purpose than having to work to make ends meet. They have challenged me to continue and make a difference until the end nears. There is nowhere in the bible that calls for retirement! Don't give up!

Ray Kroc was in his sixties when he convinced the McDonalds brothers to insert his multi-mixer into every McDonald's Restaurant and use the franchise concept.

Today his concept has reached unbelievable proportions and every child knows that name, McDonald's Hamburgers!

Colonel Harlan Sanders started 'Kentucky Fried Chicken' at 75 years of age simply because he didn't have enough money at retirement and the <u>neighbors liked his chicken. The Colonel reacted, acted and expanded! The world eats Kentucky Fried Chicken</u>

The Colonel NEVER retired!
At age 75 (1965) he was just getting started!

Sam Walton started 'Wal-Mart' in his late sixties after owning several stores, with his first Walmart store starting in 1962 with an emphasis on 'service and low price'. I could go on and on. There is not one section in my Bible that implies retirement is to do nothing or sit uselessly in a retirement center. 'All retirement should be is helping people to bring out the best of one's ability to make a difference for one another and hopefully supplement one's income accordingly. I hope to die while seemingly healthy, if at all possible.' Gary Cooper.

To date we now have three schools that assist with DUI, Defensive Driving and Alive at 25 and our school population is growing every month. Our students rave and grade our Instructors as 'Excellent'. Our agenda and instructions skill levels continue to increase with 3 more instructors coming on board very shortly with a total group of

6 instructors and we appear to be going strong. We hope to have more schools with investors/partners input before the next two years. Our basic three stranded rope holds much stronger. We have also grown personally in these endeavors over the last 4 years and my yearning for the Bail Bond business has been replaced. THANK GOD! Only HE could give me this new passionate life! Over the years we have watched our children with our 14 grandchildren! Right off the bat I want you to know I personally had no goal planning whatsoever for these results. Although I find this subject of grandchildren a great blessing as mentioned earlier we are quickly approaching reflection, happiness, thanksgiving, love and immense joy. When no one other than my wife is around I keep having warm feelings regarding this experience of having all of these beautiful youthful people and their part of me! Because of these terrific numbers I want to live as long as possible to simply see what happens! Another way to put it is if you have kids like our kids, God only knows the potential with these special youthful kinfolk. And they all know Susan and myself... *We are the Grandparents!* Let's see what happens...

*Grand Kids in Action/
3 Daughters-Mothers/
3 Sisters All Withholding
Great Additional
Baby Actions...*

*All were pregnant
at the same time.
Our grandparent total
would reach 14!*

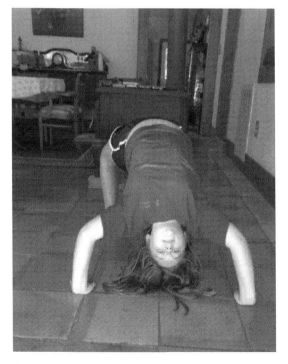

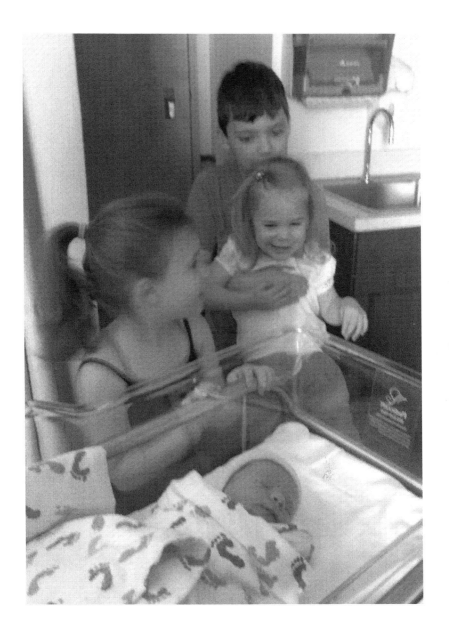

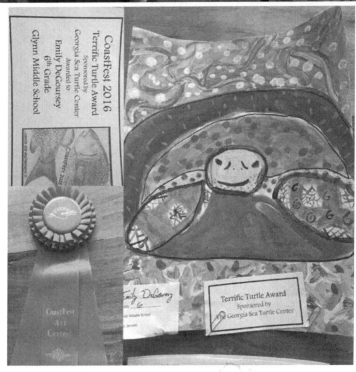

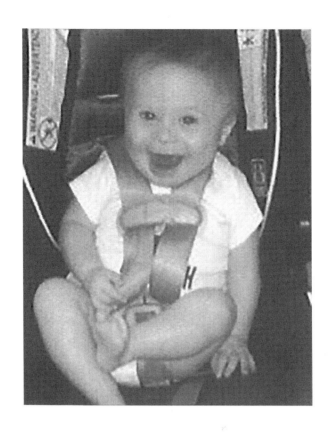

*11 Grandchildren plus three in the ovens (or shortly out) means 14!*

*Ending with NEW Beginnings...WOW!*

# What about Us?

We have to look clearly and honestly at ourselves. The mind, the body and the spirit. It's time to show what really helps make us better as we approach the ages of 60's.70's,80's, 90's.. Here's how we 'manage our lives' in these latter days of our lives.

1) We try very hard to get at least 7-8 hours of sleep. 'Less sleep- anxiety grows.'

2) We try to eat far more plant based foods than animal fatty foods.

3) We try very hard to think of the 'positive rather than the negative thougts'.

4) I practice deep breathing three/four times a week, more oxygen in the blood

   a) The breath has to be exhaled with a powerful 5-10 second burst
   b) As you steadily breathe inward refill the lungs fully- hold
   c) If you want a DVD email me at cooperzehdui@gmial.com for $25.00 plus freight. Credit or Debit is accepted. Simply note:<u>Breathing Techniques.</u>

5) We walk and/or workout daily for 1 1/2 hours '4 days-week'. Use it or lose it!

   a) Water aerobics, steam-sauna room, pushups and stretching
   b) The key to all of this in consistency and effort with moderation
   c) I also do a 'water weights' regimentation, using water allows flexibility
   d) Zumba - Testing my Hip in moderation/ Great for the heart!

6) We are liberal with vitamins and supplements (1-5 days per week)

7) A well balanced diet is what we prefer, majoring in fruits and vegetables. We rarely eat red meat ,but do eat fish and poultry. Processed food is taboo.

8) <u>Lung Problems were formally ranked as 8th reason for cause of death. By 2016 it became the 3rd reason for cause of death statistics.</u> As you've learned from my breathing problems, this may benefit you as well even if you appear to be in good condition. Please take the time to breathe deep breaths for a 10 second hold and do it again as deeply as possible. Tests the results, if you cough a great deal you need to do it more, if not occasionally. As pollution of the air increases lungs get worse off. <u>Your lungs matter!</u>

9) *Anxiety and stress comprise 80% of all illness based upon AMA-American Medical Association studies.* Because of this we try very hard to not let our emotions get out of control. Whether driving, at work or play. In a restful state I hypnotize individuals to lower anxiety. Study and act on Philippians 'Be anxious for nothing' scrolling down the scripture that simply states, 'Put your mind to dwell upon good things' We had a well known Psychiatric Professor from Washington State University tell us- at 'Instructor DUI School in Conyers, Georgia' - when we have a concern or problem that seems to dwell within us remember this: Every problem can be overcome. If you have 1 big problem replace with 3 good thoughts. <u>Remember 1 problem requires 3 good thoughts in order to recover a more positive thought process. Protect your mind!</u>

10) Spiritually speaking. Find a church, Sunday School Class or some way to acknowledge God as you meet daily with Him. Your spiritual life matters! Find a fellowship with other like minded believers. "Seek first the kingdom of GOD, all these things will be added unto you",

Look clearly at the example of *Maslow's Hierarchy of Needs at Goal and Dream Planning and look where you fit in.* Don't stress, just develop a simple faith plan and <u>try something! Make a difference for yourself and others! With one step followed by another...</u>

*Someday, maybe even today you too can create and benefit from a simple but well thought out plan. This is the first day of the rest of your life! 'Keep on smiling' for a POSITIVE CHANGE*

# AS YOU 'WRESTLE YOUR BEAR!

Start writing your plans and goals

Keep in mind that some of your greatest thoughts come in the early morning hours and don't forget your solar plexus, your gut!

Men don't trust your emotions but listen to your gut! This might save your life!

Made in the USA
Columbia, SC
21 March 2019